U-BOAT COMMANDER
A Periscope View of The Battle of the Atlantic

U-BOAT COMMANDER

**A Periscope View of
The Battle of the Atlantic**

PETER CREMER
in collaboration with Fritz Brustat-Naval

*Translated from the German by
Lawrence Wilson*

NAVAL INSTITUTE
PRESS

First Published in Great Britain as
U333 by The Bodley Head Ltd 1984

© 1982 by Verlag Ullstein GmbH, Berlin
Translation © 1984 by The Bodley Head

Published and distributed in the United States
of America by the Naval Institute Press,
Annapolis, Maryland 21402.
Library of Congress Catalog Card No. 84–61243
ISBN 0–87021–969–3
Printed in Great Britain
This edition is authorized for sale only in the
United States and its territories and possessions.

Second Impression 1984

Contents

Translator's Preface, *xi*
1. Crisis in the U-boat War, *1*
2. The Invasion of Norway, *5*
3. My First Command, *16*
4. U 333's First Kills, *30*
5. Hostilities Against America, *48*
6. Rammed by a Tanker, *56*
7. Floodlit Florida, *70*
8. Action Against Convoys, *84*
9. A Novel British Submarine, *104*
10. The Atlantic Transmitter, *113*
11. The Hunters Become the Hunted, *130*
12. Collision With a Frigate, *150*
13. The French Resistance, *165*
14. My Transfer to an Electro-Boat, *178*
15. A New Generation of U-Boats, *190*
16. The Last Days, *203*
Afterword, *214*
Appendix: German U-Boat Casualties in World War II, *215*
Select Bibliography, *239*
Index, *240*

Acknowledgements

We wish to express our thanks for their help to many former submariners, scientists, institutions and advisers, and in particular to the following:

Lt. Cmdr. P. Beesly, RN, London; Cmdr. P. R. Compton-Hall, RN (Retd.) and Mr. Gus Britton, The Royal Navy Submarine Museum, Gosport; Hans Engel, Kapitän z.S., Marburg/Lahn; Mr. Paul Hartmann, Washington, D.C.; Professor Ellic Howe, London; Frau Liselotte Lemp, Hamburg; Capt. Peter Barnsley Marriot, RN, Thetford; Mr. J. P. McDonald, Ministry of Defence, London; Mrs. Mary S. Pain, London; Professor Jürgen Rohwer, Stuttgart; Christine Schjetlein, Oslo; Günther Stiller, Hamburg; Peter Tamm, Hamburg/Berlin; Cmdr. M. R. Wilson, RN, Ministry of Defence, London; Mr. Robert Wolfe, National Archives, Washington, D.C.; and especially Frank Lynder, Berlin.

The Crown copyright material on pages 98, 107ff, 118, 163 and 183 is reproduced by permission of the Controller of Her Majesty's Stationery Office, London.

List of plates

1. Grand Admiral Dönitz, *after page* 20
2. Admiral Sir Max Horton, 20
3. Periscope watch on *U 333*, 20
4, 5. The control room in *U 570*, 52
6. HF/DF aerial on HMS *Exe*, 52
7. Cylinder for *U 333*'s Aphrodite balloons, 52
8. Radio cabin in *U 333*, 52
9. U-boat pens at La Pallice, 52
10. USS *Dallas*, 52
11, 12. *U 333* damaged by SS *British Prestige*, 52
13, 14. Tankers torpedoed off Florida, 84
15, 16. *U 333* after its encounter with HMS *Crocus*, 84
17. HMS *Crocus*, 84
18. *U 570* brought to bay, 116
19. USS *Core*, 116
20, 21. U-boats under air attack, 116
22, 23, 24. The U-boat's AA battery, and its perils, 148
25. Freighters travelling in convoy, 148
26–31. *U 333* during and after attack by HMS *Exe*, 148
32. The Schnorchel, 180
33. Prefabricated section of Type XXI U-boat, 180
34, 35. U 2519 heading for sea trials, 180

Grateful acknowledgements are due to the following for permission to reproduce photographs: to the Imperial War Museum for nos. 2, 4, 5, 6, 17, 18, 20 and 21; to the Bundesarchiv, Koblenz, for nos. 12, 15, 16 and 24; to Ullstein Bilderdienst for nos. 25 and 32; to Franzenburg for nos. 33, 34 and 35; to Kost for no. 11; to the National Archives, Washington D.C., for nos. 13, 14 and 19; to the US Naval Institute for no. 10. The remaining photographs are from the author's collection.

Translator's Preface

Towards the end of 1943 the British Admiralty's Operational Intelligence Centre produced a breakdown of German U-boat commanders according to the length of time they had served. The list then comprised 168 officers. Fifty had served for less than three months, all but sixteen for less than sixteen months, and only one for more than twenty-five months. That one was Peter Cremer. By the time of the Allied Invasion in June, 1944, among all the officers who had served with him since his first patrol in May, 1941, only one survived. Cremer himself was the only U-boat commander to have sailed from German bases in western France since that year and lived to tell of it. Such were the casualties suffered by the men of the German U-boats, such the toughness of their war.

Here, then, is one thread in this book, the severity of the U-boat battle. It was a crucial battle for the British, because a U-boat victory, cutting the lifeline with the New World, would spell starvation; and for the Germans, because it offered the best chance of bringing about a stalemate in the West. In his book, Peter Cremer (known as Ali among friends) describes the story with drastic realism, both with regard to his own experiences and to the wider context.

But he goes further, and here his personal background comes into the story, allowing him to see the U-boat war from both points of view, the Allied and the German, and presenting them with remarkable objectivity. For by his ancestry Peter Cremer had a foot in both camps. His father practised as a German lawyer, and one of his ancestors had served Frederick the Great as a Cornet. Over Peter's bed as a child hung a patriotic motto popular at that time: 'Never forget that you are a German!' But the Cremer family had come originally from Alkmaar in the Netherlands. Moreover, his mother was a French woman from Lorraine, with the maiden name of Houlé, and Peter Cremer was born in that province, at

Montigny les Metz, growing up bilingual and aware of the strong national feeling of his mother's family, which traced its ancestry back to the time of Louis XIV when an Houlé had been the king's treasurer.

But the strongest influence on his tastes and attitudes came from the English branch of his family. His father's mother, born Lucy Thursby, was the daughter of an officer in the Royal Navy. The family owned a house in Abington, Northants (now a museum) and another, Ormerod House, in Burnley, Lancashire, and could trace its descent from before the Norman Conquest. In the fourteenth century a Thursby had been Archbishop of York. From 1352 to 1373 he served Edward III as Master of the Rolls before being appointed Lord Privy Seal and finally Lord Chancellor, a position he held for seven years.

Peter Cremer was expected to become a lawyer like his father, and was sent to study at Grenoble University. But he wanted to enter the German Navy and at the age of 18 applied for training as an officer. Here, his international background told against him, but eventually, in the summer of 1932, he was accepted. In that year the German sail training ship *Niobe* turned turtle while on exercise in the Baltic with heavy loss of life among cadets on board and overnight the Navy was in urgent need of recruits. Of 4,000 applicants 54 were accepted, among them Peter Cremer. Six years later, having passed all his examinations, he was sent to sea for the first time as an officer.

Lawrence Wilson

1
Crisis in the U-boat war

May 1943. At 1730 on the 14th, Grand Admiral Dönitz, C-in-C Navy, reported to the Führer at his headquarters at Rastenburg, East Prussia. They discussed the need to keep Italy in the war. If the Anglo-Saxons freed the Mediterranean, they stood to gain two million tons of shipping space.

'. . . which our valiant U-boats will have to sink in their turn,' observed Hitler.

'Well, at the moment,' replied Dönitz, 'we are facing the greatest crisis of the U-boat war: the enemy are making it impossible for us to fight. They have new systems for locating our boats and are inflicting heavy losses on us, fifteen to seventeen U-boats a month.'

'Such losses are too high,' exclaimed Hitler. 'Things can't go on like this!'

'Besides,' added Dönitz, 'Biscay is the only attack route for the U-boat war. It is a narrow lane so charged with obstacles that it takes our U-boats ten days to overcome them.'

Two weeks later, on May 31st, matters were if anything worse. In his report to the Führer, the C-in-C Navy said: 'Losses have now risen to approximately thirty per cent of U-boats at sea. We have to husband our forces. I have withdrawn from the North Atlantic to the area west of the Azores. To enable U-boats to avoid surprise air attacks, we have to equip them with the means of picking up the emitting frequency of the aircraft we wish to locate. We possess nothing in this field. We do not even know yet what wavelength the enemy is using to locate us. We have no idea whether they are using high frequencies or whether they have some other device. A counter-measure must exist, but we have failed to find it. The enemy's defence at sea and in the air will increase. Unknown factors are involved. Nevertheless it is my opinion that the U-boat war must continue, because the enemy forces it is tying down are extraordinarily large, even though our aim of sinking large tonnages can no longer be realized.'

'There can be no question whatever of letting up in the U-boat war,' Hitler insisted. 'The Atlantic is my western buffer zone and even if I have to fight there on the defensive, that is still better than defending myself only along the coasts of Europe.'

'In that case I believe that the increase of U-boat construction hitherto envisaged must continue,' replied Dönitz, 'and that the figure of thirty boats a month is insufficient. I think the figure ought to be increased to forty boats, and request the Führer to issue an executive order to this effect.'

The Führer agreed, changed the figure of thirty U-boats to forty, and signed the order.

The Berlin headquarters of C-in-C U-boats were located in a villa near the Hotel am Steinplatz. Here in the operations room Grand Admiral Dönitz's staff officers could read the writing on the wall only too clearly. In the first forty-four months of the war, from 3 September, 1939, to 1 May, 1943, on average 4.9 U-boats had been going missing each month. In some months the loss had been as little as two. Then the number had started rising — to eight, and on one occasion to sixteen in a month, until by this May the situation was quite out of hand: as I was soon to learn, the number of boats that failed to return from patrol reached 41, more than one a day, and there was talk of 'Black May'.

Until now, the U-boats had been reporting by radio from the expanse of the Atlantic, from Iceland to Gibraltar, from Biscay to the Bermudas, but particularly from the Western Approaches, the routes taken by the Allied convoys between 43 degrees North and 43 degrees West. Suddenly the boats fell silent, disappeared from the scene without a word — unless the enemy reported their destruction. No one knew what had happened. The dead could not speak and those who had managed to survive made vague and contradictory statements.

It was an anxious feeling to watch the big situation maps and follow the boat of a fellow-skipper, somebody one knew well, with whom perhaps one had even trained. The little flag that symbolised his boat would be moved to and fro. One read and processed the radio signals of one's friend at sea. Then came the moment when contact was lost. He would be asked to report his position — once, twice, but there would be no response. Then one knew he had gone. The little flag would be removed from the map and one could only hope that he had fallen into the hands of the enemy as a prisoner. The fifth staff officer, who was responsible for the list of the missing, would put a star after the name of one's friend, and a few days later a second star. Then his name was 'put on file'.

After the resignation of Grand Admiral Raeder on 30 January, 1943, Dönitz had become C-in-C of the German Navy and had his office in the Berlin naval headquarters on the Tirpitzufer. He had retained direct command of the U-boat arm, however, and whenever he visited us at U-boat headquarters he would now spend the time pacing up and down in silence in the operations room. With every day that passed, this May, he became more reserved. The nub of the problem might be the enemy's radio location techniques. Dönitz had assured the Führer that he was collaborating with Reichsminister Speer to improve our own equipment and counter-measures. But the fact was that neither Dönitz nor his chief of staff nor we ourselves knew what was going on out there. We could only guess that, by some means thought to be technically impossible, our opponents had found a way to take our U-boats by surprise, whether they were surfaced or submerged, day or night, regardless of visibility. Had their defence tactics outmatched us to such an extent that we were close to losing the battle of the Atlantic?

Dönitz talked of the 'uncanny' and kept dwelling on possible treason—he had all his staff officers screened. After our private lives had been investigated in detail and we had been cleared, Dönitz remarked ironically to his chief of staff, Captain Godt: 'That just leaves the two of us. To unmask the traitor, one of us must go on leave.' To reduce the number of those privy to operational secrets, the Berlin staff was halved, leaving only twenty men.

I could follow these events from my office at headquarters, where I had been assigned to Grand Admiral Dönitz as second staff officer. I had only recently been discharged from hospital and still walked with a limp, though I had finally laid aside my crutches. My battered condition resulted from an encounter with a British corvette off Freetown the previous autumn during my fourth patrol with U 333: both the U-boat and I had returned to base in dire need of patching up.

At the end of May Dönitz came to us and announced: 'Experienced commanders must try to find out what is going on out there.

3

Three of you must sail again . . . Volunteers, please.' All the staff officers qualified for the new task volunteered. Dönitz took a quick look round. 'You — and you, and you!' meaning Herbert Kuppisch, Friedrich Guggenberger and me.

So it happened that I found myself on the express from Berlin via Paris to the Atlantic coast and, on 2 June, 1943, I took the repristinated U 333 out of the bomb-proof bunker at La Rochelle and sailed on my fifth patrol as commander.

But let me start the story from the beginning.

2

The invasion of Norway

On the outbreak of war in 1939 I was gunnery officer on board the
destroyer *Theodor Riedel*. Unlike many young officers who saw
fame and promotion in a trial of arms, the prospect of war did not
rejoice or excite me. At noon on 3 September, 1939, when the
wireless brought news of England entering the war, I was sitting
over coffee and ices with my mother on a café terrace in
Wilhelmshaven. We said not a word, but simply looked out over
the broad naval basin called the Jade. Since the death of my father
in 1928 I had never seen my mother looking so grave. For this
peaceable woman the war against Poland, already two days old,
was a calamity. She sensed that France would follow with a declaration of war on Germany. Naturally she was thinking of her father
in Lorraine and of all our French relations. But as a mother her
greatest concern was my fate. At this moment we felt very close to
each other.

I tried to stay cool and objective, but in fact was deeply upset.
'Never forget that you are a German!' That dictum from my
childhood kept recurring to me. But I thought, too, of my dear
French grandfather in Metz and my relations in England, a nation
against which I would now have to fight. How would it ever end?
As a naval officer I knew Weyer's *Pocket Book of Navies* too well to
be under any illusions. In the summer of 1939 the British possessed 255 destroyers, we a mere 34. True, many units of the
British fleet were spread over the ocean. Nevertheless the proportion in home waters was still roughly 1 to 8. On a football field that
would amount to 11 players having to tackle 88.

The leave-taking from my mother was brief, which was all to the
good. That very afternoon we were to sail on patrol.

The C-in-C Navy, Admiral Raeder, was then attending a conference at the naval high command on the Tirpitzufer in Berlin.
Under discussion was the deployment of the fleet against Poland

after hostilities had begun on 1 September. An officer of the intelligence service came in and laid before the admiral an intercepted radio signal. It contained only two words: 'Total Germany'. With these two words British warships all over the world were informed of the state of war with Germany.

Without comment Raeder passed on the signal, which went from hand to hand among the officers present. Then the admiral withdrew to his office and remained for a long time alone before summoning his chief of staff. About an hour and a half later he reappeared, holding a piece of paper on which he had briefly set down his thoughts on the outbreak of war.

'Today,' said the admiral to his officers, 'war has broken out against England . . . In the course of this afternoon France will also declare war on us. According to previous utterances of the Führer we should not have had to reckon with war before about 1944.' Raeder was thus emphasising that he saw Hitler alone as responsible for the fateful development. Hitler had repeatedly assured him that there would never be a war with England, and the admiral had believed him.

As for Commodore Dönitz, he had been repeatedly drawing attention to the weakness of the U-boat arm under his command. He had requested that Hitler be advised that it would not be in a position to inflict serious damage on England. As late as 22 July, about six weeks before the outbreak of war, Raeder had apprised the senior U-boat officers of Hitler's statement that under no circumstances would Germany fight a war against England. Four weeks later Dönitz was urgently recalled from leave to take personal charge of preparations against England himself.

That day, 3 September, Dönitz was sitting in his command post, a barrack on the ominous-sounding *toter Weg* (dead path) near Wilhelmshaven, when the staff officer (Intelligence) handed him the same signal: 'Total Germany!' The 47-year-old Dönitz uttered a brief curse: '*Verdammt!*' Then, having already experienced the First World War as a U-boat commander, he added: 'That this has to happen to me again!' and left the room.

In his memoirs Dönitz writes of the first hours in the Second World War: 'After the British declaration of war on 3.9.1939 and the order received at 1330 from the German naval operations division, "Commence hostilities at once", several of us met for a conference at Neuende near Wilhelmshaven. We were in a sombre

6

mood. We knew what a war against England meant. On 4.9.1939 the first British air-raid took place against the locks at Wilhelmshaven and the warships lying in the harbour. With great determination the British attacked at low level and sacrificed themselves without notable success. Owing to our own successful defence my U-boat officers were in optimistic mood, so I called them in and gave them my opinion of the coming war: "Take this war very seriously! Realise clearly that it will last a very long time, perhaps seven years, and we shall be only too glad if it ends in a compromise even then."'

When I boarded *Theodor Riedel* its name, hitherto displayed in shining brass letters on a blue ground on either side of the stern, had been removed. The entire hull had been given a chequered coat of camouflage in three colours, reminiscent of an Indian on the warpath. The ship's name had also been removed from the cap bands of the petty officers and men, and replaced with just the legend *Kriegsmarine*. The ship was but a year old, a handsome 'steamer' of 3,100 tons displacement with two high-pressure, superheated steam turbines delivering an output of not less than 70,000 h.p., which could give us a good 38 knots through the water.

Our first active duty was to escort three ships which only a few days before had been carrying carefree holiday-makers to the North Sea islands. The ships had been hastily painted grey and converted into mine-layers with the task of laying a belt of mines in seven separate lines off the Heligoland Bight.

Almost nightly we were either acting as escort or laying mines ourselves for a 'West Wall' in the North Sea, at times as far as the Channel. On dark nights we even penetrated into the Thames estuary, as into a front garden, and left a new weapon there: the magnetic mine. In contrast with the anchored mine which exploded on contact, this one lay on the bottom and was actuated by the metal mass of the ship passing over it. Its ingenious detonator could be adjusted so that four ships could pass in deceptive safety while the fifth primed and exploded the mine. It was a surprise success and Göring's Luftwaffe eventually took part in dropping these magnetic mines. On 23 November, however, a German aircraft dropped one such mine in the muddy shallows of the Thames estuary. The British fished it out and took it to pieces

— and once an enemy mine has been captured intact, a counter-measure can be found. The British surrounded their ships with electric cables to produce an anti-magnetic field which neutralised the magnetic mine, a procedure ('degaussing') which we adopted in our turn. From October 1939 to March 1940 our mining operations cost the enemy 68 merchant ships and 3 destroyers.

Less successful, to put it mildly, was a sortie aimed at British fishing vessels which we intended to seize in the old-fashioned way with boarding parties: 'Operation Viking'.

It was the evening of 22 February, 1940, and bitterly cold, which made things even more difficult. Six of our destroyers were sailing in line ahead; we were number four, and behind us came *Max Schultz* and *Leberecht Maass*, to give them their peace-time names.

As gunnery officer I was stationed on the bridge. At 1930 we sighted what appeared to be an enemy plane. For his part the pilot thought we were British warships. While we recognised the Heinkel III and its German markings in time to avoid a mistake, the aircraft went into attack and at 1944 struck the last ship, *Leberecht Maass*, between bridge and forward funnel with a 50-kilo bomb. The destroyer veered to the right, dropped out of line and lost course — a secret course intended to give us a passage clear of mines.

Leberecht Maass just had time to signal 'Am hit, need help' before it was torn apart by a massive explosion. A brilliant flash was followed by a thick cloud of smoke which hid the destroyer. For a short while bow and stern could be seen above water, then *Leberecht Maass* disappeared. Minutes later, the ship behind us, *Max Schultz*, blew up with a roar.

We all now assumed we were under attack from enemy submarines, particularly as in the listening room they claimed to be picking up typical underwater noises. When the look-out on the forward gun also reported 'bubble tracks sighted', indicating torpedoes, our captain ordered 'Make ready depth charges' and seconds later 'Fire!' Four depth charges flew overboard in a high arc and the explosions shook us. Electric fuses jumped out and, as an unexpected side-effect, the electric steering gear was momentarily jammed. *Theodor Riedel* began to rotate like a circus horse and when the captain ordered us to put on lifejackets even I had butterflies in the stomach.

The other destroyers also believed we had submarines to contend with. Finally the lead destroyer radioed the order 'Report if fit for action'. There were three affirmative answers. The rest was silence. On that ice-cold night 270 men from *Leberecht Maass* lost their lives. From *Max Schultz* there were no survivors. 308 men went down with their ship.

Theodor Riedel headed back to Wilhelmshaven. When we left the Jade the following day we steamed through fields of dead men in blue uniform with seagulls perching on them. Many people find these white birds beautiful, part and parcel of a seaside holiday; I have never particularly liked the creatures and still do not today.

As the subsequent inquiry revealed, the cause of the fatality was not British submarines but British mines with which the enemy, on the tit-for-tat principle, had fouled our waters. *Leberecht Maass* would not have been sunk by the bomb from our own air force if the attacking plane had not at the same time forced it out of line. *Max Schultz* was probably hurrying to its assistance when it suffered the same fate. Only this can explain why the last two ships were lost and not the leading ones. The German plane had known nothing of the presence of our own destroyers in this sea area.

The supposed presence of torpedo tracks could only be put down to our crews' inexperience. Such false sightings occurred repeatedly — though later, as U-boat commander, I was occasionally to find such false sightings very helpful, particularly off the Florida coast. At all events, luck seemed to be with us this time, for the blow might equally have struck *Theodor Riedel*.

A few weeks later, at the beginning of April, 1940, the invasion of Norway took place under the code name of *Weserübung* (Exercise Weser). The reason was simple: we were short of raw materials, particularly the vital Swedish iron ore, which we needed for our armaments. It is mined near the Arctic Circle at Kiruna, and in the summer months it is shipped across the Baltic from the port of Lulea. In winter large parts of the Baltic are blocked by ice and the ore is then redirected by the 'ore railways' to the ice-free Norwegian port of Narvik, which is open all the year round. For the freighters there are two routes, the 'outer' leading through the open sea, and the 'inner' or protected route passing inside the string of Norwegian islands. In peacetime the latter is favoured during the stormy season, and in war it offers the further advantage of lying within Norwegian territorial waters and therefore being neutral, outside British control.

In the first months of the war the British had already succeeded in reducing German ore imports considerably through a blockade of the outer route. But Churchill, then First Lord of the Admiralty, had returned repeatedly to the idea of mining the protected inner route, thus forcing the German freighters out of neutral waters. (The British had considered something similar in the First World War, but dropped the plan for fear of Norwegian resistance and a reluctance to use force against a small neutral nation.) Now there was less concern at infringing neutrality. In February, 1940, for instance, the British destroyer *Cossack* penetrated Norwegian territorial waters and intercepted the German tanker *Altmark* in Jössing Fjord. Finally, at the end of March, after lengthy discussion, the British decided to mine the inner route.

As a naval strategist Grand Admiral Raeder foresaw this development and writes in his memoirs: '. . . As we in the navy had not given close thought to the prospect of an imminent war at sea, the question of how far Norwegian neutrality would assure the safety of our freighter traffic with Narvik had not been considered. Neither, as I soon noticed, had the political leadership considered this matter, nor Hitler himself, to whom such questions were naturally more remote. At the end of September, 1939, Admiral Canaris, head of German counter-espionage, told me of certain signs indicating a British intention to set foot in Norway. To meet this danger the only possible course was to forestall the British intentions.'

He reported to Hitler on every aspect of the question and continues: 'In considering the date for the occupation of Norway it had to be borne in mind that the destroyers which were to take in General Dietl's mountain troops required long, dark nights . . . I suggested to Hitler the next new moon and 7 April as invasion day. On 2 April Hitler ordered the execution of "Exercise Weser" for 9 April, 1940.'

On 6 April, we in *Theodor Riedel* were in Cuxhaven with other units when at 1400 we began to embark the mountain troops. In the course of the afternoon 1,200 men boarded the heavy cruiser *Admiral Hipper*, while *Theodor Riedel* and the other destroyers took on board 200 each, with their weapons, ammunition, equipment and motorcycles. To North Germans like us the speech of the men from Upper Bavaria, Styria and Tyrol was barely comprehensible. I showed them below to their sleeping quarters — on the bare deck. Ammunition boxes and the rest were made fast on the upper deck with steel wires. None of the men knew our destination and the decisions of the High Command, which had been kept extraordinarily secret, were unknown even to us officers, so that many believed we were going *gen Engelland*, as a well-known marching song proclaimed. Hardly anyone thought of Norway.

At 2200 *Admiral Hipper*, *Theodor Riedel* and three destroyers set sail. On 7 April the battleships *Scharnhorst* and *Gneisenau* and ten destroyers joined us by the lightship off the estuary of the Weser. In Bremerhaven they too had each embarked 200 mountain troops. No one suspected that those ships had a mere six days left before they would be sunk. Those ten destroyers left behind nothing but their fame, yet worldly fame is transitory and today not even their names are remembered — *Wilhelm Heidkamp*, *Hans Lüdemann*, *Hermann Künne* and others.

Steam was raised in all boilers and the pressure gauge approached the red mark. The fleet had sailed. At 1240 on 7 April the Fleet Commander in *Gneisenau* signalled 'Increase to 27 knots.' All crews were at action stations, for it was reckoned that the British Home Fleet would waylay us. The wind was SSW Force 5, increasing, moderate visibility, sea slight also increasing. In the course of the afternoon the weather deteriorated and developed into a full storm. The seas became so rough that the destroyers began pitching heavily. It was literally 'enough to make you sick' and the poor troops were vomiting all over the ship. A powerfully built second lieutenant was staggering near me. 'Rather a hail of bullets, a bad shoot-up, but no more seafaring, thanks!'

The destroyers tossed about, shipping cascades of water. We tried repeatedly to secure the ammunition boxes with more steel wires. In vain — they broke loose and the seas swept them overboard. One box slid up and fell on our depth-charge rack at the stern, striking the last bomb which rolled off and exploded. The destroyer following close behind us in line ahead disappeared for moments in a cascade of water.

On *Bernd von Arnim*, the destroyer ahead of us, a man was standing on a gun platform. A breaking sea surged up at him and swept him overboard. One moment he was standing there, the next, the sea had wrenched him down. I could observe the whole incident and, despite the storm, hear his cries for help. He was wearing a lifejacket, but little good did that do him — the destroyer slid past him in a flash.

A sailor was washed overboard from another destroyer, too, and on some other units the raging sea carried off unsuspecting mountain troops, who were never seen again. *Bernd von Arnim* even lost a second sailor in front of my eyes. They were all left behind in our wake.

Despite the storm, however, the destroyers kept steaming north according to orders. Meanwhile the goal of 'Exercise Weser' became clear to us all: Norway.

What we did not discover until later was that a force of British destroyers was battling its way through the stormy seas at the same time, on a similar errand. After much consideration the British had finally decided to land in Norway as foreseen and, for a start, to mine the West Fjord leading to Narvik. Their operation also carried a code name, 'Wilfred', and we missed each other only by hours. The British were already on the way home when the two fleets unexpectedly came in contact, neither one aware of the size of the other. For while several of our destroyers were losing personnel, a man was washed overboard from the British destroyer *Glow-worm*, whose skipper asked permission from the force commander to carry out a search. In the process, however, he lost contact with the other units. The sky was overcast, the air misty, visibility poor, and so it came about that a British destroyer suddenly ran into our 'Exercise Weser'.

We had no inkling of British warships in the area and the destroyer took us by surprise; I caught her very quickly in my gunsights and recognised by her superstructure that she was quite definitely an enemy ship. Our opponent turned on to a parallel course, intending in the heavy seas to start a running battle. My request for permission to open fire crossed with a signal from *Admiral Hipper*: 'Destroyers forbidden to fire!' The heavy cruiser itself took *Glow-worm* in its sights and opened fire with its four 20.3 cm guns at a distance of 8,400 metres.

After the second salvo a hit was scored on the destroyer's bridge. *Glow-worm* tried to avoid the fire by altering course and hiding behind a smoke screen but was soon heavily damaged. Her speed dropped. I saw the crew running to and fro and thought: 'She's finished, now they'll take to the boats.' Far from it, they were giving no thought at all to their rescue. When the heavy cruiser pushed through the smoke screen it unexpectedly found the British destroyer in front of it, bearing down with such power as she could still muster, intent on ramming. *Hipper* had no time to avoid the collision. At full speed *Glow-worm* rammed her 10,000-ton opponent and tore a 40-metre gash in its side. The heavily damaged British destroyer then withdrew. Minutes later she blew up. The battle was over.

For the first time I had learnt what bravery meant. The conduct of the British skipper, Lieutenant-Commander Gerard Roope, was superb.

Admiral Hipper, still operational despite its damaged hull, fished up the 40 survivors of the *Glow-worm*. Nets and Jacob's ladders were hung over the side and the men, covered with oil, climbed up and heaved themselves on board in the heavy seas. I no longer looked on them as enemies but simply as seamen in distress who must be helped at all costs. The brave skipper was also pulled out but lost his hold through exhaustion and fell back. Posthumously he was awarded the Victoria Cross (conferred only 24 times in the Royal Navy between 1939 and 1945).

On the same day our battle group was detached by the Fleet Commander. *Admiral Hipper*, the 2nd destroyer flotilla including *Theodor Riedel* and three further destroyers were to capture Trondheim. Early on 9 April we set course for the approach. At 0412 the Norwegian coastal battery at Hysnes opened fire. *Hipper* replied with the two after turrets. We ourselves did not take this exchange with the coastal battery very seriously, and on completion of the passage the mountain troops were landed, still green in the face and weak at the knees. But our friends recovered quickly; the moment they felt solid ground beneath their feet they stormed in like savages and captured the guns. As that lieutenant told me an hour later (the one who had preferred to fight a battle than go to sea again) the Norwegians had been taken completely by surprise. We had disturbed them at breakfast. Their coffee was still warm and our troops had helped themselves liberally to bread and jam.

Four destroyers had suffered considerable storm damage on passage, including damaged propeller-shaft bearings, and on top of that *Theodor Riedel* had grazed an underwater rock on the approach to Trondheim and torn its outer skin. Cautiously the captain ran the ship on to a sandy bottom in Strömmen Bay where, in the event of a British thrust into the fjord, it was to defend the approach with its guns and searchlights. Most of the crew had to go ashore, leaving on board only my gun crews and the anti-aircraft and torpedo personnel. At low water the ship sat high and dry. This went on for ten days, but things could have been worse. Fortunately no enemy ships appeared, though we were attacked by Swordfish torpedo-planes. They had taken off from the aircraft carrier *Furious* and flew directly at us. I watched with mixed feelings as their torpedoes glided towards us. They missed, exploded against the cliffs and all that hit us were the columns of water. One of the torpedoes slithered on to a projecting sandbank and stayed there. Of course we salvaged it and were surprised to find the first British torpedo that had fallen into our hands; its warhead had a magnetic fuse. But the British returned with 20 planes and dived on us like hornets. We opened up on them with everything we had and I was able to shoot down one plane. For this kill, among other things, I received my first decoration: the Iron Cross.

Almost two months later, on 8 June, 1940, *Theodor Riedel* was able to leave Trondheim and set course for home. 'Exercise Weser' was now a memory. The Allies had landed at three places in Norway but then withdrawn. The battle for Narvik had been decided in our favour. Norwegian forces had capitulated at Trondheim. But all in all the navy paid a heavy price. First, it lost the heavy cruiser *Blücher* in Oslo fjord, then the light cruisers *Karlsruhe* and *Königsberg* were sunk and, only a few days after the landing in Narvik, the ten German destroyers were destroyed there by the battleship HMS *Warspite* and other British forces. As for *Admiral Hipper*, it had been put out of action for a month.

Hardly was I back in Wilhelmshaven than I received the order to report to Dönitz at once at Sengwarden. He was in his office surrounded by a number of officers who all inspected me closely. Captain and Commodore Dönitz was in command of the U-boat arm. He impressed me at once. With the familiar *du* with which he addressed all junior officers, he asked me '*Willst Du zur U-Boot-Waffe?*' (Would you like to join the U-boat arm?) Such a question leaves no scope for long consideration, let alone a request for time to think it over. Dönitz was watching every reaction and I felt the others boring into my back with their eyes. Of that meeting all I

14

remember today are Dönitz's eyes — and my answer: '*Jawoll, Herr Kap'tän!*'

My experience on board *Theodor Riedel* was by no means wasted. Its captain was very skilful at manoeuvres and under him I had learnt a lot. As officer of the watch I had often to maintain station as number two in the flotilla; according to the captain this meant keeping directly astern of the ship ahead, at a distance of only 20 metres . . . while maintaining a speed of 30 knots. This experience saved my life several times later, as a U-boat skipper, for I knew how a destroyer handled and could therefore outmanoeuvre many a British destroyer.

3

My first command

In the Anglo–German naval treaty of 1935 Germany had voluntarily undertaken to restrict its naval armaments to 35 per cent of the British tonnage in warships in order to secure the peaceful coexistence of the two powers. U-boat tonnage, however, was the exception, for the permitted maximum was 45 per cent of British submarine tonnage; in 1938 this was extended by mutual agreement to parity with British tonnage. The peacetime German naval building programme provided, in the so-called Z-plan, for the construction of 249 U-boats in the period from 1938 to 1948.

Within the framework of the total building programme, which included battleships, 'pocket' battleships, aircraft carriers, cruisers and destroyers, U-boat construction naturally occupied only a small place, and was staggered over the coming years. The shipyards were mostly taken up with the construction of capital ships, which also claimed most of the finance available. At the beginning of 1939 the Z-plan was given the highest priority; in April, Hitler abrogated the Anglo–German naval treaty, and in September the Second World War broke out. After the experiences of the first months a change came about in strategic thinking: the Z-plan was abolished. Surface ships nearing readiness were completed, those just laid down were abandoned, and from the middle of 1941 all energies were to be transferred to the construction of U-boats and aircraft. Already when I joined the U-boat arm in June 1940, new craft were being turned out at the rate of 12 a month and rising . . . to 20 a month by late 1941. Personnel recruitment was also markedly on the increase.

All this does not alter the fact that the German U-boat arm entered the war with only 57 U-boats and of very varying types and sizes, from the 250-ton surface displacement coastal U-boat to the 740-ton long-distance type. Of these 57 boats only 46 were operational and still fewer, a mere 22, were suitable for the Atlantic. So it was that, contrary to general belief, at the start of the war only five to seven boats were on patrol in the Atlantic. According to Clausewitz war is the continuation of politics by other means. But seldom has a branch of the Services gone to war with such slender means, a circumstance for which the political leadership of that time bore responsibility.

In the winter of 1938/39 the Commodore U-Boats, Captain Dönitz, set up a strategic planning game: U-boats in the Atlantic. From this it emerged that for any hope of a successful action against British merchant shipping at least 300 front-line U-boats would be needed, namely 100 on patrol, 100 refitting and 100 en route to and from the operational area. In addition, an efficient means of communication would have to be developed so that a pack of U-boats could be directed by remote control over great distances. These findings were sent in writing, in August 1939, to the C-in-C Navy. The C-in-C Fleet, Admiral Böhm, supported the demands; Raeder, however, did not respond. A planning committee appointed by him urged that the vital British supply lines in the Atlantic should be attacked primarily by battle groups comprising strong surface forces supported by giant U-cruisers in a reconnaissance role and serving as gun platforms. The conventional U-boat with its torpedoes was hardly given a chance: in the naval high command its value was disputed, and Adolf Hitler, besides being impressed by the sheer size of battleships, was continually exposed to Göring's insistence on the importance of air-power in warfare. In view of these differences of opinion it is not surprising that, right into the war, the accelerated construction of U-boats repeatedly demanded by Dönitz was not fulfilled.

The naval historian Prof. Dr. Jurgen Rohwer has studied the U-boat building programme and its alleged delays. Initially (1936) six months were wasted through dilatory placement of contracts. He concludes, however, that even with maximum use of shipyard capacity, the availability of finance, and construction to the limit allowed by treaty, only 72 boats would have been produced as compared with the 57 actually achieved (though over 40 would have been of the larger types). 'In the first half-year of the war it would thereby have been possible to keep about 15 U-boats continually in the area west of England and the Bay of Biscay. In fact for the period from September,

1939, to March, 1940, the average number of U-boats in the Atlantic operational area was somewhat more than five.'

According to Rohwer an increase to around 300 boats could not have been achieved by 1942 within the framework of the accepted peacetime restrictions, even with a crash programme of U-boat construction. It would have required the suspension of all other ship-building and in any event would not have been accepted by Britain without corresponding concessions. However that may be, whether 300 boats or none, neither Churchill's memoirs nor the historical researches of the Americans could ever find an explanation for the inadequate support given to Dönitz. Not that the British were any better off. In September, 1939, the Royal Navy possessed 58 submarines ready for operations (from the 440-ton H class to the 1,520-ton minelayers), including the H and L types built in 1918/19(!) with restricted capability. Eleven submarines were under construction; a twelfth, the *Thetis*, sunk in an accident, was salvaged and put back into service under the name *Thunderbolt*. On the other side of the Channel, too, no great importance was attached to the submarine in a modern war at sea. The tendency was to invest in strong surface forces. But the British had to grapple with strategic problems that were almost the exact opposite.

Britain's fleet was basically a defence against a threat to her existence. Britain had no need to seek a conflict, the conflict was already latent in her insular situation. With a continually increasing population long since unable to feed itself on home soil produce, dependent on the import of food and raw materials from overseas, and re-exporting the latter as the finished products of a highly developed industry, Britain could only survive by protecting her global connections, the long ocean routes leading to and from her Dominions and Colonies.

But attack is often the best means of defence, and it has to be delivered against any source of danger to these lifelines. In defence of her insular existence Britain pursued her great campaigns against Spain, Holland and France on the seven seas. And for centuries, as far as back as the days of the cinque ports, the wine fleets and the Magna Carta of 1215 which, in its 41st article, promised merchants safe escort to and from English harbours, Britain had been accustomed in times of crisis to collect her merchant ships together and protect them with armed forces. Thus the convoy system arose long ago, was perfected in two world wars, and is still of value today, as Nato manoeuvres show.

When the Second World War broke out superiority at sea still lay with the British. The German *Kriegsmarine*, with its long-term and interrupted construction plans, had little to put up against the Royal Navy. Apart from the problematical *Luftwaffe* the only means of blockading the island and to sever or interrupt Britain's supply-lines remained the U-boat. The possibility of disappearing from the surface and hiding in the depths gave the U-boat a certain advantage over surface ships.

Admittedly the days of an Otto Weddingen, whose U 9 had sunk three British armoured cruisers at a blow in 1914 (*Hogue*, *Aboukir* and *Cressy*), so giving his name to the first U-boat flotilla of the new German navy — those days were long past. Between 1918 and 1939 effective means of defence against the U-boat had been developed, and every nation closely guarded its secrets. Sensitive detection gear was developed, so was an improved depth charge; fast U-hunters and destroyers kept the U-boat from its prey and the aeroplane was ultimately to become the U-boat's most dangerous opponent. In the First World War U-boats had come more or less unconcernedly to the surface. The new weapons and systems did everything to force them down — and keep them down.

Nonetheless, the new German U-boat arm had already made its mark, both in individual actions and attacks on convoys. In the first nine months of the Second World War U-boats sank 300 enemy freighters and tankers, mostly British and French, totalling 1,137,000 gross register tons, which represented a carrying capacity of one and a half times that figure. That seemed to us at the time a lot of shipping, for no one could foresee that before long we would be sinking almost a million tons in a single month.

Some commanders had made a particular name for themselves, like Herbert Schultze, Joachim Schepke, Otto Schuhardt who sank the aircraft carrier *Courageous*, Otto Kretschmer who later became the most successful U-boat commander of the Second World War, and above all Günther Prien who achieved the greatest propaganda effect — to name only a few. On 14 October, 1939, Prien in U 47 had penetrated the base of the British Home Fleet at Scapa Flow. In this operation, which had been prepared down to the last detail by Dönitz himself, he sank the battleship *Royal Oak*. Among the 883 dead was Rear Admiral Blagrove, commanding the second British battle squadron. This sensational success soon after the outbreak of war was fully exploited by propaganda and put the U-boat arm in the centre of public interest, while it gave Prien colossal popularity and the nickname 'The Bull of Scapa Flow'.

The first false note was struck with the mistaken sinking of the British passenger liner *Athenia* by U 30 in the North Atlantic on the very day that Britain declared war. Lieutenant Fritz Lemp had taken the ship for an auxiliary cruiser and lost no time in torpedoing her. The 1,300 survivors, among them citizens of the still neutral United States, were rescued by other craft. On the German side this error was never admitted, as initially it was still desired to adhere to the prize regulations agreed by the sea-faring nations under international law. According to these, U-boats were not allowed to sink merchant ships without warning; even when they were armed they could only be sunk after examination for contraband, unless they engaged in warlike actions. After such a sinking, the U-boat had to ensure the safety of the civilian crew — how it did this was its own affair. These arrangements, however, were so impracticable that in 1937 an exemption was made: merchant ships sailing under the protection of warships of a belligerent nation might be sunk without warning. Hence the saying arose: to enter a convoy is to perish in it.

Strict adherence to prize regulations put German U-boats in grotesque situations dangerous to themselves, until matters intensified on both sides. The exceptional case became normal. Strongly armed convoys faced U-boats which attacked without hesitation, particularly after Hitler declared a total blockade of the British Isles in August, 1940. The battle of the Atlantic developed without restraint. In the first six months of 1940, 900,000 gross register tons were reported sunk.

This was the situation when I came to the U-boat arm in the summer of 1940. Of course there had been losses on both sides; in the first nine months of the war ours amounted to 23 boats. Some had struck mines, most had been sunk by British destroyers. Coldly expressed, a loss rate of 2.5 boats a month could be accepted, particularly as 13 to 20 new U-boats were coming into commission monthly, and provided that the personnel problem could be resolved — and it was resolved, despite the fact that as a matter of principle only volunteers were admitted, with high demands being made on the applicants' state of health. 'Fit for

(*above*) *1. Grand Admiral Dönitz broods on a chart at his HQ, with staff officers.*
(*below*) *2. Admiral Sir Max Horton, C-in-C, Western Approaches, in his underground office.*

3. Periscope watch aboard U 333. Peter Cremer wears his captain's emblem: a white hat.

U-boat service' really meant something. The aura of the U-boat arm, supported by propaganda which mentioned nothing of the shadow side, exerted a powerful attaction on young people.

If one speaks of a certain superiority of the submarine or *Unterseeboot* in being able to hide under water, one must in the same breath mention its weaknesses. Strictly speaking, they were not pure 'under-sea-boats' but submersibles which, for shorter or longer periods, were kept 'hovering' over a watery abyss. If this period were exceeded they were obliged to surface to gasp for air and charge the batteries. How and why, we shall see in a moment.

The U-boat has a double hull, a strong inner and a thin outer one. The inner, called the pressure hull, contains all the functional elements such as the command system in the control room, the engines, the underwater weapons, the W/T office, and space for the crew who live a boxed-in existence between all these things. The steel pressure hull is strong enough to withstand the water pressure which, for every 10 metres of depth, increases by 15 pounds per square inch, or one atmosphere. The boat is designed for a maximum diving depth, and if it exceeds this it is crushed like an egg shell. The limit of the diving depth is governed by the strength of the pressure hull. The diving depths of the different U-boat types in the Second World War ranged theoretically between 50 and 250 metres. In fact they were exceeded at times until the frame members began to crack.

The considerably thinner outer hull, which with its superstructure gives the boat its shape, mainly contains the ballast or diving tanks. For the outer hull water pressure presents no problem. When submerged, the ballast tanks are flooded and the inside pressure equals the pressure of the surrounding water. When the boat is surfaced the bottom of the ballast tank is open and air, kept in from above, prevents the water entering. The boat is floating on an air bubble. To dive, the air is allowed to escape at the top through vents. Water takes its place — the boat sinks and disappears. To surface again, one method is to blow out the tanks with compressed air. This might make the boat come up unnecessarily quickly, using up a lot of compressed air, and hence electrical energy, in the process. The other way is to proceed dynamically and steer the boat to the surface with the hydroplanes; here the diesel engines take over the work, expelling the water from the tanks with their exhaust gases. This latter, however, was not the usual way of surfacing. (The horizontal hydroplanes, fore and aft, work as in an airship, steering the boat up and down.)

So-called trimming tanks within the pressure hull, whose water content can be adjusted to bring about and compensate weight changes, hold the boat in equilibrium — hovering in the ideal neutral buoyancy state — so that it maintains its diving depth and neither tends to rise nor sink. But a U-boat is easier to keep in balance when it is moving. Control is easily lost when it is stopped and it can slowly sink to the sea-bed. At times, then, the boat is so sensitive that even a small change of weight, such as the movement of one man from bow to stern, is enough to throw it out of balance. When it is being hunted and lies still so as not to betray its presence by pumping or flooding, with consequent noises, it must be properly trimmed or 'balanced'. Its weight changes continually, through the consumption of fuel oil and fresh water alone, and at times the change is quite sudden (as after the firing of torpedoes), when it becomes lighter by a matter of tons and must be quickly stabilised so as not to surge upward and betray itself, particularly as on such occasions it is only at periscope depth. The preservation of the trim, the balancing out of the stability, calls for a whole system of pumps, circuits, valves, hand-wheels and more — and practice in their use.

The U-boat is propelled in two ways. Above water by diesel engines, below water by electric motors. On the surface the diesels charge the batteries. When submerged, the diesels cannot be used because they consume fresh air. The electric motors derive their energy from the batteries which are heavy and bulky, limited in size only by the narrowness of the boat. Under heavy loads their energy is soon exhausted and the boat is obliged to surface to recharge them. The same holds for the fresh air, which diminishes underwater and must be replenished. Those, in broad outline, are the strengths and weaknesses of the serviceable diving-boat types with which we had to deal in the Second World War.

The submerged U-boat is connected with the upper world by a periscope, a telescope 14 metres long that can be raised and lowered. There is an attack periscope with an all-round view, its disadvantages being a dead angle immediately above the boat, but in addition there is a periscope for aerial targets which covers this sector. For a close observer above water its comparatively large head makes it more easily recognised. In naval German we called the periscope *Spargel* (asparagus). Periscope depth, that is the diving depth at which a periscope could be extended above the surface, was between 12 and 14 metres. The upper edge of the conning tower, the highest point of the boat, was then about 6 metres below water.

In the second six months of 1940 U-boats sank about 1,500,000 gross register tons.

After six months' training, which included a simulated escape with life-saving apparatus, from a sunken U-boat in a basin, I was appointed commander of U 152. It was the last boat in the II-D series, an improved coastal U-boat of 314 tons displacement on the surface. These boats, 44 metres long, were on the small side and were known in naval jargon as 'canoes'. They could dive to 150 metres, were very well designed and seaworthy. At an economical speed they could cover 5,600 sea miles but at most they could only remain four weeks en route before their supplies ran out. On the U 152 I flew my first commander's pennant: a narrow white affair with the Iron Cross.

Everything was new: pennant, boat, commander. The boat lay ready at the pier in Kiel. The commander went on board to gain experience with this small type before being entrusted, perhaps, with a larger boat.

I was received on the upper deck by the chief engineer-officer. Cautiously I climbed down into the conning-tower hatch and was greeted with the characteristic U-boat fug: the stink of diesel oil mixed with cooking smells, the exhalations of fusty clothing and stale air. As soon as I held on to something my hands acquired a film of grease which it was better to leave and wipe off later with a lump of cotton waste, as every contact with pipes or other metal smeared them again.

For me, in the 'stove-pipe', a new life had begun. One's whole existence had to be adapted to the U-boat, eating, sleeping, going on watch, all in the narrowest space, in closest physical contact, in closest relationship with the steel hull. There can hardly be a branch of the services in which a man must rely so much on others, tolerate their habits and subordinate himself to the team. Comradeship and a strong feeling of solidarity were characteristic of the U-boat service and indispensable for successful operations under difficult conditions. My crew comprised 25 men, including three officers. As usual they were all volunteers, selected from serving ranks and ratings in the navy. At that time every kind of specialist skill was represented in the U-boat arm. Some of those men were with me throughout the whole war and I shall revert to this in greater detail. We were all dressed in grey–green leather, a suitable uniform which made us outwardly all alike, the commander only being distinguished from the others by his white cap. This white cap, which in the course of time became anything but white, was actually contrary to regulations, but had established itself in the navy. The commander could thereby be recognised at a distance, particularly at night on the darkened bridge.

The tests and acceptance trials of U 152 took only a few weeks. Service followed in the 24th U-flotilla, a training unit, first in Danzig, later in Memel. These harbours in the eastern Baltic were far from the actual scene of hostilities and afforded immediate access to considerable depths of over 100 metres in the comparatively shallow Baltic.

My experiences of war and the knowledge of weapons I brought with me were naturally very useful. Handling the U-boat itself, in all situations, with all the technical tricks, had to be learnt and rehearsed until one could do it in one's sleep — and these covered every conceivable eventuality from normal manoeuvres to crash dives, when water poured into the tanks and the boat disappeared from the surface in 25 seconds or less. Off the harbour of Memel, with its broad entrance flanked by a mole, a heavy ground swell would get up under a north-west wind, offering a hard test to future U-boat men trying to find their sea legs. The little U-boats pitched and rolled, and played at standing on end, while everyone inside clung on desperately to pipes and steel projections — a foretaste of how these boats would behave in the heavy storms of the North Atlantic.

On top of this, the engine-room staff chose to enjoy themselves venting the fuel oil tanks inside the boat, which helped accustom the novice commander to what lay in store: nauseating vapours in a pitching, tossing boat. In harbour, on the other hand, the entire crew lived in roomy accommodation ships, and there at least things were made as tolerable as possible for them. But the actual object of the flotilla was to train the commanders to attack. Day after day we had to toil away at attacking, running out in the morning to the firing area and returning always in the evening.

The natural U-boat weapon was the torpedo. The German torpedo had a diameter of 53 centimetres, weighed about 1½ tons and carried an explosive charge of 300 kilos. The charge was contained in a detachable warhead and the firing mechanism was primed only after the torpedo had covered a certain distance. So nothing could happen inside the boat. The torpedo propulsion no longer depended on compressed air, as formerly, but on an electric motor to turn the propeller. There were two standard types, the G7a and the G7e. While the first (oil–air) could make 44 knots over short distances, and at 30 knots could effect a long-range shot of up to 14 kilometres, the electric G7e was the most prevalent; it would make about 30 knots over 6 kilometres. Fast as an arrow in flight, it was an extraordinarily complicated and, as we shall see, sensitive instrument, looked after by specialists who serviced, regulated and set it to the required depth, etc.

The behaviour of torpedoes varied. Before they were taken on board they were tested for optimum accuracy at test stations and experimental units on measured stretches, where every deviation was recorded. In addition, every torpedo was given a service certificate or warranty, a document that accompanied it on board. There it was treated like a raw egg, to be taken out of the tube every few days and, in layman's language, have its vital parts examined. The tube lay inside the pressure hull and was shut at both ends by a bow cap and rear doors.

The price of a torpedo corresponded, in present-day terms, to that of a medium-sized house. Obviously one had to consider, when confronted with a difficult choice, whether it was worth firing a torpedo or whether, circumstances permitting, the prey could be destroyed by gunfire or other explosives.

Such considerations, however, did not concern us during training. Day after day the exercising flotilla went out to the practice area. There the individual boats spread out on to the map squares allotted them by the officer in charge and tried to plant their arrow-swift 'eels' on a target ship crossing the area. Sometimes a whole convoy was set up and the exercising flotilla became a tactical flotilla, making the assault as a pack.

Let us imagine that U152 has three bow torpedo tubes, all loaded. The tubes are rigid, and one aims with the whole boat. The boat dives, the target ship approaches, growing bigger and bigger. The commander has her in the cross-wires of the periscope. He notes the course of the enemy if she is not zig-zagging in convoy, estimates speed and distance, aims off and starts the attack . . .

'Tube One, stand by for underwater firing.'

Below in the boat the order is passed on like an echo. Otherwise there is silence, everyone listening tensely. The water pours gurgling into the tube, the pressure is equalised. There is a click — a lever falls into place showing operation completed.

'Open bow cap.'

'Bow cap open,' comes the reply.

'Tube One ready!'

'Ready!'

'Tube One — Fire!'

A slight shudder can be felt: the torpedo has left the boat. It has been mailed!

While the commander stays glued to the periscope, below him in the control room the chief quartermaster is holding the stopwatch. 'Five seconds — ten seconds — fifteen seconds — '

It seems an eternity. What's up? Did I get the figures wrong? 'This won't do . . .'

' — twenty seconds — twenty-five seconds — '

There! Target ship signals a hit. The expensive house has not missed after all.

Apart from this, nothing happens. The enemy does not go sky-high. He neither shifts nor stirs. With its easily spotted red and white dummy-practice head the torpedo has run beneath the target ship, trailing a foaming bubble-path; losing speed, it emits a cloud of smoke. Meanwhile recovery boats are following to fish out the valuable item, all one and a half tons, as soon as it has lost momentum and come to the surface.

It is only a game, nobody loses a hair — though the commander would have to face a chewing-out if he missed.

But what of a 'live' situation in which the enemy is struck by the high-explosive warhead and again nothing happens? When the enemy is not even shaken, but keeps course and speed and seems not to notice the attacking U-boat? Then the great guessing game begins: can it be sabotage?

It seems hardly credible, but such occurrences actually happened and plunged the U-boat arm at the beginning of the war into a serious crisis of confidence. When it came to the point, those extremely expensive instruments, the torpedoes, had simply failed. On 30 October, 1939, for instance, U 56 (Wilhelm Zahn) encountered the heaviest British battleships, *Rodney*, *Nelson* and *Hood*, attacked and at the most scratched their outer paint. All three escaped. After the unreliability of the torpedoes had been established in further individual actions, 'Exercise Weser', the invasion of Norway in the spring of 1940, proved a huge disappointment.

Among the 32 U-boats assigned to the Exercise, some of them under well-known commanders like Günther Prien, Otto Kretschmer and Herbert Schultze, contacts with the enemy led repeatedly to wholly negative results. U 47 (Prien) made hits on two cruisers, transports and the battleship *Warspite*, but all sailed on undamaged. The old *Warspite* even sailed into the sights of U 46, U 37 and U 38 without suffering any serious damage. Off Narvik U 25 made a fruitless attack on an entire destroyer flotilla. U 30 (Fritz Lemp) landed his torpedoes on the battleship *Barham* where the impact was even heard — but the witnesses reported that nothing happened.

In his book *Ten Years and Twenty Days*, Dönitz writes that the main weapon, the torpedo, was to a considerable extent unusable in operations. In at least 25 per cent of all shots there were torpedo failures. Many reported misses were later found to have been hits that simply failed to detonate.

Confidence in the torpedo began to fade. The nervous strain on commander and crew had its effect. Prien, the hero of Scapa Flow, had incurred a severe depth-charge pursuit on account of a torpedo failure, and exclaimed bitterly that he could not be expected 'to fight with a wooden gun'. The tried and tested men of the U-boat arm were seized for the first time by something like depression. Dönitz himself went from one flotilla to another and spoke to the crews, who all knew him personally, so that the crisis was gradually surmounted, particularly as court-martial proceedings lasting six weeks, against all the officials responsible for the technical failures, brought the causes to light — or came very close to doing so.

They were of a physical nature and concerned almost exclusively the electro-torpedo G7e with which the torpedo testing station at Eckernförde had been experimenting for years — in our latitudes, in favourable weather and calm seas. It emerged that previously unrecognised factors affected detonation and depth-keeping. Amongst other things the antimagnetic field of ships, generated as a counter to the magnetic mine, impaired the activation of the electric proximity pistol in the warhead; this was supposed to be activated by the magnetic field of the target and then detonate the torpedo, but in many cases it failed. The high air-pressure usually arising in a U-boat on long submerged passages was said to disturb the sensitive depth-keeping mechanism. The steering gear was faulty and failed to find the target; in short, the whole thing was fraught with snags.

Of course, everything was done to cure the faults. But up to 1942, even after many trials, setbacks and improvements, there were still failures. Later we were given a brand-new torpedo, certain to hit: the self-steering, acoustic 'TV' or *Zaunkönig* ('wren'). Two sounds receivers were built into the head which picked up the propeller noises of moving ships. If the sounds were louder on one side, the torpedo's rudder automatically moved to alter course towards it. The torpedo snaked of its own accord in the direction of the noises, finally to strike the ship from astern. We shall see that this eel, too, was more than capricious, often running unpredictably; I was to have no end of trouble with it.

Moreover, a 'surface-searching' torpedo with pre-programmed zig-zag course was invented. Fired at venture into a convoy, it would most probably hit one ship or another.

In May, 1941, U 152 was ordered from Memel to Trondheim in Norway, which I already knew. When the accompanying patrol boats and those that had guided us through the mine-fields had taken their leave and steamed away we were on our own for the first time — a small dot in the wide North Sea. Not an aircraft appeared, not a convoy came in sight. Only a single mine floated past and was detonated, as we had learnt to do in the destroyer. Without particular incidents we ran into Trondheim amid beautiful fjord and mountain scenery. Our new base offered enough variety but no real contact took place with the Norwegians, not at any rate as we had imagined it. The population remained reserved towards us. The attack routine proved no different than in the Baltic except that the depth of the fjords, which dropped steeply to 200 metres, had to be borne in mind, as the maximum depth for the U 152 — which remained a training boat throughout the war — was 150 metres.

Meanwhile, as though in peacetime, I had become a trained and experienced U-boat commander, and a whole year had passed. Later, when there were more new boats but also more losses, training time was curtailed — and this would have its consequences.

On 7 March, U 47 (Günther Prien) had been lost, destroyed, as emerged only later, by the British destroyer *Wolverine*. A few days after that U 99 (Otto Kretschmer) was heavily damaged by the destroyer *Walker*, but at the last moment was able to scuttle itself. At the same time and place the destroyer *Vanoc* rammed a further U-boat: U 100 (Joachim Schepke). This meant that three prominent U-boat commanders of the early days had been lost in the North Atlantic through convoy battles. Only Kretschmer, the most successful of all U-boat commanders in the Second World War, was rescued and taken prisoner.

In the first six months of 1941 German U-boats sank 1,458,232 GRT of enemy shipping.

In July, 1941, I was transferred to command the operational boat, U 333.

4
U 333's first kills

To say that I 'assumed command' of the new boat would be an over-statement, for it did not yet exist. What was taking shape on the slipway at Emden was intended to become a U-boat. At the moment it was merely a torso (strictly secret) of 20.5 millimetre-thick sheet steel, being filled up with every imaginable object: cables, power units, items ranging from the gyro compass to the torpedo-aiming gear, from the press-button steering to the tip-up bunk, not to mention the echo-sounder, signalling lamp, radio set, electric cooker, crockery, blankets, and so on. Immensely long power cables twined round one another like skeins of wool. But the experienced shipyard workers calmly sorted everything out and day by day the new boat emerged from this welter of parts.

My chief engineer and the engine-room personnel that I had personally selected climbed around inside and memorised every corner, frame and bulkhead down to the last screw. It reminded me of the box of bricks I had loved playing with as a boy and I, too, was soon finding my way around without blueprints and drawings. We all grew up, as it were, with the boat. Officially it was called 'constructional training' and was deliberate.

Twenty-four hours before the boat was due to be commissioned it was still looking like nothing on earth. Much amusement was aroused at the time by a cartoon depicting the launch of a half completed ship in which bare ribs showed where there were still missing sections of the ship's side, with the caption: 'No matter, a deadline is a deadline!' But I was not exactly in a mood for laughter, and doubted whether 'my' boat would be ready on time. Finally a posse of painters arrived and painted over everything — but everything — and the cursing crew meticulously had to scratch off the thick coat of paint from levers and wheels, switches, valves and seals.

However, this boat, which until then had been known merely as a number in the shipyard's order book, was handed over and put into service on 25 August, 1941. It was a VII-C boat, developed from the Type VII of which over 600 were built. Medium-sized, readily manoeuvrable, reliable and exceptionally seaworthy, this was *the* U-boat of the Second World War and caused the enemy a lot of headaches. (Almost twenty years later one of these boats was still on active service in Norway. Then it was returned as a gift to the German Federal Republic on the express condition that 'maintenance and fitting display would be guaranteed' to the war veteran. Today it is stationed on dry land before the naval memorial at Laboe.)

The VII-C boat displaced 760 tons on the surface, measured 66.5 metres and, with twin screws and diesel engines delivering 3,000 h.p., could make 17 knots or more on the surface; and at economical speed it had a range of about 9,500 sea miles, the distance roughly from the North Sea exit to the Panama Canal, or to Brazil or West Africa and back without refuelling. It had four bow torpedo tubes and one in the stern, and generally took 14 torpedoes on patrol. The VII-C boat was impressive, and after long months in a 'canoe' I felt like a man transferring from a VW 'beetle' to a Mercedes.

The chief engineer and I had to sign a heap of papers. With my final signature the boat was discharged from the responsibility of the shipyard and handed over to the navy, in this case to me. After the formalities of commissioning it was now called U 333. But this number could not be shown on the outside, for its identity had to be concealed, so we did like all the other boats and chose a symbol instead, only recognisable by initiates. There were already quite a few such signs, from civic coats of arms to snowmen, from unicorns to the Olympic rings. Schepke had chosen a tiger, Prien a bull, of course, and Kretschmer a horseshoe, which brought him personal luck — he survived. All these emblems on the conning tower were not strictly speaking as laid down by regulations, and before one put to sea they were supposed to disappear. For the rest, officialdom shut both eyes. My crew and I decided to have three little fishes painted on the conning tower. I cannot now remember exactly why; perhaps 'Three Little Fishes', an American hit tune popular at that time, gave us the idea — in the German navy we did not listen only to 'folk' music.

There followed a meal with the shipyard management, a delegation of workers and the garrison commander of Emden. On the following day I took U 333 from Emden through the North Sea–Baltic canal to Kiel where we were attached for the coming months to the 5th U-flotilla, again purely a training flotilla.

Next, the technical officers of the U-boat acceptance unit paid me a visit on board, headed by a naval captain who was an experienced U-boat commander from the First World War. Since the start of the new U-boat arm in 1935 he had been recalled to duty and he now set about examining the new boat in detail. Not everything endured his critical scrutiny and the engine-room staff had to change round a few things, principally in the pipelines. What most impressed our visitors was the first-class welding on the hull. It was literally vital for survival and had to withstand water pressure of up to 25 kilograms per square centimetre — that is 10 tons to the square metre, at any rate up to the set limit of 250 metres diving depth. There was *some* safety margin, and in certain circumstances some of us took a chance and reached yet greater depths without incurring damage.

Once every man had been made familiar with every possible accident and engine malfunction, and with every conceivable emergency, U 333 was passed on to the technical training group for operational U-boats. This group exercised in the Baltic between Hela, Bornholm and Eckernförde, and was intended to acclimatise newly-commissioned boats to operational conditions. Thus we were exposed (at a safe distance of course) to the detonation of a live depth charge in order to give the new hands an idea of its ear-splitting explosion. One of the drills practised again and again was the crash dive, in which the boat had to disappear from the surface in 28 seconds or less and go to a depth of 20 metres. On the 'alarm' order I always opened the air vents to the diving tanks myself, whereupon the air was expelled through the top and the water came in below to make the boat dive. The men on the bridge jumped inside through the conning-tower hatch as best they could; as commander I jumped in last, when the water was already gurgling round the edge of the tower. There were two ladders, one from the bridge to the conning tower and one from the tower into the control room; we simply let ourselves fall down them rather than take them step by step. Usually there were five men on the bridge. Anyone not sliding down fast enough got the next treading on his head. Certainly that was risky, and did not always pass off without injuries, but it was the lesser evil.

On the other hand the fall of a colleague who vanished below at top speed during an air attack in the Bay of Biscay struck a comic note. He was inboard when the boat dived but in the hurry his white cap was left behind, bobbing on the waves. The British fished it up and had to be content with that.

As I was a fully trained gunner, our target practice could teach me nothing new. U 333 carried an 88 mm gun on the upper deck, its muzzle shut off with a water-tight plug, and on the platform behind the bridge a 2 cm AA gun. Though it practised attacks on convoys and had duels with destroyers, the training group neglected anti-aircraft defence. Aircraft meant little to us at the time, and although the British had already announced the destruction of a U-boat by an aircraft fitted with radar, we doubted it, just as we also underestimated the problem of radio location which was soon to become a deadly threat to us. The wireless operators practised the transmission and receipt of coded radio signals, which were later to be the sole, tenuous link connecting us with home, and the bridle with which the C-in-C U-boats guided us from a distance.

The year 1941 was drawing to a close. In November U 81 (Friedrich Guggenberger) sank the aircraft carrier *Ark Royal*. Shortly afterwards U 331 (Hans-Dietrich von Tiesenhausen) destroyed the battleship *Barham*. These were single successes; as a whole the bag of German U-boats in the second half of 1941 was considerably less than before — 713,658 GRT. There was still a relatively small number of U-boats in the Atlantic, patrolling an extensive area, and our air reconnaissance was inadequate.

On 7 December, 1941, the Japanese attacked Pearl Harbor and the USA declared war on Japan. Four days later, Germany and Italy declared war on the USA. For the U-boats in the Atlantic this altered the situation less than might be imagined as, in practice, the USA had already been engaged against us. Not only had they handed over to the British 50 admittedly obsolete destroyers, circumvented their neutrality laws to deliver war material, extended their so-called security zone far to the east and occupied Iceland, but they had also used their naval forces to protect the convoys fetching war material from the USA. Although Germany wanted in principle to avoid war with the USA and Hitler forbade any attack on those forces, a first incident had occurred with the US destroyer *Greer*, and others followed. After the American Secretary to the Navy, Knox, had ordered German U-boats to be fired on (15 September, 1941) an open conflict was only a matter of time. American historians (Langer and Glaeson) take an ironic view of the intervening period and express surprise not at the loss of a few American ships, but at there not being many more.

Our particular problem, however, was to locate the convoys at all. Naturally the Atlantic convoys used definite routes and ones as short as possible, but the shortest were a good 3,000 sea miles. Everything had spread to a gigantic scale. The navy, which had jealously been denied an aerial reconnaissance facility of its own, possessed no long-distance aircraft to survey the area from above, and the low field of vision of a U-boat is very restricted. If, despite everything, a U-boat did succeed in latching onto a convoy, it was not itself allowed to attack but had to maintain contact and report position, course and speed by radioed short-code signal to the C-in-C U-boats, who would call up all the boats within reach. On the other hand, later, while we were still all unsuspecting, the enemy was quickly able to locate these signals transmitted on short wave and work out the position of the U-boat. Thus, not only was the boat itself endangered but the convoy could simply be diverted away from the threatened area.

To patrol the entire Atlantic Ocean would have needed shoals of U-boats which we simply did not possess. The British Ministry of Information subsequently maintained, in a brochure intended for the public (*Merchantmen at War*, HMSO, London, 1944, p. 93), that 'in the spring of 1942 over 250 [U-boats] were at the same time in the Atlantic . . . they hunted in packs of a dozen or even 20 and 25.' This incredible estimate was far from the truth. Perhaps it was exaggerated in order to justify the shipping losses to an anxious public. For us the reality looked much worse. U-boat construction had indeed been accelerated, but we also had suffered losses (67 boats since the beginning of the war, according to the official report, *United States, Submarine Losses, World War II*) and a number were still undergoing trials.

After July, 1941, when the Russian campaign seemed to have been decided in our favour, U-boat construction became a priority — together with aircraft. But as of 1 January, 1942, the navy possessed a mere 91 U-boats, of which 26 were in the Mediterranean area, 6 west of Gibraltar and 4 in Norway. This left 55 for the tonnage war in the Atlantic; of these a good 33 were under repair in the shipyard and held up owing to a labour shortage, 11 were on the way to and from the operational area, leaving 11 on active patrol in the area itself. So after more than two years of war it was not 250 U-boats that we had in the Battle of the Atlantic, as the British claimed, but a paltry 11.

At the end of 1941 I was attached to the 'Ziethen' group operating in the Atlantic. On 31 December we were north of the British Isles in the passage between the Shetlands and the Faroes which I had chosen to reach the open Atlantic from the North Sea. We were proceeding on the surface at reduced speed against a broken sea and were keeping eyes and ears open so as to meet all the dangers which might break in on us at any moment from the sea or air. At the New Year the sea's motion became so unpleasant that we were forced to proceed submerged, much to the satisfaction of the off-duty watch, though their talk quickly died away when we heard the first depth charges, which were not however meant for us. In fact, we reached the open Atlantic unmolested and steered purposefully westwards towards our goal.

Towards our goal — at least in the wider sense. I had long since opened the sealed envelope containing my orders from the C-in-C, known only to the sender. I was on my way to a map square allotted to me, an area in the North Atlantic, fairly far to the west, almost below Greenland and on the classic route of the big convoys between the USA and Britain. The Atlantic is large and three fifths of the earth are covered with water. Thinking on a large scale, therefore, the naval high command had divided all the seas into map squares and marked them with letters and numbers. The two letters of my assignment designated an area roughly the size of the Federal Republic and France put together. The individual squares were subdivided nine times, and these subdivisions again nine times, and those once more nine times so that gradually quite a dense net was created with a mesh-width of only six sea miles. An invisible net, of course, in whose meshes friend and foe would get caught. A mesh might be labelled, for instance, BC 8524. It was a method of naval warfare aiming to get a tactical grip on the ocean and everything afloat in it.

That is how it looks on paper. If, however, one looks beyond this net and faces the reality, nothing is left but a boat lost in the immensity of the ocean, a dot with a limited field of view, lonely

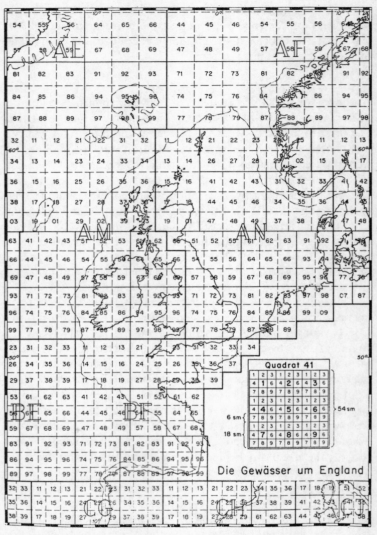

Squared chart of British waters used by U-boat captains for grid references.

as a leaf hovering over a watery abyss better not thought about: for it is 3,000 to 4,000 metres deep.

And so we sailed westwards in U 333 under a low wintery blanket of cloud, rolling and pitching while the diesels puttered monotonously and everyone was busy with his job, in the conning tower, the control room, the engine room, at the electrically-controlled helm, at the radio and sound detectors, in the torpedo space, including the cook at the electric stove; he only cooked but he was so important for the morale of the crew, for, as Napoleon remarked, an army marches on its stomach.

Meanwhile the watch was changed every four hours and some of the men going off duty crept into the still-warm bunks of those relieving them, for a permanent sleeping space was not available for everyone. And from time to time the captain glanced thoughtfully at the course marked on the chart and kept watch for the enemy. Hardly were we in the Atlantic than I heard U 701 reporting a convoy. The New Year, 1942, was starting well.

Night-time on 2 January, we surfaced again. I was standing on the bridge and could not believe my eyes when suddenly through my binoculars I saw a cloud of black smoke which quickly dispersed against the dark night sky. Visibility was good. I dried the wet lenses, looked again — and there she was again, my first opponent (Had the vessel been neutral, her display of lights, and her national colours painted on her hull would have made this clear.) Slowly the outline of a tanker revealed itself, still too far away to get in a shot. Behind me the sky was black and overcast, but the air was cold and clear, and by chance the moon came out of the clouds. I turned at maximum speed towards the tanker, offering her a slim silhouette — and then I had her about 400 metres in front of me.

A lot has been written about how a submarine commander feels when he sees his first opponent in the crosswires of his sights. He is compared to a hunter who has his first royal stag before his gun and trembles with excitement. With me it was nothing like that. I was neither excited nor ice-cold. For me it was part of a well rehearsed routine, culminating in the deadly dialogue:

'Tubes 1 to 3, stand by for spreading salvo.'

Factually, coolly, position, speed and distance are fed into the fire-control apparatus for the torpedoes, as into a computer.

'Open bow caps.'

'Bow caps open.'

'Tubes 1, 2 and 3 ready.'

'Ready.'

'Salvo — Fire!'

A shudder runs through the boat as all three 'eels' leave their tubes at two-second intervals. Suddenly the boat has become lighter by 4.5 tons and must be counter-trimmed forward at once. Everything goes like clockwork, just as it did on the attacking course in the Baltic. But what is this?

One of us is not playing the game, not sticking to the rules. The tanker has no intention of keeping still and allowing herself to be despatched. She has, to stay with huntsman's language, smelt powder. Despite the darkness her look-out probably spotted the tell-tale tracks and the captain has enough experience of war to turn towards them at once. All three torpedoes miss by a hair's breadth.

On top of that, the ship now comes towards me and I have no choice but to turn. From the new position I try to give her a stern shot and call: 'Tube 5 ready and fire!' Nothing doing — the second watch officer has 'stepped on the gas' too soon and the fourth 'eel' is already on its way. The heavy pitching and rolling of the boat prevents the tube being reloaded. Another miss.

The tanker meanwhile is so taken aback that she forgets to bring her gun to bear, but radioes continually for help, giving the signal SSS SSS SSS and her position, calling down fire and brimstone on my neck. And so, to cap it all, an aircraft of RAF Coastal Command comes at us at low level and there is nothing more to be done but dive, and creep away from the scene.

The tanker was the *Algonquin*, an American ship of 10,800 loaded displacement tons. She survived the whole war intact.

Richer by that experience, and not exactly in joyful mood, we continued the journey. The weather showed its most unfriendly side: sky dark, water as grey as lead. Not for nothing does the loading line 'Winter North Atlantic' on the sides of merchant ships allow for lighter loading than in the peaceful summer. But the U-boat was up to the neck in it and had to take everything as it came, including the heavy storm that dragged on without ceasing for over a week, during which the wind backed and veered between SW and NW, screaming and howling up to hurricane strength. Within a few hours on 8 January an enormous sea developed which threatened to smash everything, and we met squalls which tore the combs from the wave tops. Visibility closed in, rain alternated with snow, sleet and hail. As far as the eye could see there were only rolling hills with strips of foam coursing down their sides like the veins in marble. On the surface, the U-boat literally climbed the mountainous seas, plunged through the wave crests, hung for a moment with its stem in the empty air and plunged down the other side into the trough of the waves. When it buried its nose, the screws in the stern seemed to be revolving in air. Then the stern dropped down, the screws disappeared in the maelstrom and the exhaust broke off with a gurgle. In the hard thumps U 333 shuddered in every frame-member like a steel spring. Striking high up in front against the conning tower and from behind into the open bridge screen, the seas smothered us and we had to shut the conning-tower hatch for a while to prevent foundering.

Wet to the skin despite oilskins and sea-boots, the bridge watch were scarcely able to hold the heavy binoculars with their clammy hands. Wedged between periscope supports and bridge casing, they all hung on by safety belts and swivels, which did not prevent the sea tearing away a look-out during the continuing storm and hurling him to the deck, with serious injury to his eye.

Seen from below, the waves were as high as houses; they struck the deck like an avalanche and swept away the few things they could seize on. Fenders and lines under the outer casing disappeared, supports cracked like matchwood. The boat listed up to 60 degrees — as the pendulum in the control room showed — so that it seemed one could plunge one's bare hands in the water, then righted itself like a self-righting doll, owing to its low centre of gravity, only to tip over immediately to the other side. It was uncanny at night when the black hills rose and fell under a starless sky, phosphorescent combers rolled up and fell away. Far and wide, not the sign of a ship.

Wind Force 8 was the least, then the storm rose to Force 10, and in breath-taking squalls reached a full 11 to 12: a hurricane! The Beaufort scale ends at 12: wind speeds of over 65 knots, air filled with foam and spray, sea completely white, all distant visibility ceases, wave lengths 300 metres and more . . .

The inside of the boat was like a dice cup with everything whirling about. Those who had something to do groped from support to support. Sleeping was hardly possible, one just dozed. Those lying in the hammocks swayed to and fro like washing hung to dry; those in the wire bunks buckled themselves in. Anything lying on the tables had long since fallen off despite the surrounding fiddles, more than half our crockery was also long since broken; here metal would have been more practical than china. Nothing would stay put on the cooker, including, of course, hot food. The air in the boat was thick with smells and cold as well, but still more tolerable than after a long period submerged.

North Atlantic winter! In such weather waging war stops of its own accord because everyone has enough on his hands without it — even when we unexpectedly sighted a tanker about 3,000 metres away. I tried to keep contact and went onto a parallel course to attack after nightfall, it being impossible to attack straight away because of the high seas and colossal swell. Wind Force 10. At one moment the tanker was on a mountainous wave, the next she had disappeared into the valley. Then I lost sight of her altogether. Snowfall and visibility between 1,000 and 100 metres. Later, in the afternoon, when we encountered one another again the tanker at once turned towards me. This captain was no greenhorn either. Snow squalls separated us again. I tried a run-in again at high speed, but had to break off as the breaking seas threatened to carry away the bridge watch. Heaved-to, to ride out the hurricane, that meant marking time, making little more than one knot.

The same thing happened the following day when a steamer appeared dimly through a curtain of snow, disappeared in the rhythm of the sea, reappeared and again disappeared. I turned towards her but could not get close and the steamer ran off in front of my nose. When I tried to follow her at still higher speed the sea tore a look-out from his metal safety belt and wounded him.

So it went on, day after day. Between times, when it could no longer be endured, I ordered 'all hands to diving stations' and went to the cellar. The wild movements diminished, but at 40 metres the boat was still rocking and it was only at 50 metres that it lay still. We cleared up. The cook brought a delicious-smelling stew to table and everyone fell to. Eat and sleep, hear nothing, see nothing. Music — ? No music at any price! It would have been a source of noise. The crew needed rest.

When we surfaced again, after some hours, the captain enjoyed the privilege of opening the conning-tower hatch and being the first to get wet. Now he was standing again on the bridge, a towel knotted round his neck, and the water ran in through the top of his oilskins and out again at the bottom. To wipe dry the dripping binoculars was hardly possible and there was little point in using them. In that weather there was no need to look at the sky, not an aircraft was to be seen. Eventually the storm abated, the snow squalls ceased and the sun even appeared again for a few minutes.

The C-in-C U-boats directed us to an attack area. On 18 January, in square BC 65 a steamer of 5,861 GRT crossed our path with a large-calibre gun on the stern. This time everything was over in a trice. She only showed herself for seconds at a time and in these brief intervals I fired a double shot at her. The time was 1315. Shortly afterwards, two detonations — and a third, probably from her boiler exploding. The ship blew off steam and went down by the stern.

U 333's first kill. As we learnt from the radio signals, it was the British freighter *Caledonian Monarch* with a cargo of wheat on the way from Halifax to London. She belonged to a convoy with the code number SC 63 which the heavy weather had scattered together with its escort, three Canadian corvettes and four British destroyers. When the convoy formed up again *Caledonian Monarch* was missing. The captain's name was Valentine Steward. Unfortunately in the high seas still prevailing not a single man could be saved.

We were in no mood for rejoicing, though when I compared the construction costs of U 333 (about 1½ million Reichsmarks) with the damage inflicted I could see that the U-boat had already almost paid for itself. The only question was, who could last out longer in this business.

Four days later we were able to clock up our second steamer, the *Vassilios A. Polemis*, a 35-year-old Greek ship of 3,429 GRT. She was sailing in ballast and heading for Glasgow, a straggler from a convoy of 30. I had observed the *Polemis* through the periscope, was in firing position at 0700, dived and fired the torpedo at 700 metres. As I had been able to determine her speed precisely, according to the stop-watch the torpedo struck in exactly 57 seconds.

The ship broke in two in the middle, the funnel tipped over onto the bridge and in 10 minutes the Greek had disappeared. I surfaced and approached the lifeboats. For the first time as commander I experienced the misery of shipwrecked crews. In one of the boats a man with burns lay across a thwart. I had bandages and burn dressings handed across and supplied them with biscuits and cigarettes. After we had seen them step the mast and set sail we gave them a course for Halifax — about 250 nautical miles. As I heard later, 12 of the 33 crewmen were picked up by the steamer *Lionidas M. Kondylis* and taken to Halifax.

The night of 24 January, 1942, was slightly hazy but the stars were clear. We were again proceeding on the surface when in the forenoon my third steamer appeared. The look-out beside me, an experienced merchant seaman, estimated the laden weight at between 10,000 and 12,000 tons. I submerged for an underwater attack and delivered a shot from Tube 1. The torpedo ran at three metres depth and struck. The steamer, a Norwegian by name *Ringstad*, stopped, settled by the bow and blew off steam. Shortly afterwards she slid stem-first into the depths.

I saw the crew getting into the boats and surfaced. The men seemed extraordinarily calm and had already dressed their wounded. The lifeboats were large, well equipped and provided with a quenched-spark transmitter which they were using. We gathered they were reporting their torpedoing and exact position, so I could not stop any longer but had to make a quick get-away.

It was not until 1979, more than 37 years later, that I heard more details of the affair in Norway. The captain of the *Ringstad* had died meanwhile, but another eye-witness, aged 20 at the time, the stoker Roar Boye Börrensen, reported on the sinking: 'It was my second trip aboard the *Ringstad*. I remember it clearly. It was a Sunday morning and I had come from the coffee break. We intended to clean the oil tanks above the engines so as to be ready for the port of St. John which we were due to reach on Monday. Below in the engine room we did not feel the explosion, only something like a heavy bump. The torpedo must have crashed into the cargo of china clay we had with us. It is used, I think, in the armament industry. Our second officer was afraid of a second torpedo and chased us at once into the lifeboats. The ship sank inside 20 minutes.

'We were sitting in the lifeboat when the U-boat came towards us. I can see it today. At that moment our captain said, "Behave yourselves like Norwegians, they are going to shoot us," and in fact I saw the barrel of a machine-gun aimed at us. But there was no shot. Instead, a man — I am sure it was the commander — called over to us and asked our nationality, where we came from, what was our destination and cargo. He spoke English and offered us food and drinking water.

'Our captain declined, saying we had what we needed. The U-boat commander showed us the direction for East Newfoundland and said we were about 85 nautical miles from land. Then he wished us luck and said he hoped we would be fished up and soon reach land, and then vanished as quickly as he had come. The man was very humane. I still don't believe he was a Nazi though by his age he might have been one of those fanatical killers trained up under Hitler. Rather, he was a seaman, one of the type that we produce. He behaved according to the code of seamen who take no oath on it but know: help one another when in trouble at sea!'

U-boat captains tended to train their guns on lifeboats containing shipwrecked crews as a precaution, in case hand-grenades were thrown. For us U-boat commanders, nonetheless, the humane treatment of shipwrecked seamen of the enemy powers was a matter of course. They were not enemies any more — but simply shipwrecked and had to be helped as far as possible. (Both sides had the problem, however, that a vessel stopped at sea for rescue operations could itself be a sitting target.)

With the *Ringstad* U 333 had now sunk three ships on its first patrol. My crew were pleased with their captain and I, too, naturally felt a certain satisfaction. But I was well aware that those merchant ships had fallen to us as fairly easy booty. It had all happened so quickly and their gun crews had had no time to get in a single shot. Moreover I had despatched them when sailing singly and not in convoy; here the bad weather had helped me by breaking up the convoy formations. But the satisfaction of having so quickly 'fulfilled my quota' was all too soon effaced when I came to sink my fourth freighter. My log relates:

'31 January, 1942. 1516. Steamer in sight, distance 5,000 to 6,000 metres. Order submerge. Intention, approach as close as possible under water to establish character of ship. From 1,000 to 350 metres precisely observe steamer in periscope with high- and low-power magnification. Definitely enemy ship: a zig-zag general course which would lead to Ireland. A British ship with slim masts, no cross-trees, only found on British ships. One gun at the stern. No neutrality marks, no flag. The meat bag at the foremast shows she is not a Swede as the Swedes only have salt meat on board. At a distance of 500 metres I had the first lieutenant confirm all these facts through the periscope. Two men see more than one.

'1648. Shot from torpedo tube 1. Hit amidships. Ship lists to port, not sinking yet. I get my chief quartermaster and the helmsman on watch, both experienced merchant seamen, to estimate and confirm the type and size of the ship. Both declare they recognise a British ship. No possibility of doubt. Fog comes up and I lose sight of the ship. Dive, at first I intend to finish off the ship, lying 2,000 metres away on the port beam, with gunfire in order to save my last torpedo. I give up my intention: the steamer is signalling on the 600-metre wavelength (for international distress calls) in English, stating its position.

'I dive to deliver the death blow. Close in to 400 metres again. Shot from tube 5, hit abreast funnel. When the smoke disperses, superstructure is burning around funnel. The forecastle is already awash. Quite thick fog suddenly sets in. Steamer sinking, can be reported destroyed.

'Move off on course for home. Radio success to C-in-C U-boats: In square BE 7114 just sunk passenger-carrying freighter with last torpedo. Two hits at 350 metres . . .'

All this took place west of Biscay. We now headed home for France.

I had fired the second torpedo at 1833. But at 1800, as previously mentioned, the ship had already called for help and reported in clear that it had been torpedoed and was burning. And this call for help had not only been picked up in England by the radio station at Land's End but also of course at Dönitz's command post in Kerneval, near Lorient, where he had established his headquarters since the occupation of France. In the SOS call in English the sinking ship had at first reported itself as the English *Brittany*, but later announced its true identity — which we did not hear: it was the German steamer *Spreewald*, a blockade-runner travelling from East Asia to Bordeaux . . .

Meanwhile Dönitz's operation staff had quickly realised what had happened. And while I was still signalling my proud success story, they had set everything in motion to save what could be saved, and that, in the last resort, was not much. Only slowly did it dawn on me what I had actually done. I had torpedoed a German ship and not only that, as ill luck would have it, the ship had a

44

considerable number of English prisoners on board. The incredible had happened and could no longer be remedied.

The whole Biscay area was alerted. From every side Dönitz called U-boats together, nine in all including mine, to search feverishly for survivors of the *Spreewald*, but next day only one, U 105, could report finding three lifeboats and three rafts with 24 German merchant seamen and 58 British prisoners. We continued until the massive search was broken off on 4 February at 1600. Fortunately almost all those involved were saved.

And I was the cause of it all.

We returned to the U-boat base of La Pallice near La Rochelle. My 45-day patrol was at an end, but there were no flowers, none of the usual pleasant reception. Just as I was, dirty and unshaven, log book and radio book under my arm, I had to get into an official car which rushed me to Dönitz's command post. The duty staff officer greeted me briefly and coolly: 'The court martial is waiting for you.' The charge read: 'Disobedience in action, manslaughter and damage to military property.'

How far my actions corresponded to the individual points in the charge escapes me, and today my memory of the proceedings themselves is blurred. Staff officers and other U-boat commanders sat at a long table. A judge advocate presided.

To understand the story, here is the background: the motor ship *Spreewald* of the Hamburg–America Line was one of many German merchant ships surprised by the outbreak of war in distant waters. For this eventuality their skipper carried sealed orders with precise instructions. Most of them sailed for neutral harbours and were interned. The *Spreewald* had been off the American west coast. The captain disguised his ship as a Dutchman, had the name *Ena* and Rotterdam as home port painted on, and fled across the Pacific. At the end of September, 1939, he reached Yokohama and from there the Manchurian port of Dairen (known throughout the world as Port Arthur, today Lüta). There the ship, a freighter with accommodation for passengers, lay for two years and waited.

Then *Spreewald* was loaded with valuable goods (crude rubber, wolfram, quinine) and became one of those 'rubber-carriers' which were to attempt to run the blockade and reach a German or French base. Despite the enemy forces, quite a number of ships sailing singly slipped through to their goal. From 1941 to May, 1942, a dozen ships got through out of a total of 16. Later, conditions became more difficult and eventually impossible. Out of the next 15 German ships to sail from the Far East only 4 reached Europe: 7 were sunk and the remaining 4 returned to Japan.

An additional task awaited the blockade-runner *Spreewald*. Through the German naval attaché in Tokyo instructions were received to embark more than 300 British civilian prisoners. These were transferred at sea from the supply ship *Kulmerland* and comprised the crews of enemy steamers which had been intercepted by the German auxiliary cruiser *Cormoran*. The *Spreewald* alias *Ena* now became the Norwegian ship *Elg*. Blockade-runners used every trick of disguise to cover their tracks. They also preferred lonely routes whenever possible, and in particular only sent radio signals in certain prescribed positions so as not to betray their whereabouts. But they heard everything they could pick up and decipher. Towards the end of the voyage, when they had reached a certain sea area, they had to announce themselves with a specific radio call. Thereupon an escort was sent out to them from the German Atlantic bases.

The German naval command was informed of the *Spreewald's* departure from the Far East, knew roughly what route she would follow and also knew how the ship would look as she approached the French coast. A U-boat, U 575, was detached to act as escort and the commander was told how to recognise the ship. All that remained was for the *Spreewald* to radio her position. We U-boat commanders knew that German blockade-runners occasionally passed through certain squares on the chart and were always alert to the possibility of seeing one of them. But square BE 7142, where I found myself on the last day of January, was not such a square, so I had no reason to anticipate meeting such a ship. As neither the U-boat standing by for escort duty nor anyone on Dönitz's staff had any idea of the *Spreewald's* present position, none of us could receive a warning. Probably the *Spreewald*, which had been lucky so far, did not wish to endanger herself and hesitated to send out the radio call as ordered.

So it came about that while U 575 waited in vain for the blockade-runner in quite a different square, she came into my sights as just another unknown enemy ship . . . with the result described.

I made my statements before the court martial in brief, military style. Finally I was acquitted as Hessler, Dönitz's son-in-law, was able to lay the blame on the *Spreewald* for failing to report her position and thus disobeying orders.

This instance was by no means unique. There was the German bomber which attacked the destroyer *Leberecht Maass*, as already described, and the loss of three mine-layers resulting from inadequate information. Or the German E-boat in the Bay of Danzig which torpedoed the steamer *Neuwerk* loaded with 800 refugees. And I was not to be the only U-boat skipper to sink a German ship, though for me that is poor consolation.

Of course my crew got wind of what had happened, but kept their mouths shut, for at that time the *Spreewald* affair was a closely guarded secret. In a radio signal on 4 February, 1942, to the U-boats searching for survivors, Dönitz ordered: 'Shipwrecked personnel and those in lifeboats are not to be told that a German U-boat was responsible for the sinking.' This could be one of the reasons why, till now, virtually nothing has reached the public about this tragedy.

5

Hostilities against America

U 333 was now detached from the 5th U-boat flotilla at Kiel and assigned as a front-line boat to the 3rd flotilla stationed at La Pallice/La Rochelle. The operational advantages of these new bases were considerable; not least, they were naturally a thorn in the flesh of the British, saving as they did the front-line boats a long, dangerous outward trip from Kiel round the north of Scotland to the actual area of operations, and the same long risky return from the Atlantic to home — continually exposed to the British aircraft above them which kept constant patrols from their island bases.

The two medieval bastions flanking the harbour entrance of La Rochelle have for long been a favourite motif for painters. After the German occupation the appearance of the landscape was impaired by massive, concrete colossi that were in no way picturesque. These were the U-boat bunkers of La Pallice, bomb-proof 'pens' in which two, if necessary three, Type VII-C boats could find shelter and undergo repair.

The construction of these gigantic, six-metre-thick concrete bunkers had been started immediately after the armistice with France in June, 1940, and was completed first at Lorient and, a few weeks before our arrival, at La Pallice. The work had gone forward at great speed and the technical *Organisation Todt* (O.T. for short) had left nothing undone. Everything that the U-boats needed, from a torpedo to a screw for a replacement part, had been fetched from Germany. Whole sections of the naval dockyard at Wilhelmshaven were transferred to Lorient. Every one of these bunkers had swallowed 6,000 tons of steel and cost 125 million marks at the prevailing prices. Hitler, who had a weakness for gigantic structures and fortifications, kept himself continuously informed about the development of the German U-boat bases.

The British had omitted to bomb these bunkers during construction when they would have been vulnerable and offered a worthwhile target. Once they were completed there were as yet no bombs which could have penetrated those great hunks of concrete. By the time the British had made up their mind to mount air-raids on the bases of Brest, Lorient, St. Nazaire, La Rochelle and Bordeaux, the Foreign Office vetoed the plan, a veto respected by the war cabinet, which was concerned to avoid endangering the French dockyard workers and the civilian population. It was not to be until 7 January, 1943, with the battle of the Atlantic approaching its peak, that Churchill would lift the embargo and the bombs would start raining down, after the population was given advanced warning. The first target was to be Lorient, on the night of 14–15 January, 1943.

We were to find a home from home in our new patrol base of La Pallice/La Rochelle until the summer of 1944. The U-boat officers were housed in the hotels 'D'Angleterre' and 'De L'Etranger' while the men lodged in well equipped wooden huts. The hard-pressed U-boat crews were at least to lack for nothing in harbour. After its first patrol U 333 lay in its bunker for about 50 days for repair. A general overhaul was also needed, some damaged components having been found, as is frequently the case with new boats. The crew went on home leave in two shifts and used Dönitz's train to take them to Germany.

It is understandable that the U-boat men favoured a long period in dock, an attitude which also influenced the dockyard workers themselves. Earlier, on 26 November, 1941, Dönitz had issued an appeal in his 'Considerations on increasing the effectiveness of the U-boat war': 'I hold the view that the length of time a U-boat needs in dock after each patrol should not correspond to a predetermined norm of one day in port for each day at sea, but that an effort must be made (unless major repairs are needed) to achieve material preparation within no more than the period the crew needs in order to return to sea physically restored and ready for battle.'

But where were the trained, fast working craftsmen and technicians to come from? As far as available, the specialists from the home dockyards had already been drawn off to the Atlantic bases and were working as civilians side by side with our military technical personnel. Thus, increasing numbers of French auxiliary workers had to be used, which naturally brought with it the danger of espionage and sabotage. They had to be carefully watched.

The British naval intelligence service, of course, knew the problems of long periods in dock from personal experience, for English submarine crews also enjoyed their home leave. With his psychological experience the enemy used this situation for propaganda purposes, skilfully combining it with a call to our U-boat crews to sabotage their own craft. Out of a clear sky, as it were, small leaflets no bigger than the palm of a man's hand appeared in the bases along the Atlantic coast and in the new U-boat base in Bergen, Norway. They lay on the ground in the bunker, were found in tool boxes or on the canteen table. One of these leaflets, printed in German and produced apparently in England, read as follows:

SIX WEEKS LEAVE
for the whole U-boat crew

if a comrade at the base causes a ballast tank to split through excess air pressure.

It's a sure and simple matter:
If a comrade closes the air vent and the flooding flap of a ballast tank, then slightly turns the corresponding air valve, as though to test whether the pressure delivery pipe is airtight, he can simply go away and wait for the 'accident' to occur.

It is best done during the stationary test at the pier or on trimming trial.

It's simple:
First, it has happened often enough without assistance. Secondly, no one can prove who has done it. Any stoker or dockyard worker coming on board can have turned the air valve.
Thirdly, quite a time passes after the opening of the valve before the pressure becomes too great and the ballast tank bursts. No one can say precisely when it happened.
One thing is certain: the boat will have to go into dock — and the crew has increased time ashore!

In the first years of the war it was highly improbable that German U-boat men were ready to sabotage their own boat. The British probably did not expect that they would, but counted rather on generating a certain mistrust, particularly between the chief engineer and his mechanics. Whether the British ever succeeded I cannot say. In U 333 the relationship between the chief engineer and his petty officers was rather that of professional colleagues.

However that may be, these leaflets of the British were the overture to a form of psychological warfare which now became a deliberate infiltration into the U-boat arm.

The coast of Florida, USA, was to be the operational area for my second patrol. We were in the spring of 1942 and, as I heard to my amazement, the Americans were not yet to be taken seriously. On the east coast they seemed to be asleep, to put it mildly. I was shown radio signals, including one from my colleague Reinhard Hardegen, from which it emerged that the lights and buoys were not blacked out but shining as in deepest peacetime, for the guidance of friend and foe alike. Admittedly these signals were some two months old, but they had been confirmed only a few days previously by returning commanders. Apparently my future operational area off the coast of Florida left nothing to be desired.

So the American war machine had not yet got into gear. The striking force of a country with the greatest industrial potential in the world, full of abundance and overwhelming power — that force was not yet stirring. Until this giant raised itself to its full height we could enjoy a breathing space. 'We' in the narrower sense: for once more, of course, everything depended on the U-boats. Already in the First World War German U-boats had operated singly off the American east coast. But now of all times, in the spring of 1942, when it was really crucial, we lacked the numbers to exploit the opportunity.

Admiral Dönitz needed only a few days to adjust to the American situation. In mid-December he had asked permission to send 12 of the so-called long-distance 1,100-ton boats of Type IX to the east coast of the USA. Unexpectedly only six were approved. The chief of the operations section, Captain (later Rear Admiral) Godt, had prepared in minute detail a venture that was to go down in the history of naval warfare under the code name 'Drum beat' (*Paukenschlag*). It was to be not simply a drum beat but a full roll of the kettle drums in which I was to take part.

One attack area comprised the seas off Cape Hatteras and the St. Lawrence River, the other the Caribbean area round Trinidad, Aruba and Curaçao, the main distribution centres for crude oil. The distances were between 2,200 and 4,000 nautical miles. On 13 January the first lightning attack had been approved, and the successes were very great. In January, 1942, alone, 62 ships totalling 327,357 GRT had been sunk.

The historian Stephen Roskill writes in his book *The War at Sea* (p. 96): 'When one considers the devastation wrought in the first days of 1942 off the American coast, it is one of the most surprising facts that never more than about 12 U-boats were operating at the same time.'

But Roskill, too, was wrong. In fact there were not even that many. The first drum beat was carried out with only 5 boats, which were replaced piecemeal. How the number of U-boats contrived to remain so small requires a full explanation. It is a piece of history which one has to have experienced to believe.

To recapitulate: around the turn of the year 1941/42 the U-boat arm possessed 91 operational U-boats. Beside the units employed in the Mediterranean, off Gibraltar and in Norwegian waters 55 remained for the tonnage war in the Atlantic. Of these, 60 per cent were undergoing lengthy repairs in dockyards and bases and, as half of the remaining 22 were on the way to and from the battle area, that left ultimately only 10 to 12 boats in direct contact with the enemy.

Quite unexpectedly Admiral Dönitz was instructed to divert some of these few operational U-boats to the Norwegian area. On 12 January, 1942, in a discussion with the naval C-in-C Grand Admiral Raeder, Adolf Hitler had suddenly required heavy naval forces to be collected in the Norwegian area as 'on the basis of information received and of an increasing deterioration in the Swedish attitude, he feared a large-scale Anglo–Russian action in the area of Norway.' 'He is of the opinion,' noted Raeder, 'that a strong battle group of battleships and cruisers off the Norwegian coast, practically the whole German fleet, in cooperation with the German Luftwaffe, would make a decisive contribution to the security of the Norwegian area. Therefore he wishes the preponderance of German naval forces to be transferred to this area at all costs.'

4, 5. *The control room in U 570, a Type VII-C boat
similar to U 333. (above) 4. The trimming panel and
hydroplane control. (below) 5. The blowing panel.*

(above) 6. *HF/DF radio locating aerial on the mainmast of HMS* Exe. *(below left) 7. Aphrod[...] tin-foil balloons filled from this hydrogen cylinder, were supposed to give false echoes and confuse the radar scanners. (below right) 8. Radio cabin in U 333. Sound waves from destroyers can be picked up, counter-measures taken, convoy positions detected.*

(above) 9. *Bomb-proof U-boat pens at La Pallice, French Atlantic coast.*
(below) 10. *USS* Dallas, *the destroyer which depth-charged U* 333 *after the torpedoing of SS* Java Arrow.

(below) *11. Jury repairs to* U 333 *after ramming by SS* British Prestige *off Florida.*
12. Rammed, depth-charged, U 333 *limps back to base after crossing the Atlantic.*

In Hitler's headquarters they apparently had no exact conception of the boats available or of the numbers needed for operations. In spite of Dönitz's objections, instead of 4 U-boats as previously, a total of 20 were now to be kept permanently in the Norwegian area for defensive purposes. Because the severe winter of 1941/42 had delayed new construction the Atlantic boats had to make up the numbers. The order came from the highest authority via the Naval Command and could not be evaded.

Thus, four days later, on 16 January, our new battleship *Tirpitz* arrived in Trondheim. The heavy cruisers *Prinz Eugen* and *Admiral Scheer* followed on 23 February and afterwards the heavy cruisers *Admiral Hipper* and *Lützow*, plus 8 destroyers and 4 torpedo boats. Twenty U-boats completed Hitler's intuitive order and disrupted Dönitz's planning.

Today it is not yet known in detail what or who it was that aroused Hitler's fears. Only a British commando raid had given cause for concern. On the night of 26–27 December, 1941, a mixed commando had landed by surprise on the orders of Lord Louis Mountbatten at two places in Norway to the south of Alesund. It had set fire to German ammunition and food dumps, blown up two small factories, oil tanks and military vehicles, and had also sunk 21,000 tons of German shipping. In the course of the operation 120 German soldiers were killed, 98 taken prisoner and brought back with 200 young Norwegian volunteers to England. The British, who withdrew to a steamer under cover of two destroyers, lost 3 officers and 17 men.

This raid, though a mere pinprick in the context of the war as a whole, probably contributed to Hitler's conviction that an invasion of Norway was imminent. Although Churchill did consider the idea of a landing in Norway in April, 1942 (Roskill, *The War at Sea*, II, pp. 100–101), this was never seriously planned, as the Allies were bent on the occupation of North Africa. Nevertheless, the result of this was that the number of our front-line U-boats, which in the spring of 1942 were ordered to operate at will off the east coast of America, was drastically reduced. From the middle of March, 1942, to the end of April only 6 to 8 boats were deployed.

Dönitz had to think again, not only with regard to numbers but also to size of craft. A Type VII boat like U 333 of about 750 tons displacement (surfaced) was called a 'medium high-seas boat'.

With a radius of action of 7,000–8,000 nautical miles it had been designed for employment against convoys in the Atlantic, in contrast to the 1,100 ton long-distance ocean-going Type IX. To keep up with large, fast convoys on the surface and get into a firing position, large quantities of fuel were necessary. The staff had therefore become used to the idea that, in practice, Type VII boats could only reach mid-Atlantic, operate there, and then return. We commanders, however, were of a different opinion. The distance from La Pallice/La Rochelle to the Florida coast and back is about 8,000 miles. Added to this are the miles covered on patrol. Yet at an economical and carefully calculated speed we believed we could stretch the fuel intended for 7,000 miles, possibly by increasing our fuel-carrying capacity. The chief engineers were inventive in this respect and my chief had the idea of filling parts of the drinking and washing water tanks with diesel oil. That could only be done with the agreement of the crew, who had to restrict themselves to the tolerable limits. The longer the patrol, too, the greater the food supplies to be carried. To a great extent we did without any spare room, took with us everything we could lay hands on, and even stacked our food in the toilet. The few free bunks were stuffed full of ammunition boxes and spare machinery parts. We inserted three additional torpedoes under the decking outside the pressure hull, so instead of 14 we carried 17. And this whole assortment in its apparent confusion had to be expertly stowed and properly balanced out so as to preserve the trim of the U-boat and not interfere with diving.

At a meeting with the flotilla commander Herbert Schultze, when I told him how we had crammed the boat, he smiled and remarked: 'Besides, when everything you've organised has been used up you'll get even more out there.' Herbert Schultze was one of the most successful U-boat commanders in the Second World War, known to young officers as 'Vati' (Pop) for his friendly, paternal attitude. I learnt to my surprise that, as one of the first U-boats, U 333 would be looked after by a 'Milch Cow'. These new 1,700-ton 'ocean-going transporters' of Type IX were intended to supply the U-boats at sea with everything they needed, so allowing them to stay longer in the operational area. At an agreed map reference I would meet one of these U-tankers (ten were built) to take on food, but particularly fuel.

Schultze's great successes had been achieved in the less difficult times of 1940–41 when enemy defence was not so precise and effective. Since then the anti-U-boat actions in the Atlantic had been marked more and more by what the Americans called 'the scissors effect'. Whereas at the beginning the two blades of the scissors were still far apart, leaving a more or less safe area in the middle of the ocean, 'the gap', with the USA's entry into the war the blades were starting to close. The gap became smaller and smaller until by 1943 the scissors were shut completely to cut off the U-boats' lifeline.

6

Rammed by a tanker

On the afternoon of 30 March, 1942, U 333 left the protective bunker of La Pallice for the great trip to America. A ship of the mine-sweeping flotilla guided us into the open fairway which we reached that evening. After this we were on our own. Ahead of us the dark, wide Atlantic appeared empty. A weak SW wind brought layers of fog. The boat was rocking in a gentle swell, as though coming awake. Inside, the routine began.

In its element every ship's hull shows a characteristic behaviour. But it only comes alive when the commander's temperament is transferred to the dead rump and gets the most out of it. To wake up U 333 completely and shake off the idleness of the weeks in dock I practised operational training for the whole of the next day. Simulated emergency situations, failure of equipment, crash dives, deep dives, until the crew once more managed everything by instinct.

We sailed as long as possible on the surface. The safety of the boat when surfaced depends of course on the alertness of the men on the bridge. The eye-level height of a U-boat conning tower is about 5 metres, and mastheads are visible in clear air at best at 10,000 to 12,000 metres. Four look-outs each observed a sector of the horizon. The officer of the watch, the chief quartermaster (or I) as fifth man on the bridge, kept an eye on the other four, on the sky and sea.

Every look-out had his own binoculars and took great care of them. These were the valuable rubber-cushioned U-boat glasses protected against knocks. For daylight attacks the commander used binoculars with particularly strong magnification, but they were awkward and heavy. To wipe the lens clean of spray and deposit, a leather was always kept ready and in bad weather a dry, absorbent cloth was handed up from the control room when needed. These are admittedly incidental details, but are worth mentioning as important for survival.

As for the men's eyes, these were tested thoroughly before

appointment to the U-boat service. But out in the Atlantic everything was different and even a good eye did not always see what it
should, for one not only sees with the eye but must know how to
interpret what has been seen, and that is a matter of experience. At
the beginning of patrols the young sailor with his normal
'peacetime eyes' saw simply nothing and had to be instructed.
Fantastic cloud formations deceived the novice, the redness of a
rising moon conjured a fire, extremes of temperature produced
mirages. Thin streaks or faint smoke trails were the first signs of
masts and convoys. The small dot far away on the horizon might be
an enemy aircraft which would reach the boat within minutes.
Then again, a hazy atmosphere would wipe out all contours and
seamlessly melt sea and sky into one. The recognition of night-
time shadows also rested on experience. At the beginning of the
war the U-boat with its slim silhouette had the advantage over a
destroyer and was hard to make out even when face to face, or as it
were eye to eye.

Noteworthy, also, is the capacity for adjustment to light and
dark; for the eyes work with a time-lag. When at night I climbed
down out of the darkness into the boat to take a look at the chart, I
put on glasses with tinted lenses which protected the eyes from the
harsh lamplight, so enabling them to adjust more quickly to the
darkness when I went aloft again, for the contrast would not be so
great. Stress and emergencies impair vision, or judgement, or
create hallucinations for psychological reasons. As captain I was
always the first to climb through the conning-tower hatch when
surfacing. If we had had to endure a never-ending depth-charge
pursuit, had been forced to stay down for fifteen hours or so and
resort to bottled oxygen, which created excess pressure inside the
boat, the tension became almost unbearable. I could hardly wait
for the telegraphist to help me into sea-boots and leather jacket, tie
the towel round my neck, hang the binoculars on me and finally
shove me up the ladder.

My breathing was always heavy and I had to summon all my
strength to loosen the wheel-lock of the hatch without knowing
what awaited me behind it. At last a sharp blow against the catch,
and owing to the excess internal pressure, the heavy round steel lid
almost blew open by itself. At that moment it seemed to me that my
eardrums would burst. With one leap I was up and out and ought to
have adjusted myself at once to the darkness. But nature will not be

compelled. More slowly than usual I recognised the surroundings, saw perhaps an empty sea — or the death-dealing shadow of an attacker nearby. That was the Achilles heel, and for long, anxious seconds I felt myself defenceless.

My eyes were in top form, the look-outs on the bridge were wide awake, there was good visibility with gathering cumulus clouds, and even so we were surprised, our third day at sea, when from those very clouds an aircraft descended with total suddenness, and came directly at us. 'Dive!'

Air vents opened, U 333 sank bubbling down, leaving behind a swirl of water to mark the spot. We were not a minute below, at about 30 metres depth, when we heard 'plump — plump' and moments later two bombs exploded beside the boat with a deafening roar. The impact threw everything into confusion. Boxes and crates fell crashing down, all electric lights went out, bulbs and fuses jumped from their sockets. The repeater compass on the control-room bulkhead smashed into fragments, flap valves and hull valves sprang a leak and a stream of oil three fingers broad poured from a crack. The hydroplanes and rudder were out of action but the boat could be steadied at 80 metres and controlled by hand. That was the first impression. The scare passed as quickly as it had come and was not repeated.

Now my practices with the crew paid off. Everyone knew what he had to do, and despite the dark went straight to his task. We could start the clearing up. First, emergency flap valves and hull valves were made secure. The electric light snapped on again, raising spirits at once, but also revealing the wide extent of the damage.

The fresh-water plant had ceased to function. In addition, the drinking water transfer valve had split and a whole quantity of seawater had flowed into the fresh water, which afterwards gave us salty coffee. Further, the leaking oil had poured over part of our food, seeped through the loose lids of tins with flour, sugar and fruit and spoilt the contents. But what matter, we were after all at war. Apparently nothing had happened to the outer skin, just the conning-tower hatch had taken a knock so that from then on a crash dive brought a stream of water into the boat as from a shower — something we got used to however. All in all the air attack had not caused any considerable damage; I confined myself to a few sentences in the log and made no radio report.

At that time I could not have done so in any case, for radio contact was temporarily interrupted. At the same time a dead direction-finding receiver and damaged echo-sounder caused little worry to us over the deep Atlantic, but the short-wave receiver and long-wave transmitter had also been broken, thereby cutting our link with home. In the radio cabin all the valves had jumped out owing to the heavy explosions — not a matter of great concern as we carried sufficient replacements with us. The telegraphists were able to repair their apparatus and resume radio traffic.

All the same, two aircraft bombs had sufficed to bring us these embarrassments. A conventional bomb works with a percussion fuse which causes detonation on contact with the water-surface. With a submerged U-boat it would be ineffective, 'blowing-off' in the empty air above it. In our case we were clearly dealing with a new kind of depth charge for aircraft, with a delayed-action fuse not activated above a depth of 8 metres and then detonating. For us that was something new.

Our main concern, however, was the surprise attack itself. Six pairs of eyes on the bridge — the look-outs, the officer of the watch and myself — but none of us had seen the aircraft in time. On the other hand it must have spotted us long before — but with what? It had not, after all, come down on us from a clear sky. In my diminutive 'cabin' (which was nothing more in fact than a space divided off by a curtain from the central gangway of the boat) I discussed the phenomenon again with the officer of the watch, a one-time pilot. Had the plane been equipped with radar? That would have explained the aimed approach and confirmed rumours which spoke of radio-location sets in British aircraft. Because of the presumably large dimensions of such equipment this did not seem to us technically possible, or at any rate only in the larger aircraft type. Had we encountered one of these? Frankly, amid the drama we had been unable to recognise the type of aircraft. So everything remained conjecture. We did suspect though that, somehow, the epoch of the bare eye, however good, was coming to an end and that the new era of technology, or electronics to be more precise, was upon us. War is the father of all things, and electronics developed in such a way that the U-boats were harried ever more closely, and with ever greater certainty of aim.

Meanwhile my colleague Freiherr von Tiesenhausen, who operated in the Mediterranean with U 331, had noted in his log on

28 February, 1942, ' . . . during the whole night various types of aircraft with white lights or without lights . . . Suspect some aircraft are fitted with locating apparatus. Suggest urgent need of an apparatus to register approaching aircraft so U-boat can dive in time . . . '

Such a set was in fact soon created. It was a simple frame aerial and so primitive that it could be put together on the spot: a rectangular, rotating lattice frame standing on edge, roughly wound round with wire. This product had the expressive name 'Biscay Cross', received on 1.4 to 1.8 metre wavelengths, and registered radar impulses from the air at up to 30 kilometres' distance with a whistling or humming noise. Every time a U-boat dived the fragile affair had to be dismantled, however, and the improved French Metox aerial, with a range of 100 kilometres, was shortly to replace it.

These relatively simple contraptions confirmed that enemy aircraft were hunting U-boats with airborne location devices, something which our technicians in the naval high command had hitherto thought impossible: U-boats coming under surprise attack, they insisted, were merely negligent. The device in question was the Allied ASV radar (Air to Surface Vessel) on the 1.5 metre wavelength.

Recovering from this attack, we resumed our journey westwards. The days' runs, i.e. the distances covered from noon to noon, were kept within moderate bounds. We were cooking on a low flame, as it were, to save fuel. Despite this, and to add to all the imponderables of the U-boat war with which we had to cope, one of our main engines (the port diesel) eventually stopped. For a merchant ship in peacetime engine failure is usually no great problem, but a U-boat's loss of manoeuvrability when on the warpath in the Atlantic . . .

In such circumstances the skipper can do nothing but contain himself in patience. The rest is better left to the technical section of the crew, and to lift it from its former shadow existence into the proper light the youngest of our stokers (the old-fashioned term survived into the U-boat service) shall tell the story:

'In March, 1942, after four months of U-boat School, stuffed full of knowledge about engines, auxiliary engines and other U-boat technicalities, I came on board U 333 as the youngest stoker. At first my job had nothing to do with the technical side and involved bringing a bright shine to the floor plates with emery paper, cotton waste and diesel oil and freeing all exposed parts from rust.

'Every hour during the watch of four hours on, four hours off the rocker arms of the engines had to be lubricated with the oil can, and at the same time the temperature of the cooling water was read and entered in the engine-room log. For hours at cruising speed — as on the long journey to America — only the monotonous hammering of the diesels could be heard; all the same, one felt a shared sense of responsibility for their smooth performance, on which everything during operations depended.

'What happened otherwise on board we usually heard only when the watch was changed, as information was seldom passed aft to the engine compartment from the bridge or control room. But woe to us if an irregularity suddenly occurred or a diesel stopped. Then a query came at once from above, from the captain perhaps to the chief engineer, as to what was the matter.

'This happened on my first patrol, which began on 30.3.1942. Suddenly, after a few weeks, the port diesel packed up and refused to start again. Big discussion between chief engineer, engine-room artificer (E.R.A.) and mechanics. Result: communication to captain that a cylinder liner and a piston needed changing. Time required, about two days — in mid-Atlantic, in shifting seas and contact with the enemy, not to mention the confined space and bad air. At times we had to dive to steady the boat while we removed the heavy parts like the piston, connecting rod, cylinder head and valves with block and tackle and stowed them securely. As the youngest stoker I had to bale out the used oil with my head in the crankcase and then give assistance, wedged behind the diesel.

'So it went on for a full three days and nights. There was no going off watch. When possible, everyone from stoker to chief engineer took a capful of sleep, otherwise we just drudged, in the truest sense of the word, thinking neither of the war nor of home, but only one hopeful thought: that we would soon be finished and the diesel running again. Meanwhile, the captain was asking repeatedly: how much longer will you need?

'At last the final screw, the final nut were tightened. The E.R.A. stood at the controls, beside him the chief engineer and around him petty officers and stokers in tense expectation. The starting valve was opened, there was a hiss of compressed air and a heavy rumbling sound. The tension grew — and then relief as the diesel ran again as though nothing had happened. Those on watch stayed up, all the rest lay down to sleep.

'In the rhythm of going on and off watch everything was soon forgotten. Only occasionally did we yarn and think of that three-day grind. Through this experience we had become welded closer together and knew we could rely on one another. In the engine room we were always subjected to strong physical stress, in the smallest space, at high speeds, cut off from everything behind a closed bulkhead and receiving orders only by telegraph — pretty remote from what was actually happening.'

We had covered two thirds of the distance to the American east coast. On 20 April, U 333 was in the map square where it was to meet the supply U-boat and take on fuel. Our rendezvous lay in the 'gap', the secure space in the Atlantic which at that time could not yet be reached by land-based aircraft. Our opponents' aircraft carriers were cruising in far distant war zones in the Pacific and elsewhere. We were simply marking time on 22 April when U 459, the new large 'Milch Cow', surfaced beside us.

Its skipper, Commander Graf Georg von Wilamowitz-Möllendorf was to us 'an old gentleman from the Kaiser's time', especially by the strict British standards which spoke of submarine captains as 'too old at 35'. He would rather have been commander of a fighting U-boat than a 'pump attendant' as my crew called him. As it was, in 1943 he was to lose his life with his 'Milch Cow' west of Biscay, and in fact none of these large, somewhat ponderous, 1,700-ton boats survived the war. They submerged too slowly and were soon destroyed, one after another, from the air.

At our meeting neither side had the faintest idea how U-boats should be supplied at sea, yet although we were the first customer of the first 'Milch Cow' the operation went extremely smoothly. We received fuel and lubricating oil, replacement parts and, to the delight of my people, 'murdered cockerels, arthritic cutlets, deep frozen pig's arse and almost fresh, only slightly incubated eggs'. As we had neither sick nor wounded we could decline with thanks a visit from the naval doctor.

After the few weeks at economical speed our fuel supply of 120 tons and more of diesel oil had not been much reduced. Nevertheless we were tanked up again, if only for the experience, and were asked to suggest improvements. All in all it was a risky undertaking as both boats, being connected with pipelines and ropes, were restricted in their movements and endangered. Neither would have been able to dive away immediately if an aircraft had shown itself or if a destroyer had appeared on the horizon. In war anything can happen.

When the work was finished the boats disappeared on their different courses in the wide spaces of the western Atlantic. The great ocean, under summer skies, spread in almost pastoral peace from horizon to horizon. And yet over the blue depths we never felt alone, but rather as a tightly knit family continually connected with the great U-boat clan on shore.

While the ocean floor stretched 5,000 metres below the keel of the U-boat, the air was humming in the short-wave band from 100 to 40 metres and in the long-distance traffic from 40 to 13 metres. For the traffic with U-boats, particularly when submerged, an ultra-long-wave transmitter was built in central Germany at Kalbe on the Milbe. It could be heard loud and clear under water off New York and in the Caribbean at a depth of 25 metres, mainly on the 10,000-metre band.

At this time a lot still went out by radio and, besides tactical short-code signals and other enciphered directions concerning particular operations, one received messages of a highly private nature, such as for Chief Mechanic Heber on board U 333: 'Healthy girl arrived. Mother and child well.' Or personal congratulations from the deputy admiral, U-boats, our head of personnel Admiral von Friedeburg: 'Small sailor with periscope arrived.' Such direct communications meant a great deal to the crew and showed that their interests as human beings were considered.

Glowing hot, sunny days alternated with shining star-lit nights and made us forget the war for a while until, east of the Bermudas and outside the customary steamer routes, it unexpectedly appeared over the horizon in the shape of two mast-heads. The fair illusion was destroyed and reality drained the Atlantic dream of its magic.

After the masts the funnel appeared. I made do with this scanty picture and on account of the mirror-smooth sea kept my distance so as not to be spotted. I tried to intercept her on the surface, although that was not easy. As it later transpired, she was the

British Prestige, a motor ship of the British Tanker Co., London, of 11,000 tons laden. What she was laden with will presently be told. Alone and unprotected, the ship was clearly bound for Europe, her continual and confusing zig-zags notwithstanding.

Slowly stalking closer, I pursued the tanker into the afternoon without her noticing us. Perhaps she was blinded by the setting sun, but it was not until twilight that I succeeded in starting the attack. The range was down to 1,200 metres. Everything seemed set for a copybook performance. So — 'Tube 3 — Stand by to fire.'

'Tube 3 — Fire!'

The stop-watch ticked and nothing happened. The seconds became longer and longer — as did my face. Damnation! — missed. The next tube . . .

There seemed to be a jinx. The second torpedo missed as well. How could these two failures be explained? For the time being I disappeared from the surface, had the tubes reloaded under water, surfaced again and set off after the tanker, which had not been standing still either. Just as I had caught up with her and was intending to start the third attack, she performed one of her incalculable zig-zags and everything had to begin all over again. The moon, meanwhile, had risen and was lighting up U 333 in every detail. We had no option but to submerge — particularly as in these very minutes the tanker laid herself wide open. It was now or never. Stand by to attack!

Down periscope, briefly, feed in the firing data, up periscope again. It was the shorter aerial search periscope, the one with the wider field of vision. The dark form of the tanker stood in the blinding moonlight, totally exposed on the silver sea. A splendid target, close enough to touch! But then, quite suddenly, the scene was wiped out and through the lens I saw nothing but blackness. The gigantic side of the tanker, as tall as a house, was coming straight towards us, so close that it was too late for evasion. There were grinding and crashing noises which sounded as though a goods train was passing over us . . .

As the captain of *British Prestige*, Ernest W. Hill from Canterbury, later described it, he had just ordered another change of course of 90 degrees and was about to sit as his desk to write to his wife when the tanker was shaken from stem to stern by a massive shock, as though she had run at full speed over a reef. In a flash he was back on the bridge where the first officer shouted to him:

'Torpedo track to starboard!' But the captain guessed right and said: 'That will be the U-boat we rammed when turning, and now pressed down under our keel.' Later, they thought they spotted a long shadow in the moonlight and made off at maximum speed.

In U 333 we had been hurled to and fro. In the control room we stood in a fountain of water, jets coming from everywhere. Water was pouring from the periscope well and from the ventilation ducting. This heavy break-in of water pointed to a gash in the pressure hull. There was only one thing to do: surface!

The conning-tower hatch refused to open so we had to climb out through the galley hatch and clear the conning-tower hatch from outside. Then we saw the extent of the damage: the tanker had first hit us at the bow, twisted our nose to port and then, with the turning of her screws acting like a chopper, shaved off the bridge and mangled our 'three little fishes'. The watertight stem was torn open, the forward net-cutter had gone and something was also missing from the stern one. The steel casing of the conning tower was dented, the periscope snapped, the D/F set and torpedo aiming sight destroyed. The bow caps of tubes two and four were jammed and could not be opened. So much for our damage.

British Prestige had torn open the whole length of her own double hull but luckily for her the inner hull remained intact and she was able to resume way. After the encounter a certain amount was written in England about this ship and her captain. It was said that *British Prestige* had lived up to her name, and emphasis was placed on the shrewd tactics of the captain, who had incidentally been kept on the alert by continual cries for help from ships sinking in different places. His lone voyage on unfrequented routes was remarked upon, and all the things it was customary to say in those days, when someone had once again survived, were said. Certainly, *nomen est omen*, but it had been a chance encounter and the unpredictable change of course must have been a decision of the moment. What appeared to be forgotten in the euphoria was that Captain Hill was a sober-minded sailor, whose sole concern must have been for his cargo — the most dangerous that could be imagined: aviation spirit. One spark would have sufficed to blast him and his ship to pieces — and at such close quarters, us into the bargain. So it could be said 'All's well that ends well' . . . and today we exchange Christmas greetings.

Seen in daylight, things were bad enough for us and we lost no time in effecting jury repairs with whatever lay to hand. In the National Socialist state, 1 May was known as *Tag der Arbeit* (Work Day) which it had certainly become for U 333. While the sun shone down on us and a fresh breeze aired the surfaced boat my people toiled away until the sweat ran down their naked chests. Two thirds of the conning-tower casing, which had crumpled like paper, was burnt off, the rotating direction-finder was made watertight with wooden pegs and cement, the conduit in the conning tower was welded together, and various other repairs carried out. In our area of operations we hardly needed net cutters, direction-finding off the Spanish coast lay a long time ahead and by then I would have thought of something. In place of the underwater aiming sight I set some binoculars on top facing forward, meaning to aim with the whole boat and hoping that the greater accuracy would enable me to get within a stone's throw of the enemy.

Although the crew's manual abilities proved themselves once again and we were fully optimistic, a subsequent test dive produced an uncontrollable leak. From somewhere there was a continual trickle which collected below in the bilges and required constant pumping, without which it would have built up dangerously — and increased the weight of the boat. We could hardly think of lengthy passages underwater or lying on the bottom, and at greater depths the pumps would barely be able to work against the outside pressure. On top of this, we had only three torpedo tubes in working order, numbers one, three and five. The other two refused to budge.

Strictly speaking we were only operational to a limited extent. No one would have reproached me if I had broken off the patrol and turned back. It had not been my fault. All the same, in war one may count on some luck and I had already heard so much about the Straits of Florida that I hoped to recapture it there. This was the summary of my thoughts and I wrote briefly in the log: 'Intention — ahead into the Straits of Florida. Surfaced by day, in no circumstances return home without steamer.' Nothing was going to deter me from my assignment.

I could rely on my crew. The course of previous operations had shown that. They followed me through thick and thin, gave of their best, and did not appear to worry their heads. But did they? No thought-reader, I cannot tell what goes through the heads of a U-boat crew undergoing bombing, a harassment with depth-charges, or a collision. What do the very young ones feel, those on their first mission? Some, full of the courage of ignorance, hardly change expression and seem to grasp the danger not at all. Others show fear over their faces and clearly believe the end has come. But nobody cries out; perhaps they press a clenched fist to their mouth. They are still young — very young — around twenty, and less. But they do not cry out. They take their example from the older ones, who in turn model their behaviour on that of the officers, while together all look to the captain, the 'old man', who is not yet thirty.

U-boat captains did not, of course, recruit their own crews, but a word in the right quarter could achieve what was required, and I believe I had a lucky knack in the choice of my own crew. 'What have you learnt, do you play games?' were the usual questions I asked of applicants for U 333, of whom there were enough. I addressed the very young ones with the familiar 'du'. If in civilian life they were locksmiths, plumbers, electricians, mechanics or professional sailors who had taken up corresponding careers in the navy I looked on them as valuable recruits. In itself I did not take sport so seriously, but if by chance the man played football he would probably develop a feeling for teamwork and fit in. And if, in addition, someone could produce a bit of music on the squeeze-box or mouth organ, he was my man. Music does not solve every problem, but it's a help on many occasions, and on many occasions we were going to need all the help we could get.

I did everything possible, stood up for them, and when necessary got them out of trouble, as in the case of Ernst, one of my stokers, barely twenty. When drunk in La Pallice he had got into a brawl and been sentenced by a court martial to six months' imprisonment 'for conduct harmful to the reputation of the German armed forces abroad'. To the supreme military commander in that area this had seemed too severe, and being the legal authority, he had changed the sentence to six weeks 'severe arrest'. Severe arrest meant two days bread and water, on the third day soup, then bread and water again, and so on — with work at the same time. The boy had to help build a swimming pool in La Rochelle. I was driving past the building site when he shot out of the hole and leapt right in front of my radiator. Dirty, emaciated, and with eyes lying deep in their sockets, he was barely recognisable, and could not produce a word. I took him with me at once and persuaded the drafting office to commute his sentence to probation, which of course would be remitted after the next patrol.

Admittedly I did not do that for purely humanitarian reasons. He happened to be the best man in the control room I could get — a man I had to have.

My half-wrecked U 333 continued on towards its goal, the Florida coast. With the Florida peninsula the United States stretches down to the subtropics, breaking up at the bottom end into a number of small islands and islets, the so-called Florida Keys, Key West being the most southerly point of the United States. Between Florida, Cuba and the Bahamas lie the Straits of Florida, a sea passage about 100 miles wide connecting the Gulf of Mexico with the Atlantic. Being the shortest route, it is of the greatest value to the considerable American coastal shipping and is constantly used by the big tankers on their way to the Texan oil ports and the Mississippi, the ships taking advantage here of the Gulf Stream flowing northwards at up to five knots, or avoiding it by sailing close to land.

Operation 'Drum beat' had begun on 13 January, 1942, and from the day of the declaration of war the United States had had almost five weeks in which to adjust to the new conditions. If she had not thought it necessary to do so, the next seven days were to demonstrate the seriousness of the situation. In that week, from 13 to 19 January, 1942, seven of my comrades sank 17 ships totalling 110,000 tons between New York and Key West. That should have been enough to wake up the Americans. When U 333 arrived it was already 4 May, and it was thanks to the skill of our excellent chief quartermaster that after three and a half thousand miles of sea and sky we found the exact point we had been aiming for, the Bethel Shoal Buoy.

Directly off Florida, we were in one of the loveliest holiday paradises in the world. As in quiet times, the fairway in the strait was marked with buoys, so navigation was not difficult. Everything seemed to me inexpressibly peaceful and I let my officers look through the periscope. When evening came we surfaced and, one after another, the men came up to the bridge for a breath of fresh air — and rubbed their eyes in disbelief.

We had left a blacked-out Europe behind us. Whether in Stettin, Berlin, Paris, Hamburg, Lorient or La Rochelle — everywhere had been pitch dark. At sea we tried not to show any light, even hiding the glowing cigarette in the hollow of the hand when smoking was allowed on the bridge. Not a ray of light came through the conning-tower hatch. Yet here the buoys were blinking as normal, the famous lighthouse at Jupiter Inlet was sweeping its luminous cone far over the sea. We were cruising off a brightly lit coastal road with darting headlights from innumerable cars. We went in so close that through the night glasses we could distinguish equally the big hotels and the cheap dives, and read the flickering neon signs. Not only that: from Miami and and its luxurious suburbs a mile-wide band of light was being thrown upwards to glow like an aureole against the underside of the cloud layer, visible from far below the horizon. All this after nearly five months of war!

Before this sea of light, against this footlight glare of a carefree new world, were passing the silhouettes of ships recognisable in every detail and sharp as the outlines in a sales catalogue. Here they were formally presented to us on a plate: please help yourselves! All we had to do was press the button.

7
Floodlit Florida

There was no time, however, for lengthy considerations about cause and effect. 'Drum beat' continued and I had to think how to get rid of my torpedoes as quickly and effectively as possible from the three tubes remaining to me, and bring my damaged U-boat home. Within three times twenty-four hours it was to be all over. In that time two other U-boats were operating in the same region while a third had recently left. But we had no contact with one another.

Measured by our previous experiences the Straits of Florida were only lightly guarded. Many of the American convoy escorts and U-boat hunters had been drawn off to the Pacific, only a few obsolescent warships remained. All the same, things did not look all that favourable for us U-boats. We no longer had the bottomless ocean depths under the keel. Here the ocean comes up from below and meets the continental shelf; in these extremely shallow coastal waters we had only a few metres to play with — on the other hand no one expected to find us here, for our inexperienced pursuers were watching only the deeps.

The following three days were memorable. We were lying surfaced in only 8 metres of water by the Bethel Shoals' lighted whistle buoy when just after midnight a large ship came in sight heading south. It was the tanker *Java Arrow*, 13,325 tons laden, belonging to Socony Vacuum Oil. As officialdom later revealed, despite repeated calls to hurry, the tanker had simply dawdled along the whole way down from New York as a straggler from a convoy. I manoeuvred into a firing position and sent off two torpedoes which struck *Java Arrow* amidships and set her burning furiously. The 45 crewmen rowed away in the boats. While tugs and escort ships were directed to *Java Arrow*, the air was humming with a new call for help from the south. The few guard ships were shuttled to and fro and confusion mounted.

It was bright moonlight and everything was visible for miles. Ignoring the danger, a few hours later a freighter approached: the *Amazone*, a mere 2,000-tonner from the Royal Dutch Shipping Company of Amsterdam. Why waste words? — another double shot. The stern broke off, the steamer was burning and the crew took to the boats. We got the names of all the ships from the SOS calls and kept ourselves informed of all the measures taken. They were using the radio here without restraint as in peacetime and apparently cared nothing about 'careless talk'.

The moon still shone, and day was not far off. I crossed the fairway. On the other side I put the boat on the bottom and waited for the next ship. Soon the sound-detector was recording strong propeller noises. Surface again! Before us the tanker *Halsey*, an 11,000-tonner from the Farr Spinning Co. of Wilmington, Delaware. Once more a double shot and a hit amidships. The explosion rent the waning night with a thunderous roar. Before the escorts' eyes the tanker disappeared in a jet-black cloud. When the smoke dispersed only the burning superstructure and upper deck appeared above the water. The life-saving station at Lake Inlet managed to bring to safety 31 survivors from the burning wreck.

The sinkings had taken place as quickly as they are described here, in almost copybook style. None of us had imagined it to be so easy, and it could not and would not continue. Another tanker came in view. I turned U 333 and fired a shot from the stern tube — or, more accurately, I meant to, but the firing-rod stuck. By the time we had cleared the tube, the tanker had gone. I fired a final shot at the burning *Halsey* to destroy her completely. Bad luck: after a straight, phosphorescent track marvellous to follow, the torpedo ran aground in shallow water and was seen no more. The night filled with the shadows of more ships which were all hurrying northward and were soon out of reach.

A local American report described the fairway as littered with wreckage of every kind and the sea as covered with a film of oil which periodically caught fire, giving off thick clouds of smoke. Twelve hours later and throughout the day these banks of smoke lay like black flags above the horizon, darkening the sun.

And still the coastal lights were shining from Atlantic City down to Florida. What we did not know was that the tourist season had started and the hotel owners, bar keepers, those that ran the bathing beaches and the travel bureaux, in brief the tourist industry, were insisting that they stayed burning. Too much money was at stake. And so, while the visitors amused themselves, we sank their ships outside their own front door. That did not seem to bother them and even officialdom was no more alert. At his interrogation before the Marine Investigation Board, New York, the captain of the *Halsey*, H. K. Johnson, complained that his ship had been regularly lit up by the rotating searchlight at Jupiter Inlet airfield, so that the U-boats had got a good look at him. He himself had been blinded by the light and seen neither the enemy, nor a torpedo track. Again and again, like all other captains, he had also suggested the convoy system should be improved, but so far nothing had been done.

After the torpedoing of the *Halsey* east of St. Lucie Inlet the agitation reached its peak. All escorts and air squadrons as well were put in the picture and as the survivors from the sunken ships swore black and blue that they had been attacked by two U-boats (because of torpedo tracks allegedly seen from different directions), and every shipwrecked sailor gave his own version of sighting whole U-boat flotillas, complete confusion arose in the Straits of Florida.

The last straw was an attack made by Reinhard Suhren against the *Eclipse*, a ship with important war material. Hence, that night, Coast Guard patrol boats ran to and fro, up and down, trying to be everywhere at once. There were few enough of them, only three, plus the destroyer *Vigilant*. But all they found were lifeboats with survivors — and an old wreck that they took for a U-boat and attacked with depth charges.

Now it was 6 May, 1942. I laid the boat on the bottom by the St. Lucie Shoal lighted whistle buoy in only 30 metres of water, comfortable enough. Reloaded the tubes in peace and started listening again. Heard propeller noises, approaching. Lifted off the bottom and saw a steamer. But at the same time much finer sounds were reaching our ears at seconds' intervals: the ping-ping-ping-ping from the impulses of an Asdic sonar transmitting apparatus with which a pursuer was on our trail. And the moderate revolutions of the freighter were suddenly blended with the higher-pitched sounds of rapidly turning screws. My periscope was still only patched up but so much I could recognise at once: on the flat calm surface a patrol boat was coming towards me with foaming bow wave. It was PC 451 from the Coast Guard which had been withdrawn elsewhere after my attacks and ordered at maximum speed to the Bethel Shoals. Later PC 450 and the destroyer *Vigilant* also arrived.

On an encounter such as this one does not wait for identification but goes straight at one another. Hit first, hit hard. All references from the enemy side are taken from the American operational reports which deal in detail with the 'U-boat kill'. They were after me, had reached and cornered me at last. The attacker had become the quarry and now they set about despatching U 333. The kill began and the blows all came from one side.

I lowered the periscope and went at once to 20 metres, but before I got there the first depth charge crashed, making us stagger. The hydroplanes failed, the boat went down by the stern, on its knees as it were, and for a few terrible moments tried to break surface bow-first and show itself. We were just able to prevent that by flooding, but overdid it so that the boat sank like a stone to the bottom.

And now the depth charges followed in series. To judge by the propeller noises we now had two opponents to deal with. They came forward cautiously and deliberately. Then we heard their obsolete depth charges go overboard, *klatsch — klatsch — klatsch*. And now suddenly their propellers were revolving faster, rising to a high-pitched singing noise which moved away from above us. The attackers were running from the explosive power of their own depth charges which detonated in their wake and hit us like punches in the pit of the stomach. And between whiles, in quiet moments, again the 'ping' of the locator echoing against the hull which, on coming closer, turned to a brief pattering noise like rain drops on a tin roof.

One series followed another. These old depth charges of the Americans left over from 1918 were not precisely accurate, but with their 200 kilos of explosive they gave us considerable shocks. Diving tanks and oil bunkers were torn open, fuel ran out and marked the surface with iridescent slicks into which more depth charges crashed.

Our lighting had mostly failed again. We crouched in the dark and awaited the next present with beating heart. We could hear it coming closer, made bets, held our breath — now! Over and past — until the next time. Depth gauge and rudder indicator came loose, the engine-room telegraph broke, the diesel air supply mast was leaking and the valves were not watertight. There were trickles everywhere. The minutes became eternity, all sense of time was lost. And the enemy would not give up.

We had to get away, but an attempt to get off the bottom failed. Although the boat was trimmed bow-heavy, the forward hydroplanes turned hard-a-dive and the motors were running, the stern would not come up. And only by flooding in time could we prevent the bow surging up again. The stern again bumped on the bottom and soon U 333 lay full length on the sea-bed. And still the depth charges exploded.

Eventually, the enemy would run out of ammunition. Until then we had to keep our nerve. I tried to change our position and as gently as possible slip into deeper water. It seemed to succeed. Trimmed to nearly neutral buoyancy as far as circumstances allowed, with very little extra ballast and moving slowly, U 333 glided over the ocean floor. After seven hours (!) we at last reached 60 metres.

It was late at night (as I later discovered) when the destroyer *Vigilant* and the two Coast Guard patrol boats were at last withdrawn to accompany a convoy from Fort Pierce to the north. When their hopes of a definite U-boat kill had not been fulfilled and neither items of uniform nor lifebelts, let alone fixtures, had come to the surface, they began to doubt whether they had flushed out a U-boat at all. It could have been an old wreck sunk in a hurricane. But no one dared to admit that openly and, believing in his U-boat to the last and remembering the oil slicks, the captain of PC 451 wrote in his log: 'It was assumed that the U-boat may have been damaged.'

In fact they had depth-charged us persistently for 15 hours, as they confirmed. We ourselves had forgotten time. Below deck day and night were the same and equally dangerous, but according to the chronometer it was now 7 May.

We had to surface. Meanwhile, however, a further destroyer had arrived at the scene of action, the *Dallas* from the Underwater Defence School at Key West. The destroyer had orders to take part in the hunt and finish off the U-boat allegedly damaged by PC 451. A reconnaissance plane was cooperating, had found our oil track in the crystal clear Gulf Stream and dropped a smoke bomb to mark it. *Dallas* got a good Asdic contact and now powerfully joined in the depth-charging, at first groping forward with single throws and then following with series. Fortunately they were no better than the previous ones and, besides, I already had deeper water around me. *Dallas* fell victim to an illusion when we were believed to be seen surfacing and all guns were trained on my supposed conning tower, which then — according to the log of the *Dallas* — turned out to be the 'boil of the depth charges' and collapsed on itself.

The destroyer reported 'the submarine manoeuvred at fairly good speed and agility' and she followed our trailing oil slick which described a circle and finally a broad straight line, drawing from *Dallas* a further series of depth charges. After several attacks the captain thought we were on the bottom, unable to move. He tried to obtain an oil sample but gave up, not daring to stop the ship. Then his Asdic located us about 3,000 metres ahead of the oil slick. The current was two knots and the depth was 91 fathoms or about 160 metres. This was beyond the effective depth of his charges which at the most exploded at 120 metres whatever adjustments were made. When at 1930 a depth charge failed to explode *Dallas* ceased her attacks against us, circled the oil patch which had increased considerably and concluded that the U-boat had been further damaged.

We had to surface whether I wanted to or not. There was too much water in the boat. The diving tanks were waterlogged, we were floating only on tank no. 1. The oxygen bottles were empty, we could get no more air and were at the end of our physical strength, shut in a steel cage with the roof threatening to cave in on top of us at any moment. We breathed in gasps and jerks, were bathed in sweat, and not only because the high water temperature of the Gulf Stream turned the interior of the boat into a suffocating tube. So I ordered hydroplanes hard-a-rise, motors full ahead. Painfully the boat came up with its leaking tanks. The casing stayed completely under water, only the battered conning tower appeared. Night and darkness had come. *Dallas* lay about 2,000 metres off and did not notice us. I showed a slim silhouette and moved away cautiously. It was exactly 2200. We escaped by a hair's breadth.

Five minutes later, at 2205, *Dallas* reported by radio to headquarters: 'Submarine bottomed in ninety fathoms . . . made eight attacks total twenty-five charges. After second attack no further movement of sub noted indicating probable positive results. Suggest plane investigate spot tomorrow to determine whether slick is still present. *Dallas* proceeding to Charleston.'

And convinced of having dealt deadly blows to the enemy submarine, the destroyer steamed away at 20 knots.

Those were the three times twenty-four hours. In the same period Suhren with U 564 had sunk three ships. Schacht, who with U 507 had rounded Key West to the other side of Florida, as many as six. With my bag of three that made a full dozen, not including three more from U 109 (Bleichrodt) which had gone off to Cape Canaveral.

When, according to her log book, the destroyer *Dallas* moored port side to pier 3 at the Navy Yard, Charleston, South Carolina, at 1621 on 8 May, to escort a group of four tankers southward next day, U 333, believed to be lying destroyed on the sea-bed, was already a good way on the homeward journey to western France. After the incidents on the journey out and the continuous depth-charge attacks we had to be considered severely damaged. My engine-room staff, so well played in as a team, had more worries than spare parts. But we had kept something in reserve — namely torpedoes. We had not fired them all. And that was all to the good.

On the dark and rainy morning of 10 May a lone ship crossed our path, the *Clan Skene*, a freighter of 7,500 tons from the Clan Line, Glasgow. Two torpedoes left the still functioning bow tubes — double shot! The ship's bridge and the entire superstructure went sky high. The crew took to the boats and the ship sank on an even keel.

Behind us the indefatigable Coast Guard tried to save what could still be saved. One sortie followed another. This organisation was only incorporated in the navy as a subsidiary force in wartime and was overshadowed by its big brother, so that its effectiveness was often obscured by more dramatic events. It was hardly mentioned, although its activities in defence of human life and material deserved more respect and gratitude; as far as human life was concerned this also was true of U-boat men, for if we tried indeed to destroy tonnage, we were never indifferent to the fate of the shipwrecked crews; their rescue always took a weight off our minds.

We had heard that within two weeks alone 151 survivors from ships torpedoed in the Straits of Florida had been saved. The Cape Canaveral lighthouse, which was still blinking, became a refuge for the shipwrecked and supplied them with necessities, while an officer of the Coast Guard went searching for survivors with a sea-plane among burning oil and thick clouds of smoke and found a boat with 13 completely exhausted men who had been drifting for a week under the hot sun in the Gulf Stream.

After we had left, their efforts turned to the *Eclipse*, a freighter loaded with essential war supplies which Suhren had torpedoed and her captain had run aground. The Coast Guard was quickly on the spot and, as it was reported, 'the spectators on land had a splendid show watching the salvage operation, full of curiosity as at a movie.' Apparently the greatest trouble came from the civilian tug captains who did not regard themselves as under military discipline, and only after much argument took the ship to Port Everglades. Similar treatment was tried with the *Java Arrow*. The ship had been abandoned by the crew and lay at anchor. Under orders from the Coast Guard two tugs brought the crew back along with an acetylene torch operator who was to burn through the anchor chain so that *Java Arrow* could be towed away. The blue acetylene flame and flashlights lit up the scene conveying the impression 'of a firework display laid on to amuse the holidaymakers.' This was too much for the crew of the tanker, who had no desire to be torpedoed yet again or left swimming in a sea of burning oil, and they demanded to be returned to the beach. Eventually the burnt out wreck was towed to Port Everglades.

And still the lights were burning. Not until 15 May was a total black-out ordered. From then on, this idyllic coast as well was subjected to the darkness of war — a war which it had taken long enough to comprehend. Florida's once so golden beaches were dark. Dead fish and the oil-smeared corpses of countless sea birds poisoned the air. Where bathers once found refreshment everything was now begrimed with the crude oil from sunken tankers and fuel oil from steamers' bunkers. Where children had once played in the shallows, dead sailors were found and the surf threw up smashed lifeboats, lifejackets and belts.

Professor Samuel Eliot Morison, editor of the official *History of the United States Naval Operations in World War II*, Vol. 1, calls the sinking of ships off New York and the Florida coast 'a merry massacre' and writes: ' . . . not till three months after the start of Drum beat were some lights extinguished along the coast. But the clamour from Atlantic City to South Florida that the tourist season had been ruined continued. And so ships were sunk and sailors drowned so that the citizens could continue to enjoy their business and their pleasure as before . . . '

The survivors of the sunken steamers and tankers were often hailed by the men on the conning tower of the U-boats and asked for the name of their ship and the cargo. Sometimes they even told. In most cases they were then dismissed with the joke customary in the U-boat arm at that time: 'Send the bill to Roosevelt!'

Some historians were firmly convinced that the German U-boats worked with agents in the USA itself and received fresh food and diesel oil from sailing ships in the Caribbean. The head of the F.B.I., J. Edgar Hoover, wrote in the *American Magazine* 10/42, that in the period January to May 1942 his office 'had been obliged to investigate more than 500 reports of enemy U-boats surfacing off our coasts, of which every single one was false.'

Patriotic amateur airmen had got together and obtained permission to set up their own flying corps. These unofficial operations increased the confusion by reporting U-boats everywhere, which almost always turned out to be driftwood or portions of wrecks. And of course enthusiastic yachtsmen in particular felt moved to offer themselves and their often luxurious motor and sailing yachts. Hundreds of these craft were given a lick of camouflage paint and their owners the naval rank of petty officer, like Ernest Hemingway, for instance, who in his yacht *Pilar*, equipped with a machine-gun, hunting rifle, revolver and explosives, dreamt of casting hand grenades into the conning tower of a U-boat. These flotillas of 'bloody amateurs', or 'hooligan navy' as they were called, created complete chaos by also seeing U-boats everywhere and sending the few destroyers to chase hither and thither and find nothing. Though their value was precisely nil the participants had fun, besides receiving a boost to their morale, and had an opportunity to indulge their love of air and sea travel free of charge, with Uncle Sam providing the fuel and food.

When the so-called 'Drum beat' started, a sharp press and radio censorship had immediately been imposed in the USA, which suppressed all undesired news. Neither the number of ships sunk nor the place of sinking could be revealed in the media. To quieten the public, fictitious dates were published and reports of 'U-boats sunk en masse'. On one day alone, 25 February, Navy Minister Franklin William Knox, himself a successful newspaper publisher, announced three German U-boats destroyed and four heavily damaged. On 1 April he reported that a total of 28 U-boats had been sunk since the middle of January off the east coast of America. Nobody had checked these figures. Coastal dwellers still saw only the smoke from burning tankers, wounded men, oil-smeared survivors stumbling ashore, wrecks run aground. They saw the heavily damaged ships, some barely floating, which were towed to the nearest ports. And they wanted to know what was going on.

The American press agencies, Associated Press and United Press, soon saw through the Navy Minister's tactic and made their own calculations. In fact not one single German U-boat had so far been destroyed. Not until 14 April, 1942, did the destroyer *Roper* sink U 85 off Cape Hatteras. And then some bitterly angry commentaries appeared in many newspapers. For although the mass media themselves already suspected that sailing in convoy was the best, if not the only, possibility of protecting merchant shipping against U-boats, the highest naval authorities were still divided on the issue.

We U-boat men knew well enough that a big convoy of let us say 40 ships, escorted by even only a few destroyers and corvettes, could not be attacked even by a whole pack of U-boats without loss to ourselves, and this applied even more so to the coastal convoys protected by air reconnaissance. But cooperation between the US Navy and Air Force was impaired, as with us, by questions of demarcation. If a German U-boat was sighted off Palm Beach, for instance, the area naval command in Key West had to ring up the bomber command of the 3rd Army in Charleston by private telephone and request a machine from Miami. That would be the equivalent, in the case of an enemy submarine being sighted off Heligoland, to the German Admiral (North Sea) having to ask Munich for a fighter bomber stationed in Cuxhaven. Being spacious, America is accustomed to think of distances in different terms.

Nor was the American naval command inclined to entertain the very thorough British experiments with the convoy system, let alone adopt them. When the British maintained that 'a weakly protected convoy is better than no convoy at all' the Americans countered that 'an inadequately protected convoy is worse than no convoy'. Or to simplify: does not a number of scattered ships, sailing alone, run a smaller risk than a concentration of ships in an only weakly protected convoy? That was the question at issue.

Finally the Chief of Staff of the American armed forces, General George Marshall, informed the C-in-C Navy, Admiral Ernest J. King, that 'the losses through U-boats off our Atlantic coast and in the Caribbean threaten our entire war effort.' For his part King again drew attention to the shortage of U-hunters and escort vessels, but promised a change. 'Since 15 May our waters off the east coast enjoy a high degree of security,' and he continued: 'I would like to say in this connection that the convoy is not just one way of dealing with the U-boat danger. It is the only way that promises success. The so-called patrol and hunter operations have proved increasingly useless.' Under the pressure of events he had changed his mind.

Samuel Eliot Morison says in retrospect: 'Admiral Tirpitz's attack on our east coast with six U-boats from April to November, 1918, had given only a very slight foretaste of the stinking medicine which Admiral Dönitz prescribed for us in 1942 . . . the massacre which the U-boats were able to "enjoy" along the Atlantic coast in 1942 was as great a national disaster as if saboteurs had blown up half a dozen of our biggest munition factories.'

On 14 May Admiral Dönitz was taken to Hitler's headquarters by the C-in-C Navy, Grand Admiral Raeder, to deliver a situation report. The text is contained in the war diary of the naval command, and states *inter alia*: ' . . . On 1 May, 1942, 124 boats were operational [i.e. including those on the way to or from operations, or in dock. P.C.] of which 85 were in the Atlantic, 19 in the Mediterranean, 20 in the North Sea. U-boat war is war against enemy merchant tonnage. American and British tonnage are jointly controlled and are therefore to be treated as one. It is therefore correct to sink where it can be done in the greatest numbers possible and cheaply, that means with minimal loss. The C-in-C U-boats intends to continue operations in America so long as that area remains fruitful. Their effectiveness is therefore carefully checked every month, i.e. the average tonnage sunk per U-boat at sea per day is ascertained. In January this was 209 GRT, in February 387, in March 409 and in April 412 GRT. Up to now a small increase is to be noted. We are still correct therefore in conducting U-boat operations in the American zone.

'One day the situation will change. There are already signs that the Americans are making every effort to stem the heavy losses . . . '

They did so quicker than expected. After the colossal exercise 'Drum beat' there was a temporary pause. Though ships were still falling victim to the U-boats, the losses could not be compared with those in the first months of 1942. Anti-U-boat defence had been strengthened. More destroyers had been drafted to the support of the initial Coast Guard units, more CG aircraft were stationed at St. Petersburg (Florida). Air Force units patrolled the area of Miami and Palm Beach, there were bomber bases at Jacksonville and Tampa. Aircraft which, unknown to us, were equipped with radar, hunted at night between Cape Canaveral and Fowey Rocks. Tactical search groups were formed, forerunners of the later Hunter Killer Task Groups intended to make U-hunting deadly certain — deadly for the U-boat, of course.

Within the next twelve months every deficiency was to be made good. The inexperience of the crews, tactical weaknesses, strategic indecision, all this was to be made up for by dint of a real breakthrough in technical developments, which was effectively to close the 'mid-Atlantic gap' and nullify our previous superiority, leading eventually to the 'black May' of 1943. Thereafter, from being the hunters, the U-boats were to become the hunted.

The capacity of the American shipyards, totally underestimated by our high command (which means by Hitler), and their new method of building Henry Kaiser's Liberty and Victory ships in sections, threw out all our calculations. Although in 1942 we were still confident of destroying 700,000 tons a month and outstripping new additions, we had in fact already lost the race between sinkings and new construction — the cardinal factor of the U-boat war. They built faster than we could sink. And as for the durability of these 'off-the-peg' ships, built in a few months on the conveyor-belt system, Dr. Josef Goebbels, Reich Minister for Popular Enlightenment and Propaganda, might maintain they would break to pieces in a storm, but they were still to be found decades later on every sea, under every possible flag. Against such 'superiority' we could simply do nothing with our few U-boats.

As far as our own U-boat building programme was concerned, Dönitz was still confident that May, 1942, when he continued: ' . . . by virtue of the large U-boat numbers which we are expecting, we shall have sufficient forces to make inroads into increased and more distant areas of traffic, with attacks now made possible by the availability of U-boat tankers . . . With tanker support we are in a position to operate in the Gulf of Mexico and off Panama or down to Cape Town and Bahia . . . and to go for two-week operations to La Plata and Cape Town. U-boat losses are now extraordinarily small. They will doubtless grow as a result of attacks on convoys and in strongly defended areas. The U-boat arm has faith in its material and faith in its capacity to fight. It is a matter now of bringing out the (new) boats from the Baltic as fast as possible and of having as many boats as possible at sea, on patrol.'

In command of British submarines, and soon to be Commander-in-Chief Western Approaches, was the 59-year-old Admiral Sir Max Horton. In a strategic analysis 'Sea Power and the RAF' of 26 February, 1942, he had demanded close cooperation between Navy and Air Force. ' . . . the only way to ensure us final victory is to employ our Air Force where it is most needed, i.e. in cooperation with the Navy to master and break up the present sea offensive of the Axis . . . If we are to last through this eventful year and tire the enemy before we ourselves are exhausted it will be necessary for our naval and air forces to be thrown together into the battle for command of the sea. If we lose command of the sea, we lose the war.'

According to Horton the U-boats had sunk up to May 1942 a total of 8,719,000 tons of merchant shipping. By the end of this period they were sinking three ships a day. They were approaching the peak of their success.

As U 333 set out on its voyage home after its operations off the Florida coast, we were honoured with a special announcement on the radio and mentioned in the official war report. The mood on board shot up. After completing the trip to Florida in 35 days — which is no faster than a sailing ship in the trade wind and reflects our economical fuel consumption — we did the return journey in less than three weeks. On 26 May, the 58th day of our 'journey to America' we slipped in towards La Rochelle with fluttering flag and a pennant on the raised periscope for every ship sunk, the last short distance under escort. At 0815 hours we were tied up in the bunker at La Pallice.

The boat was photographed from front and rear. So much damage had hardly been seen before. We were fêted. Most German newspapers carried column-long reports on the front page under headlines like 'On Atlantic Patrol with barely submersible U-boat' or 'Tanker rams U-boat and tears off conning tower' or 'Depth-charged for hours then: operation continued'. Moreover, Dönitz wrote of 'two particularly capable U-boat commanders operating [off the coast of Florida], Lieutenant-Commanders Cremer in U 333 and Suhren in U 564. Both achieved the same successes in their attacks as previously, even in shallow water and the presence of strong sea and air surveillance.' My crew were very proud of their commander, for fame rubs off.

On 5 June, 1942, I became the 48th member of the armed forces to be decorated with the Knight's Cross to the Iron Cross. It was entirely welcome to me, but did not go to my head. There can hardly be a soldier in the whole world, whether friend or foe, who would not be proud of merited decorations. In the further course of the war a captain with the Knight's Cross was particularly valued by U-boat crews: he offered a certain security, because a young and inexperienced commander, who wanted at all costs to clock up the 50,000 GRT of enemy shipping which entitled him to his Knight's Cross, would often act over-hastily and could put his crew at needless risk, especially under the intensified defence measures of the enemy. This at any rate was how the ordinary crewman saw it, which is understandable, for whatever his readiness to fight, or because of it, everyone wants to survive.

8

Action against convoys

The long repairs after our Florida patrol made it possible to send the entire 52-man crew home on three weeks' leave in two alternate shifts. I myself went to my mother's. Strange as it may sound, despite the happy anticipation, there were men on board who preferred to travel to Germany in the second shift. They came mainly from the engine room and had hardly been able to get a breath of fresh air during the patrol, let alone a glimpse of the sun. They almost always produced the same excuse: 'I just can't show my face at home looking as pale as this, Sir. My mother would have a fit.' Admittedly, none of us was looking fresh as a daisy, and we all needed to recuperate. Even the normal round of duties, the tiring bridge watch in the wet and cold, the confined work around the diesels and electric motors, the shortage of oxygen when submerged, the lack of exercise and loss of appetite which occurred despite every culinary art, all this made extreme physical demands. Add to this the interminable depth-charge attacks to which we had been helplessly exposed when submerged, and even the strongest men emerged exhausted.

Our appearance, furthermore, gave us the look of pirates rather than military men, and unintentionally marked us off from the personnel at the base with their military bearing. It was not merely the matted growth of hair and unkempt beards which inevitably arose in the conditions on board (where cosmetics were not our first consideration) and which usually resulted in the hairdresser being our first call once ashore. It was also the uniform. We went to sea with only a kit bag containing a change of underclothes, socks, handkerchiefs and little else. During a patrol all other effects were crammed into a bag that stayed behind at the base, and it can be imagined what the contents came to look like. When the blue number one suit came to light it would be crumpled (if not musty), anything but corresponding to regulations, and would need

(above) *13. Tanker torpedoed off the Florida coast (background), May 1942.*
(below) *14. Torpedoed tanker engulfed in flame, May 1942.*

(above) *15. U 333's conning tower riddled with Oerlikon fire from HMS* Crocus. (*The three little fishes, however, keep swimming.*) (inset) *16. The U-boat after its collision with the corvette . . .* (below) *17. HMS* Crocus.

ironing. But the U-boat man, with the sea and its storms behind him, would be above such niceties. Why bother, and with what? He felt good now and at ease through the mere contrast between war and peace.

Only the military police, intent on good order, had to shut both eyes when they came across a U-boat man, whom they could recognise a hundred yards off. There was not much they could say — after all, he was living out of his kit bag. And if he did not return from patrol, which might happen quite soon, his bagful of personal effects would be sent to the next of kin: your husband is dead . . .

But for the time being the U-boat man wanted to recuperate and forget. In the big canteen which was open for U-boat men from mid-day to seven there were only sausages, cakes and weak coffee. But he was allowed to dance with the young German girls on the staff. Afterwards, at any rate so long as the towns with their dives had not been bombed out, he would go to his favourite bar to enjoy a stiff drink and the girls behind the counter. Things tended to become even more uninhibited until occasionally someone got out of hand and tried to smash up everything within reach — as our leading seaman Waldemar did, for instance, when he created so much devastation that willy-nilly I had to stop his leave.

He was working in the bunker when Admiral Dönitz came in with a group of staff officers, unexpectedly. 'Why such a grumpy expression?' asked Dönitz. Waldemar stood to attention and described his excesses and his stopped leave in loving detail, whereupon Dönitz shook his head and replied: 'I think you could have spared me the details.' 'But you did ask me, Sir!' Waldemar countered. The C-in-C U-boats turned briefly to me and said with emphasis: 'Cremer, make a note! If there's time, send the man on leave after the second shift.' And covered now from on high, I did that all the more readily because, on the job, Waldemar was the most reliable man, who allowed nothing to disturb his calm. Another man who had sold items of uniform to get money for schnaps I got released on probation. There was plenty of opportunity to prove oneself and whatever iniquities the men might have committed ashore, on board they were above reproach. On board, there were no longer insignia of rank because everyone went around in leather suits, oilskins or unconventional mufti, and saluting was no longer required because we lived together round the clock and everyone knew everyone else. On board, duty was performed, not according to the big-ship rule book 'Behaviour towards superiors', but according to circumstances, and the commander was always 'the old man' regardless of how young he might be.

When we put to sea again it was already mid-August, 1942. It had taken 77 days to patch up U 333 — and I mean to patch up, but in view of the many plates welded on top of one another we believed we now had a particularly strong boat under our feet. Moreover, we were psychologically back in condition for battle. Leave was over and port lay behind us.

By August 1942 our enemy had recently been showing a noticeable increase in the air surveillance of Biscay, and at night out of the darkness he would home in on surfaced U-boats quite inexplicably. In compliance with standing orders (later rescinded) we therefore made the voyage out by day, 'as the danger of surprise by locating aircraft is greater at night than by day.' (The success of Allied night-time air surveillance methods, as experienced by U 333, is described in Chapter 10, p. 116.)

There it was again — the latent danger of location which always hung over us and was shortly to give trouble to U 333, but not in the way we expected. The first day at sea passed without incident and gave us an opportunity to practise the usual manoeuvres: emergency dives, more emergency dives, and yet more emergency dives, until every function was performed as in sleep and the boat disappeared from the surface in less than half a minute. Difficulties, on the other hand, arose with the 'Biscay Cross', already mentioned, which gave us early warning of the locating beam of hostile aircraft. Each time we dived it had to be dismantled, so that I noted in the log: 'With the great cross aerial the boat is not ready for emergency dive!' The disadvantage outweighed the advantage. So what was the point of it?

On this our third patrol we were not ordered to operate alone but had to join a group of U-boats code-named *Blücher*. In the course of the war there were numerous groups comprising a varying number of U-boats ordered to bar the way to the enemy convoys and intercept them. These operations often covered wide areas, the boats being spaced out at intervals of up to 10 miles. The *Blücher* group consisted of seven boats, and U 333 was stationed off the Azores.

On 17 August the group made contact with the British convoy

SL 118. As the identification number indicated, it consisted of ships which had come up from the South Atlantic and formed into a convoy off Freetown, Sierra Leone. It comprised 33 merchant ships beside an armed merchant cruiser, the auxiliary cruiser *Cheshire*, a 10,500 ton passenger liner of the Bibby Line, Liverpool. The mass of the ships was divided into nine columns which sailed on a broad front in line abreast. The convoy was flanked by four escorts: *Folkestone*, *Gorleston*, *Pentstemon*, and *Wellington*. These details of a typical convoy are taken from a British account. For a single U-boat with its comparatively narrow field of vision it is almost impossible to survey everything at once. It sees only individual parts or significant detail. An overall view only arises from the cooperation of the group — if it is not forced to scatter. The attack on SL 118 lasted three days and brought U 333 no success. We did not even get a shot in. Instead we gathered practical experience which, on the German side, we were unable to recognise at the time for what it was, let alone to interpret its full scope.

As usual I was in touch with Dönitz's headquarters and exchanged several signals on short wave. A position had been assigned to me on a map square and I had reported again after arriving there. Presumably I was the last to join the group and was its wing man. Of course we were particularly on the *qui vive* after the long interval and, with our binoculars trained on the horizon, we were eagerly looking for the enemy. The boat was surfaced and we managed to out-manoeuvre several aircraft. We did not have long to wait — it was afternoon when there came a sudden cry: 'Smoke ahoy!'

Was it a convoy? I turned towards the smoke and sent off another radio signal. I tried to get closer, had to avoid a bi-plane flying up from astern, and along with the thickening smoke-cloud I caught sight of the tripod mast of a warship. The mast was very massive and at first sight suggested a cruiser. At the masthead she carried a strange latticed contraption I had never seen before and took to be a crow's nest. It was not till years later that I discovered its real significance. I closed in to maintain contact and discover more, and saw a second warship with the same mast. That is, only the mast, the ships themselves still lay below the horizon. For that reason I was thinking it extremely improbable that the enemy could have spotted us yet, when suddenly a Liberator flew up and forced us to crash-dive to periscope depth.

But no bombs were dropped. Instead, rapid propeller noises as from destroyers made me prick up my ears. Then came depth charges — about a dozen exploded really close, shaking the boat to breaking point. That, I suddenly thought, could only be the two warships with the peculiar masthead baskets. I lost no time in dropping to 90 metres.

Unwittingly I had decoyed two of the four convoy escorts towards me so that another U-boat succeeded in attacking and picking off the first ship out of the convoy at 1756, followed by others in the next two days until the series of successes broke off on 19 August. Meanwhile I was being so stubbornly pursued, I had no time to wonder how I had been located. Eventually I seemed to have shaken off my pursuers, for after some hours the depth charges were falling further and further away. U 333 was once again taking in water, of all places through the hull valve of the WC. The water was tipped with buckets into the main bilge where it was pumped out. Other leakages occurred as well until a few tons of Atlantic had collected. It was not till after midnight that circumstances allowed us to surface. From ahead came the rumble of gunfire and the night was eerily lit up by star-shells. The convoy was engaged with the other U-boats.

With us a strong grinding noise, a very loud screeching appeared in the starboard clutch. The depth charges that exploded astern had apparently thrust the propeller shaft upwards. Nevertheless, I tried to renew contact with the convoy and under cover of darkness followed it on the surface. Between whiles I reported our damage to the C-in-C in detail on short wave. Frequently I was deflected by escort vessels and forced to dive — and of course depth-charged. One pursuer (probably a destroyer) made a sharp turn towards me, but I was able to trick him. As she surged past, I turned back and put myself behind her stern. Following in her wake I continued my effort to maintain contact but saw nothing of the convoy. Then the destroyer turned the tables on me, forcing me to submerge again, but she did not pursue. It was a game of hide and seek. Surfaced once more, I was yet again forced down by a Liberator which, in the excitement, I only noticed from the splashes of his bombs. Crash dive!

All this agitation had noticeably affected U 333, and new dangers threatened us from within the boat. There was a corrosive smell. The heavy shocks had shaken up the batteries to such an extent that gas was escaping. If this mixture spread in sufficient quantity and concentration, a spark would suffice to send us sky-high. And there were more than enough sparks at the stern, where the grating of the bent propeller shaft was increasing audibly. On quick dives, particularly, it gave off a veritable rain of sparks like a grindstone. The cooling jacket of the exhaust pipe of the starboard engines showed cracks which were increasing. The boat's speed was dropping continually. Maximum performance was now out of the question.

In short it was becoming ever clearer that we could not catch up with the convoy however much we tried. SL 118 was simply running away from us as it slogged it out with the other U-boats, while U 333 dropped ever further behind, exposed to increased air attack. The brief, alas all too true résumé in my log read: 'In practice my three-day effort to maintain contact with the convoy was in vain . . .'

The damage could not be repaired with the materials on board. We had to return to base. But that was easier said than done. The noise and the grating sound in the boat became so bad that the youngest crewmen got frightened. The propeller shaft was glowing hot. To keep the boat moving at all we continually dripped oil onto the rotating steel and its bearing, hoping devoutly it would not begin to smoke or even catch fire like an overheated frying pan. To help us we used the only oil can small enough to reach the site. Because of the cramped attitude the men relieved one another in quick succession. This time, apart from the commander, everyone had to take part, even the off-duty wireless operators, although the sensitivity of their fingers to the rhythm of the Morse alphabet ought to have been spared.

So we arrived off our home base, announced ourselves, were picked up by patrol boats outside the mine fields and were led in as far as the lock. That was at noon on 24 August. My decision to abort our mission was approved in a brief comment by Dönitz: 'Patrol discontinued on account of malfunctioning machinery or depth-charge damage. Restricted movement obviated promise of operational success.'

But one question remained. What had drawn the convoy escorts so quickly and unerringly towards me, when nothing was as yet to be seen of the convoy but plumes of smoke and mast heads, while the slim silhouette of U 333 was still beyond the horizon so far as the warships were concerned? I assumed that in the circumstances I could not have been detected with radar. So how had they done it?

The answer to the riddle was one which nobody hit upon at the time. It was, again, strictly technical and, we had thought, beyond the bounds of possibility. This was in 1942. While two years later our scientists were still discussing methods of ship location, taking into consideration active or passive infra-red, ultra violet, heat-seeking and such like techniques, the Allies had long since achieved the apparently impossible and in 1942 anticipated the simplest technical solution — namely, extending radio location to short wave.

In other words they had constructed a short-wave set, the High Frequency Direction Finder HF/DF, commonly known as Huff-Duff. This set was able to determine the direction of a short-wave transmitter . . . and U-boats signalled on short wave! In general the boats maintained radio silence, but when reporting position or damage, above all on sighting a convoy, a lively exchange of information took place with the C-in-C. This was a danger we created for ourselves without recognising it.

While we went on exchanging our short-wave signals, with the aid of Huff-Duff our opponent was quietly preparing his ships and convoys for anti-U-boat defence. With this relatively simple direction-finder the radio signals of the U-boats were located in the area of the ground wave at up to 25 miles. Thus the escort vessels using the bearing ray as a guide were in a position to intercept the U-boat and turn it aside. It must again be mentioned that Huff-Duff required a particularly characteristic aerial which was unknown to us, namely the basket-like construction such as was carried by those escorts which so unexpectedly descended on me.

This had been the situation, then, when SL 118 ran into the *Blücher* U-boat pack on 17 August. The British report — and we shall frequently be using these sources which are now available — the British report states that 'during the day frequent Huff-Duff reception indicated that there was more than one U-boat in the vicinity of the convoy.' At 1558 the steamer *Nurani*, presumably on sighting torpedo tracks, gave twelve short blasts and turned to port. The torpedoes went past and struck the Norwegian *Triton* on the port side. The ship, which was heading from Sydney for Avonmouth, sank within eight minutes while the crew were picked up by the British *Dunmore*. The convoy turned 45 degrees to starboard and after an hour returned to the original course.

While the corvette *Wellington* was zig-zagging at the head of the convoy, *Folkestone* and *Pentstemon* had bared their flank cover and gone over to attack U 333. Shortly after 1600 the first series of depth charges plastered the U-boat in tens. Five minutes later came the second attack, with a third and fourth following at 1645 and 1649. Only because the British were dependent on 'poor Asdic conditions' on account of radio silence did they miss me by a hair's breadth. All the same, some of the charges exploded so close behind the stern while the boat was still at shallow periscope depth that, as already mentioned, they bent the starboard propeller shaft. Finally contact broke off completely and, with the addition of *Gorleston*, my pursuers returned to their stations with the convoy, which they reached at 1907.

When I had reported my contact with the enemy and its consequences to the C-in-C, our opponent noted that 'at 1815 a U-boat transmitted near the convoy and there was little doubt that this time two U-boats were involved.' The true size of the group remained as before undetectable and could not be ascertained even by repeated radar searches. The following night the convoy frequently sighted surfaced U-boats, near and far, altered course several times and opened fire together with star shells. But they were merely beating the water. Pursuit was fruitless as the U-boats took evasive action or submerged. Between 2000 and 2300 further depth-charge series were dropped until the ammunition apparently ran short, when only single depth charges were thrown to frighten us off.

The few escort vessels seemed to scatter, so that at times only *Gorleston* stayed with the convoy, which continued on its way undeterred. Partly owing to radar direction-finding, partly to sound location, the agitation continued on the forenoon of 18 August when the presence of three U-boats was definitely established. At 1144 a Huff-Duff bearing indicated a U-boat closing up nearby, which apparently dissolved into nothing. Then a few miles away another one came in sight. The escorts took up pursuit at maximum speed 'but despite every effort on the part of the engine-room staff, the U-boat was able to hold its own.' In other words, it ran away from them. A single gun salvo fell short.

This developing action, described in broad outline from the

British viewpoint, in which four U-boats were involved, should give an impression of the varied moves in a small convoy battle. Similarly the spatial dimensions in which everything takes place become clear when one reads that in its pursuit the corvette *Pentstemon* covered 17 miles away from the convoy, that firing took place over distances of between 3,000 and 13,000 yards, and that the U-boats for their part approached the convoy to within 70 yards(!) when their periscopes were spotted. As the mass of the ships went steaming on without pause and the rescue of ship-wrecked men was left to a 'bone gatherer', the whole 'battlefield' moved continually northwards towards England.

On the afternoon of 18 August at 1655 the auxiliary cruiser *Cheshire*, stationed behind the leading line of ships, noticed a 'disturbance' on the port side, despite air cover from a Catalina. About a minute later the steamer *Hatarana* (7,500 tons GRT) of the British India Co. was torpedoed on the port side. One minute later still, at 1657, the *Cheshire* herself received a hit to port and, as in a chain reaction, after one further minute the Dutch East Indies ship *Balingkar* (6,000 GRT) was also struck on the port side by two torpedoes, of which the first apparently ran under the *Cheshire*. All torpedoes came from U 214.

While the convoy zig-zagged, *Balingkar* sank half an hour later, her survivors being rescued by three other ships following astern. The weather was still good, the sea only slight. *Cheshire* had been struck at no. 1 hatch. The detonation had made a big hole, visible also above water. The space filled with water but the ship was able to keep up with the moderate speed of the convoy and continue the voyage. There had been no wounded on board.

In the late afternoon three armed merchant ships fired without result at a periscope. While the escorts busied themselves with the *Hatarana*, which was still afloat, a new torpedo track was observed. The listening set gave a contact, a new series of depth charges was dropped. As it did not seem advisable to stay around any longer with the *Hatarana*, all secret papers were removed and the wreck finally sunk by gunfire on the waterline. So it continued till after dark.

Just after midnight the escorts obtained radar contact with a surfaced U-boat. This was U 333 which was limping along and now dived. At 0630 next morning the same U-boat was attacked by a Liberator with gunfire and depth charges and escaped by a crash dive 'at an unusually steep angle'. Later a Catalina from Gibraltar discovered U 333 which this time, because of the defective propeller shaft, 'submerged very slowly'. It received one depth charge 'just for luck'. In the early afternoon the convoy got additional protection from the destroyer HMS *Zetland*. But further U-boat signals showed that into the third day the danger was not yet over.

On the contrary! At 1430 on 19 August the British steamer *City of Manila* (7,500 GRT) of the Ellerman Line, en route to the Clyde, was torpedoed by U 406. This time the shot came from starboard. Only ten minutes later the *Defoe* and the *Silver Sandal* reported a periscope only 75 yards astern. The ensuing wild pursuit blotted out all sound contacts, which were lost in the louder churning of propellers, and allowed the U-boat to escape. The weather was still fine and a slight swell was running.

The *Empire Voice*, a merchant ship of the British War Emergency type, took off the people from the *City of Manila*, which sank so slowly that salvage was considered, and the *Gorleston* stood by the damaged ship. But during the night the 26-year-old steamer dipped alarmingly by the bow until at last, repeatedly distracted by anti-U-boat duties, the *Gorleston* took off as many usable commodities as possible and left the sinking ship to her fate. The *City of Manila* vanished from the surface at noon on 20 August. The corvette followed the convoy as a straggler, catching up with it late on the evening of the 21st — which shows how far it had moved away. The *Cheshire*, too, had become a straggler. The damaged auxiliary cruiser had not after all been able to keep up speed and had dropped astern. But, escorted by the destroyer HMS *Zetland*, she reached Belfast Loch without further incident.

Thus ended the last attack on the convoy SL 118, in which four boats of the *Blücher* group, including U 333, had taken part. The nearer the convoy came to the British Isles the more protection it received, partly from surface craft, partly from the air. Here again, it is significant and gives an idea of the space involved, that a Liberator S/120 that had been ordered out missed the convoy. In the last stretch, almost 'before the front door', the fastest ships were taken out and fetched into port in a high-speed convoy, both parts of the original convoy covering the rest of the journey 'without incident', as we are told, and reached home waters on 25 August.

As an analysis subsequently instituted by British command

sources states, the British had located three to four U-boats following the convoy on both sides. It was at first hard to differentiate between contacts, i.e. to establish whether the signals came from several boats or one and the same. The Huff-Duff contacts on 19 August had been ascribed to several boats. But circumstances showed that they definitely came from the same boat, namely from U 333 again, which had reported damage in a long radio signal to Dönitz and in so doing was located.

The British résumé states: 'Once it is established that U-boats are in the vicinity of a convoy, HF/DF bearings obtained by the escort are invaluable in assisting the Senior Officer to estimate the probable disposition of the enemy and to make his plans accordingly.'

It closes with the qualification: 'While the value of HF/DF in escorts cannot be too highly stressed, there may be a tendency, as a result of its use, to overestimate the number of U-boats actually involved and thus to confuse the picture.'

Our opponent had outstripped us with this aid. While we were struggling to determine direction and distance, the mere direction from which the enemy approached was enough for him. From mid-May, 1942, the value of the simple apparatus was fully recognised and it was installed in naval and merchant ships. By the end of the year it was part of the standard equipment of all escort vessels. And although the accuracy of the Huff-Duff bearings decreased with distance (one spoke of 300 sea miles), a whole chain of Huff-Duff shore stations was established which could detect over great distances the presence of a U-boat in a certain area. Through the intersection of two and more Huff-Duff bearings from different stations it was finally possible to determine not only the U-boat's direction but its exact position.

So it was not surprising that until the end of the war we ascribed a large part of the U-boat losses to radar without being in the least aware of the existence of Huff-Duff. At the same time our counter-espionage had succeeded in taking telephotos of British warships with the characteristic Huff-Duff aerials. The ships had lain off Gibraltar and had been photographed by agents in Spanish Algeciras. And here is the joke: to conceal the provenance of the photos in case they fell into enemy hands, the ignorant interpreters had re-touched the background or trimmed off the top edge . . . and the typical aerials had fallen victim to this procedure!

Huff-Duff, the Allies' short-wave direction finder, was a new means of defence against the U-boats. Not by itself a war winner, admittedly, but one thing added to another: Asdic-sonar-echo-location, the ASV radar on the centimetre wavelength in aircraft, Huff-Duff and other inventions — until our opponent gained the upper hand.

(Of the seven boats in the *Blücher* group all were sunk in the further course of the war, four of them with all hands — as we say, with man and mouse. U 333 was not spared either. Only I was to survive, though at the time this looked most improbable: as far as I was concerned prospects then could not have looked worse. But I anticipate.)

Troubles seldom come singly. A run of bad luck is not so quickly ended. Our repairs were completed in a few days. U 333 was once more ready for patrol and on the way to West Africa where the *Iltis* group was stationed, and we had the task of keeping the harbour of Freetown under observation: here enemy ships coming up singly from the south were formed into convoys.

As far as crew and material were concerned everything seemed fine. Things went smoothly until after a few days we had to crash dive to escape a British land-based aircraft. Suddenly water burst into the engine room, at the same moment the inner exhaust valve fractured and flew out. Looking for the cause of the flooding, one of the petty officers found a screw as thick as a thumb in the cover of the cooling-water chamber. The cover would not shut and the water poured in. We made everything watertight with caulking and, after repairs lasting four hours, surfaced again.

These events gave rise to long technical discussions with the chief engineer. He thought the fatal screw had been 'forgotten' by a dockyard worker. During the routine manoeuvres at the start of the patrol this screw had slipped a little and, on diving away from the aircraft, it had jammed the cover and let in the water. When the water was then pumped out via the bilges it was dirty and con-taminated with oil, showing a clear track on the surface and serving the enemy as a marker to unload his depth charges accurately on our heads. Whether the exhaust valve had jumped out owing to weakness in the material or whether it had been partially sawn through in the dockyard could not be determined at sea. But there was undoubtedly intention behind the 'forgotten' screw.

95

Now the word 'sabotage' hung in the air. That nobody from our own crew was responsible seemed logical as he would have risked losing his own life. But espionage and sabotage on French soil were on the increase, encouraged by British psychological warfare which had begun with leaflets and their short-wave Atlantic transmitter. As we U-boat officers had learnt at flotilla conferences, our counter-espionage in Angers had recently succeeded in breaking a French sabotage ring. Its leader had been the French naval commander d'Estienne d'Orves. He was shot. Even without his sparse statements, it was a fair assumption that among the French dockyard workers enough men were to be found who sympathised with the awakening resistance movement and were willing to commit sabotage. Not least among them were the coloured Frenchmen employed since mid-1942 as auxiliary workers in the dockyards — Moroccans, Tunisians and other former members of French colonial territories, now dissolved, who were necessarily opposed to the Third Reich on racial grounds. And were there not political opponents among the German workers themselves? They all came under the Todt Organisation, which did not mean much and was no guarantee of their reliability. After all, one could not investigate every worker and craftsman. They had opportunity a-plenty for sabotage.

The safety of the U-boat bases was not guaranteed even by the high priority accorded to them by counter-espionage: in occupied France in 1942 only about a thousand personnel of Admiral Canaris' *Abwehr* were active, including administrative staff, drivers and radio operators. So it is in fact surprising that only this one case of sabotage occurred in U 333. For the exhaust valve had indeed been partially sawn through, as we were later to discover back at base. The matter of the 'forgotten' screw, on the other hand, was never cleared up.

After we had tanked up from a 'Milch Cow' again en route, we reached our operation area on 6 October, 1942, and approached the Freetown roads, the collecting point of convoys in the middle Atlantic. We were to ascertain the number of merchant ships with their escorts and report to the U-boat command. Shortly after 0500 we had crossed the 100 metre depth line off Freetown to reconnoitre. What happened then is recorded in my log and subsequent notes: '0400, dark night, poor visibility, rain and sheet lightning, squally. Sea slight. Shortly before 0500 I left the bridge to check the navigation and soundings. Minutes later came the shout "Captain on the bridge!" About 500 metres astern a shadow was coming towards us at maximum speed. Visibility was about two miles, the moon was covered by cloud. Escape was impossible; had we dived, the corvette (as it turned out to be) would have rammed us.

'As I reached the bridge, the corvette opened up on us with guns and machine-guns. I turned hard-a-starboard and went full ahead. Because of the close range, everyone on the bridge, including the commander, was immediately wounded and incapacitated. The first watch officer and I at once got to our feet again. I had several splinters in the arm and the officer had one through the throat. The explosion threw us both down the conning-tower hatch, but we managed to climb back onto the bridge. When my companion was hit several more times in the arm and leg, I ordered him to leave me alone on the bridge. With my one sound arm I helped the wounded lying on the bridge to get back down into the conning tower.'

One man, a bosun's mate, had apparently slipped overboard and disappeared without trace.

'. . . Meanwhile the corvette kept up continuous fire and I received yet more shell splinters. I put the rudder hard over to avoid being rammed, and tried everything to get into position to fire my torpedoes, while the corvette kept turning towards us and trying to ram. We were circling one another so tightly that their searchlight was lighting up my conning tower from above. We kept closing in until there was a crash. My manoeuvres deadened the impact of the collision but we remained locked together for what seemed an eternity.

'When it looked as though I might not be able to fire a shot or even to save the boat I gave the order "stand by lifejackets and escape gear". Meanwhile I was wounded in the head and my vision was impaired by blood running into my left eye. Owing to the short range (50 metres or less) the corvette's shells were overshooting, and several times their blast as they passed over spun me round. Then a splinter lodged in my breast-bone. Time and again I tried to evade, but the corvette followed my every movement. Weakened by loss of blood, and with blood sealing up my left eye, I decided to dive as a drastic measure to save the boat. I took up a parallel course and proceeded slowly ahead of the corvette. My boat had such a heavy list that our opponent assumed we were about to capsize, and set about ramming us again. I turned hard-a-starboard at the best speed we could muster so that she only went over our stern. Having suffered damage herself, the corvette could not follow up fast enough and, bow first, I dived at a steep angle.

'With our riddled bridge, a battered bow, two and a half metres of our stern crushed and a heavy list, we must have looked as though we were sinking. I ordered a depth of 20 metres, then blacked out. The boat slumped to the sea-bed. When the corvette rammed, she tore the bow cap off a torpedo tube; with the stern tube leaking, water was pouring into the electric motor compartment and could not be kept under control by pumping. Meanwhile the corvette was dropping depth charges. We had to get off the bottom. I decided to surface and make off under cover of darkness. The corvette fired star shells but did not notice me. Damage to U 333 could not yet be assessed, but we were still able to dive. Owing to loss of blood, however, I was not in full possession of my faculties and the second watch officer asked the C-in-C for a medical boat.'

This duel to the death was graphically described from the British side in the British Monthly Anti-Submarine Report. 'A U-boat was detected at a distance of 2,800 yards. Ten minutes later *Crocus* sighted the enemy. She rammed and struck him on the starboard side between conning tower and stern. For about two minutes the U-boat hung on the bow of the corvette and then scraped along the starboard side. Illuminated by searchlights, it was under constant Oerlikon fire. The conning tower was hit several times. After an explosion great pieces of metal flew through the air . . . and in the searchlight beam the damaged conning tower looked like a piece of nibbled cheese.

'The boat tried to escape by diving, but soon came to the surface again. After a chase lasting nearly a quarter of an hour *Crocus* caught up with the U-boat and again rammed it under full helm, this time very close to the stern. The boat passed down the starboard side under continuous fire from the Oerlikons, Pom-Pom and Hotchkiss. When it was on the beam both depth-charge throwers were fired to starboard. The U-boat was listing heavily, disappeared under the shower of water from the explosions and was seen no more . . . Until 0419 nine further depth charges were dropped, set between 50 and 100 metres. After several attacks contact was lost at 0427. *Crocus* spent the next five hours in a careful search . . .' The discrepancy between the times in my log and those in the British reports results from a one-hour's difference between German and Greenwich Time.

Years later the *Crocus*'s skipper, the New Zealand Lieutenant-Commander J. F. Holm, sent me his own account of the action, which rounds off the picture. He had returned to Freetown on the afternoon of 6 October, 1942, after a long deployment to South America and the Caribbean as a convoy escort, happy to have a quiet night in front of him . . . until he received a radio signal from his flotilla commander: 'Sail immediately. Several U-boats off Freetown, probably seven.' He sailed at about 2200. Around 0400 his wireless officer reported an object on the radar screen. He was certain it was the conning tower of a submarine.

'My intention,' Holm wrote to me, 'was to intercept the boat as quickly as possible and ram it before it could dive. All guns were manned, but I did not want to shoot too soon for fear of giving away our approach. Ten minutes later we suddenly spotted the boat. Things then moved at lightning speed. The Oerlikons on either side of the bridge opened fire at the same moment, and they were hitting the target, as I could see from the tracer. I ordered continuous fire so as to prevent the crew getting out of the conning tower and manning the 88 mm gun. My sole thought the whole time was to ram you as hard and fast as possible before you could get into a torpedo firing position. As your evasive actions showed, you guessed as much. If my coxswain with his thirty years in the Royal Navy had not been so quick in carrying out my orders we would not even have touched you at our first attempt. But at least we achieved a slight bump.'

This brief impact sent the U-boat scraping along the side of the corvette and tore her open below the waterline for a length of almost two metres. Her bows quickly flooded and all pumps had to be used to keep her afloat.

'Meanwhile,' he went on, 'I was trying everything to catch you again, and this time properly. But you were twisting and turning. Our ship's turning circle was always greater than yours and so we danced round one another. Each tried to outmanoeuvre the other. Finally I succeeded in ramming you a second time. You heeled over sharply and suddenly dived. My men on the bridge thought you had capsized and sunk.

'. . . *Crocus* was in continuous radio contact with Freetown and at dawn asked for an aircraft to search for evidence of the sinking, but it found only oil slicks. Our search apparatus was functioning very badly, having been damaged when the bow was gashed. At any rate,' *Crocus*'s skipper concluded, 'you out-tricked me with your handling.'

Action reports are not literature and tend to be pretty bald. In the midst of tracer and whistling splinters, in the metallic crash of shell hits, in powder smoke and searchlight glare, it is as though one were on a stage, staggering for support, disregarding personal pain, and finding it hard to hold the five senses together.

On the day after the battle our dead (the first lieutenant and two able seamen) were buried at sea according to naval custom. I myself had a finger-long shell splinter, sharp as a razor blade, stuck in my chest. Every breath was painful. The thing had to come out at once, but how? U-boats carrying no doctor did carry a medical handbook; I and one of the wireless operators could consult it for anything from a toothache to an inflamed appendix. We had not yet met the supply U-boat and the wireless operator did not dare perform an operation — he said his hands would tremble — so my chief engineer undertook the surgery. I was encrusted with blood and my body was black from falling into a pool of diesel oil. My uniform was slit open, my 'surgeon' disinfected his hands, as far as that was possible in a U-boat, and fetched a great pair of pincers from a tool box.

A few days before sailing I had celebrated with other U-boat commanders at the 'Schéhérazade' in Paris and the host had given me a bottle of the best French rum from Martinique. This now had to do its duty and I gulped down two mugs full. Of what followed I remember only that three men held me down while the chief applied the pincers and twisted out the splinter.

It was not till seventy-two hours later that we made our twilight rendezvous with the 'Milch Cow', U 459, skippered by Commander Georg von Wilamowitz-Möllendorf. U 459 could supply not only fuel, food, spare parts, but also medical assistance. Doctor Kirmse came across and probably saved my life. His report stated: 'Three men in the crew died of severe wounds. One man was missing. Although Lieutenant-Commander Cremer was bleeding heavily from all his wounds, particularly the head wound, he passed the dead and wounded down into the conning tower and only had himself bandaged twenty minutes later when boat and crew had been saved. This explains the heavy loss of blood and general weakness. Findings on 9.10.42:

1. Marked cardiac weakness through prolonged loss of blood (barely perceptible, irregular pulse).
2. Bruising of the chest and lumbar spine accompanied by stiffness.
3. Bruising of abdomen.
4. Swelling and haemorrhage of the left upper and lower arm, total immobility of the whole left extremity.
5. Penetrating wound in left upper arm.
6. Splinter wound in left temple and forehead.
7. Splinter wound chest.
8. Splinter wound right hip.
9. Splinter wound left knee joint.
10. Splinter wound left lower leg.
11. Splinter wound right shoulder.
12. Splinter wound left upper arm, elbow and lower arm.
13. Grazing and bruising of left cheek with parotitis (inflammation of ear).
14. Grazing of spine.

Seventy-two hours after the engagement, when we met up with the supply boat and I was lying in my bunk, incapable of movement, we were sent a replacement officer, Lieutenant Kasch, to bring U 333 home. I let him carry on but I was really in command of the boat. The nearer we came to the base at La Pallice/La Rochelle the more I forced myself to stay awake despite my deplorable, sedated condition, particularly as the last hours of a patrol are often the most dangerous. The bridge watch are already thinking of leave and somewhat careless because at any moment the protective escort vessel must come to lead the U-boat through the danger zone like a mother her child. The look-outs are no longer completely alert.

The enemy is well aware of this, his experience being exactly the same. We therefore had to expect British submarines which would try to intercept us at the last moment, outside our front door. And — even if I had not said it, it would still have happened . . . We had good visibility, a calm sea with slight swell when, late afternoon on the last day but one, on 21 October, 1942, the bridge watch shouted 'torpedo track to starboard'. At first only foam was to be seen and we turned hard a-port. Then four torpedo tracks were recognised close together. They had apparently been fired without angle of spread. The salvo of four went past close astern. In the boat we could hear the high-pitched hum of the screws becoming louder and louder and, after they had passed us, four colossal explosions at the end of the run.

Every movement was reported to me at once in my bunk, and I gave orders accordingly, going onto a zig-zag course at maximum speed. A radio signal informed Dönitz about this attack by an enemy submarine in the Bay.

As if that was not enough, before the escort took us over we had to dive to avoid three enemy fighters. And on top of that, a mine went up in front of our escort. On 23 October we ran into La Rochelle. We entered the lock with three dead, two severely wounded and a wrecked boat. One man had disappeared without trace. The mysterious British submarine, of which more later, for it is a story worth the telling, had reported us sunk.

My first watch-keeping officer was dead. My second W.O. and the replacement officer were still alive, but enjoyed only a respite: death was to catch up with them on other U-boats. Lieutenant Pohl, the officer who had been shot in the throat, and I survived. Pohl paid with the loss of his voice and even today, so long afterwards, he can only whisper. I myself was to spend long months in hospital.

And what of my friend Lieutenant-Commander Holm?

After the war I learnt a great deal about my former opponent whom I had previously known only as a tough customer. This New Zealander was a splendid fellow: he had heard of the hard times in Germany and wanted to give a little help with food parcels, so he got in touch with my mother. Great was his surprise to find me among the living and he wrote to me on his own initiative:

'Dear Sir, I hope you read English better than I German. After many attempts I got your address through the British Admiralty in London. I was more than surprised to learn that I did not sink U 333 and I am glad you managed to bring your heavily damaged boat back to the French base.'

Two men who had been at each other's throats without setting eyes on one another became friends. He came from a sea-going family from Wellington and was a captain in the merchant navy. His letter to me continued:

'Until the end of the war I commanded the corvette *Crocus* with the rank of lieutenant in the reserve. I am married and have four children. I agree with you: war is a damned nasty business. In fact it seems completely idiotic that in those days you and I had no other desire than to do away with each other. I consider you to be a fine fellow, as you do me. It simply amounts to this: we both did our duty for our country.'

The captain of HMS *Crocus* had reported me as sunk, and the British Admiralty recognised this U-boat 'kill'; King George VI therefore conferred the Distinguished Service Cross on him, though not for this operation alone.

9

A novel British submarine

Back from our fourth patrol in U 333 and our savage encounter with HMS *Crocus*, Pohl and I went to hospital in La Rochelle. Two days later Dönitz appeared with a staff officer, his son-in-law Commander Hessler. I had the feeling that their visit was not solely compassionate and the searching questions were not merely the routine ones following an attack by an enemy submarine, seeing that up till now, October 1942, eight German U-boats had been sunk by enemy submarines. There must be more to it than meets the eye. Over a glass of champagne every detail was raked over exhaustively, but nothing more emerged than what was already entered in the log: an unexpected salvo of four, tracks of four torpedoes coming suddenly out of the blue and whipping past close to the stern only because of our quick port manoeuvre and increased speed. 'And was nothing else seen? Think it over.' No, really not. Neither I nor my people could report anything more. Only one thing was established. On 21 October, 1942, at 1657 Central European Time a submerged submarine had fired at me. And frankly I had always expected something of the sort in that phase of the homeward run. What submarine had been involved remained hidden from us for a long time. When we finally found out we were not a little surprised.

It was not until 1980 that, on looking through a British wartime log book, that of Lieutenant Peter Barnsley Marriot, I was able through detailed comparisons to recognise that it was the British submarine HMS *Graph* which had tried to torpedo us in 1942. The British made up their log books even more precisely than we did in the U-boat arm. Its movements in time corresponded exactly with mine. His drawing of the attack corresponded exactly with my own sketch. There could be no mistake. Everything had taken place in sight of the north Spanish coast and the ridge of the Cantabrian mountains lying behind, which give their name to this part of the Bay, the Cantabrian Sea.

Returning U-boat men of the Biscay flotillas sometimes preferred the proximity of the Spanish coast as enabling them to swim to land if things went wrong, even stepping outside legality to make a small detour through the safe Spanish territorial waters. The neutral Spaniards could not place guards everywhere and Franco had enough to do keeping Spain out of the war. Naturally the British knew our habits, and so *Graph* was lying in wait exactly at the right spot off the north Spanish coast, in the Cantabrian Sea.

On that 21 October, 1942, a Wednesday, Lieutenant Marriot described in his log how, mixed up with the sounds of the torpedo explosions, his underwater listening gear picked up a series of loud, continuous noises, difficult to describe. These noises continued after the explosions, and sounded like the rattling of biscuit tins, then much creaking and cracking.

Everyone in the British submarine heard the noises, and almost everyone heard something different, ranging from bangs to tinkles. Nobody could explain them, but it was assumed that the German U-boat must have been sunk and a signal was sent off to that effect.

In fact the battered hull of U 333 had produced the noises. When the boat went to maximum speed on a zig-zag course everything not firmly in place had begun to rattle, including part of the hull of HMS *Crocus* still draped round the conning tower. The water that normally flowed round the tower was now pouring through all the holes in the superstructure and upper deck, producing more noises which were accentuated under water and which none of the British submariners could explain.

Our encounter with the British submarine conceals, like the doll within a doll, an inside story. Not till after the war did it appear that behind the name *Graph* was one of the best kept secrets of the Royal Navy, namely the former German submarine U 570. A Type VII-C boat and hence a sister ship of U 333, it was one of the few German units that fell almost without a fight into enemy hands. On 27 August, 1941, it had been captured in the North Atlantic by the British.

On that day U 570, while diving about 80 miles south of Iceland, had been spotted by a British Hudson aircraft, without the U-boat's knowledge. The plane dropped smoke markers and made a sighting report. Two hours later another Hudson saw the same

U-boat surfacing directly beneath it. The U-boat commander had omitted to give a preparatory glance through the air periscope. It was very late to dive again and before the boat could reach a suitable depth the other Hudson, flown by Squadron Leader J. Thompson, had well and truly surrounded it with depth charges. The splintering of instruments, the failure of all the lights, water breaking in forward, batteries destroyed and the danger of chlorine gas generated a panic on board. The commander writes:

'. . . we dropped lower, how low we did not know as our instruments were no longer functioning. We only knew that sooner or later the point would be reached when the surrounding water pressure would crush the boat. In that situation the only course was to blow out the ballast tanks immediately with compressed air. I gave the order for this and brought the boat to the surface.

'What was the situation now? The boat was no longer fit to submerge and hence robbed of its effective strength . . . On the surface we could not escape the aircraft which kept contact with us and was later relieved by another aircraft, until the arrival of the first patrol boat. If we had attempted to escape we would not even have known in what direction we were going as the depth-charge attack had destroyed our compass installation. I therefore decided to scuttle the boat . . .'

But apparently circumstances were against him. It was still possible to destroy the secret papers or throw them overboard, but no more than that. The crew were at odds. Then British patrol boats and a destroyer appeared, whose machine-gun fire wounded half a dozen U-boat men and prevented scuttling. The loss of the crew's life-saving gear in the sea-way and the British threat to abandon the men to their fate if they scuttled made it impossible to sink the U-boat. U 570 was surrounded by planes and ships and towed away, to be beached on the south coast of Iceland that same afternoon as an easy prize for the British.

In the autumn of 1941 the British Admiralty compiled a top-secret document that dealt very thoroughly with the capture of U 570. It was the product of the available evidence and detailed interrogations, and it was impressive in its objectivity. This document of 15 November, 1941, described how U 570 left Norway for its very first patrol on 24 August and the troubles which arose from the start: cooling system not functioning, water breaking in through one of the torpedo tubes and some of the crew hopelessly seasick. At 0830 on 27 August the commander (R) submerged to give his inexperienced crew relief from the heavy seas, surfacing again after two hours at the precise moment when a Hudson of 269 Squadron was immediately overhead.

After describing the explosion of the depth charges and the consequences, the British document continued:

'Convinced that all was lost, R. ordered his crew to put on lifejackets and collect in the control room. One minute after the water thrown up by the explosion had calmed, the aircraft saw the U-boat with its bow slightly under water and men coming on deck. The Hudson opened fire and the Germans jumped back into the boat. A sharp fight developed between those who wanted to get out from inside the boat because of the presumed danger of chlorine gas and those who were equally determined to escape the machine-gun fire from above. That generated pressure and finally forced men from below onto the bridge. They had a white flag and — to exclude any misunderstanding — in addition laid a large white board on the deck.

'Crouching in and around the conning tower in a high sea which made it impossible to go to the guns or even lower the boats, 80 miles from the nearest land, with nothing else in sight than a well armed aircraft which flew round and round, the crew spent a miserable day. In the afternoon the Hudson was relieved by a Catalina flying boat (209 Squadron) which kept the enemy in check with its guns. Towards evening the U-boat officers seemed to have recovered something of their nerve and some of the crew members were bold enough to go down again into the boat. A signal was despatched to the C-in-C U-boats stating that U 570 was no longer able to submerge and had been captured by the enemy. Secret papers were torn up, the coding machine was destroyed and thrown overboard and very inexpert attempts were made to smash instruments with a hammer. The prisoners stated that the water in the control room had risen. It seemed there was a leak in the bows and it was sealed.

'At 2250 the patrol vessel *Northern Chief* arrived and signalled: "If you attempt to sink yourselves we will not save anyone and your floats will be fired at." R. replied, "Can neither sink ourselves nor leave the boat. Please rescue us tomorrow." He was instructed to set a small white light so that the patrol ship could keep in contact. In their agitation the crew began to throw ballast overboard in the form of ammunition and food, while others collected personal possessions. Some of the bolder ones went below decks to sleep through the night.

'At 0330 on 28 August, the patrol ships HMS *Kingston Agate* and *Northern Prince* arrived, followed two hours later by *Burwell*, *Wastwater* and *Windermere* as well as the Canadian ship *Niagara*. Around 0800 an aircraft suddenly appeared and dropped bombs which fell into the water near the boat (Note: error of a British pilot). This caused R. to inform us that his boat was letting in water aft. But all observers on the adjacent ships did not believe him as the U-boat lay in the same trim as before.

'A helpless U-boat in a heavy sea must be an extremely uncomfortable prison and the Germans who had been in it for 24 hours began to complain. They were promised that if they could keep their ship up they would be saved, otherwise not. A little later an attempt was made to take U 570 in tow. *Burwell* threw a hawser and *Windermere*, lying to windward, pumped out oil to calm the sea. Three times the manoeuvre failed. At 1030 U 570 lay with the bow deeper in the water. The crew were now signalling continually that they could not hold the ship any longer, but did nothing to remedy the trouble. So it finally became necessary to underline the order to blow the ballast tanks and pump out oil with a few machine-gun bullets. In this unfortunately five Germans were wounded owing to the movement of the ships.

'Extremely disturbed, the Germans now not only showed another white flag but, more practically, they discharged oil and water. Now for the first time U 570 appeared in the full, surfaced trim. At 1350 *Kingston Agate*, which was especially equipped for towing, sent two officers and two men with a hawser to the U-boat. The wounded were fetched away. But it was not until 1600 that U 570 could be taken in tow, stern first, and the whole crew taken over. Three and a half hours later the hawser parted. But finally *Northern Chief* succeeded in beaching the German U-boat off Thorlakshafn, Iceland. The wounded were taken to Reykjavik.

'The first examination of the boat showed that the pressure hull was undamaged and not leaking. One of the main tanks had a hole. Only a little water was found in the forward part. In the control room and the engine room there was hardly more water than is normally to be found in the bilges. It is doubtful whether chlorine gas had developed. Diesels and electric motors were pumping, compressors, auxiliary machinery etc. were all working. The batteries, though almost empty, gave sufficient light.

'On 30 August, 1941, a sub-lieutenant, a petty officer and two sailors, all four submariners, flew to Iceland for a further and more detailed examination of U 570. They found the inside of the boat in a chaotic condition. Oil and sea water were washing to and fro, in them broken glass, food such as flour, dried peas, beans, tinned fruit, articles of clothing and bed coverings. Together with many loaves of bread the whole formed a repellent mass reaching up to the knees. The men established that the German crew had turned the single lavatory into a store room for food. They worked day and night into the early hours of 5 September. Then at last the boat was ready and could be taken off Red Beach near Thorlock. The work had consisted in getting out the ooze with buckets, sealing the leaks, blowing out the tanks and finally pumping out the bilges. The boat was towed into Hvalfjord, once again thoroughly examined and made ready for the crossing to England.

'The pressure hull showed only minor fissures. How far these were attributable to the depth-charge attack or the beaching of the boat could no longer be ascertained. In the forward tank 21 of the 62 battery cells were fractured, aft 26 cells were out of action. All in all, the depth charges had caused little damage.' (The document lists seven items which were soon repaired.)

'According to the summary of damage the boat is able to submerge, no salt water could be detected in the after batteries . . . When one considers that after their capitulation the German crew were on board for another 24 hours, they undertook extraordinarily little to make their boat unusable.'

The secret document draws the conclusion that a reasonably practised crew would have had no difficulty in diving with that boat, and asks the question why did not U 570 dive after the Hudson attack? Was it the consequence of inadequate training and lack of U-boat experience? Chief petty officers and petty officers of the crew who had served for some years 'made no attempt to conceal from us the incompetence of the crew, and the officers were seriously criticised.'

The document continues: 'Success and failure of a U-boat depend chiefly on the competence of the commander . . . If the commander fails in a crisis it is usually not the case that the younger officers fill the breach . . .

'The impression we gained was that propaganda had raised the morale of the crew to a high level. But it had been built on sand and when the storm came up it fell, and it was a long fall. After the willing surrender the crew forgot both the glamour of the U-boat service and the dangers of underwater warfare. In a somewhat childish manner they turned to the more domestic problems of their captivity. In comparison with other prisoners they had shed their Nazidom more easily.

'The quantity and variety of foodstuffs in England astonished the prisoners and obliged them to admit that their U-boat blockade could not be as effective as Dr. Goebbels maintained. Although they hardly made an effort to refute that, thereby, the U-boat war had not achieved its goal, they all defended Admiral Dönitz, the C-in-C U-boats, as a man of enterprise and vitality who was free of the spirit of the narrow "traditional and out-of-date officers of the naval high command".'

To the British U 570 must have been a gift of the gods. For the first time they had one of the 'grey wolves' of Admiral Dönitz on the lead and with determination they went to work on it. They lost no time in including the German U-boat in His Majesty's fleet. The take-over of a foreign warship is usually not simple, as it is tied to the different technical norms of its class and the spare-parts question is also not easily solved. But up to mid-1941 the British submarine arm had lost a total of 31 boats and, 'in need of anything that could dive and fire a torpedo' (Horton), it now possessed eight Dutch, five Greek, three French, one Norwegian and one or two other foreign boats as well. But in the case of U 570 it was not just a matter of an additional submarine but of the 'great unknown'. . . .

Under the name HMS *Graph* it was assigned as an experimental boat to the 3rd Submarine Flotilla and received as captain the previously mentioned Lieutenant Peter Barnsley Marriot. The vessel's name, relating to graphical demonstrations and diagrams, probably symbolised the experimental character of the boat and was later retained.

On many trial runs the former German U-boat had now to show what it could do and above all what it could withstand. The captain was very satisfied with its behaviour. On the other hand his crew found fault with the narrow and uncomfortable interior. The British submarines they were familiar with were larger and offered more room. From the technical point of view, too, the VII-C boat was a gift for the British in offering an up-to-date lesson on German submarine technology, and they set to work to extract all its secrets. Submarine experts taken on board as observers wrote, it is said, whole books about the speed of the boat. The wireless officer tested the range on all wavelengths above and below water and handed in a long scientific analysis. Shipbuilding engineers praised the carefully executed riveting and welding work. The greatest attention was naturally paid to the pressure hull; they were astonished to find that it was made of steel plates 20.5 millimetres thick and would withstand a water pressure of 15 atmospheres at a depth of 150 metres (in fact considerably more). That caused the British speedily to adapt their depth charges to the previously underestimated German diving depths. The priming could now be adjusted deeper than previously, to 200 and up to 300 metres.

A full year passed before HMS *Graph*, formerly U 570, started on its first operation on 8 October, 1942, against the enemy, the so-called Biscay Patrol. Apart from a 'chastity belt' twenty miles wide kept open (as long as that was possible) by the British off the north Spanish coast, Biscay was a 'sink at sight' area. Because of the shortage of British submarines and their deployment in other theatres of war, only a few were available for this task. It could hardly be thought possible, but as late as 1941 it was said of the Admiral, Submarines, 'as a general rule he kept two of his best submarines in these turbulent waters' — two! It was a matter of directing them effectively.

The German approach routes to Brest (1st and 9th flotillas), Lorient (10th), Saint Nazaire (6th and 7th), La Pallice/La Rochelle (3rd) and to Bordeaux (12th) had many branches, were sealed by complicated mine fields and controlled more easily from the air than the sea. Of course the British guessed that German U-boats, particularly when damaged, would try to move along the secure north Spanish coast and they must have been hopeful, given time and patience, of intercepting them there.

On 15 October the submarine HMS *Graph*, looking like a German U-boat, which made it doubly dangerous, was at diving stations 15 miles north of Cape Ortegal, observing dozens of Spanish fishing vessels. One day later a Spanish tanker crossed its path. A few days more passed in sailing to and fro until on 21 October came the encounter with U 333 . . .

On its return the boat was suitably praised for its apparent success.

Meanwhile, Allied air bases were being established in Newfoundland and Labrador, the range of aircraft was increasing — and the Gap in the Atlantic was becoming smaller and smaller.

But in November, 1942, the shipping losses of the enemy reached their high point. German U-boats sank 117 ships with 700,000 tons on all oceans. In the same month the British Prime Minister established the Anti-U-boat Committee, upgrading the question to the highest level of priorities. In the same month, too, Admiral Sir Max Horton was appointed Commander-in-Chief Western Approaches. As such, he was, in brief, 'responsible for the safe and punctual arrival of convoys'. Or, as the Admiralty order more fully described it, responsible 'for the protection of trade, of the convoy routes, for supervision of all convoys and measures for combatting attacks of any kind by U-boats or enemy aircraft within the area of his command.'

The area of his command comprised that extensive part of the ocean bounded by latitude 43 degrees North (Cape Finisterre in Spain) and longitude 43 degrees West (Cape Farwell in Greenland), from the North Sea to Biscay. And if it should so be, beyond.

And therewith the Battle of the Atlantic entered its decisive phase.

10
The Atlantic transmitter

When I was finally able to leave hospital I was limping with a stick. U 333 had acquired a new conning tower and a few other things and was under way with Lieutenant Schwaff. Until my complete recovery I myself was ordered to the staff of C-in-C U-boats. Time had not stood still. It was early spring 1943, the dynamic of war had developed further and things had happened, some of them unforeseen.

Grand Admiral Raeder had resigned at the end of January and Karl Dönitz had become his successor and therewith Commander-in-Chief of the *Kriegsmarine*. He had sought this responsibility as little as he would later seek that of last head of the German Reich. The mantle had fallen onto his shoulders. Grand Admiral Raeder had recommended Admiral Carls and Dönitz as possible successors, and Hitler played the U-boat card.

The quarrel leading to Raeder's resignation derived not least from an obviously mistaken strategy for the capital ships (the mistake resulted from Hitler's premature opening of hostilities); these ships lay around, blockaded and inactive, while the handful of U-boats had more and more become the actual instrument of the war at sea. The abortive attack of a German naval formation on the British convoy JW 51 in the North Sea (Operation Rainbow) was the last straw; Hitler had flown into a rage and threatened to scrap the rest of the high seas fleet.

It was in the nature of things that the new commander of the *Kriegsmarine* should remain a U-boat man from personal preference, conducting operations himself, while the former deputy admiral of U-boats, von Friedeburg, now commanding admiral of U-boats, should relieve him of all non-operational tasks.

Dönitz's headquarters had also been changed and were no longer on the Atlantic coast. After the surprise British attack on St. Nazaire in March, 1942, which raised the fear of kidnap among the staff, they had moved to Paris and later to Berlin, where the naval command headquarters were already established on the Tirpitzufer. Every morning the new C-in-C Navy left his desk and turned up shortly after at our HQ in the Steinplatz.

The front-line commanders attached to Dönitz lived in the Hotel am Steinplatz and worked in a neighbouring building where, in rooms off limits to outsiders, the battles were fought at the legendary green-baize table. There were no fixed hours of duty. We relieved one another, but individual operations often lasted for days. At night our work was interrupted more and more often by single British 'Mosquitos'. Later whole formations forced us into the air-raid shelter — the place, according to eye-witnesses, was 'swarming with Knight's Crosses'.

From an office desk I now followed the movements of the U-boats. Their positions were symbolised by little flags and plotted on big situation charts, the oceans on paper. A glance was enough to put one in the picture, usually — unless there was radio silence, for instance, and the boat concerned did not report.

This was the case with Lieutenant-Commander Heinz Franke who in April, 1943, was under way in U 262. On receipt of the code word 'Elster' he had opened a sealed envelope, found himself ordered on a special mission, and then in a literal sense submerged. The order read:

'As announced by secret letter code, some of our boys held prisoner in Canada are planning a break-out from their camp, which lies in the area of New Brunswick. They are hoping to be at a certain point on the coast of the western Gulf of St. Lawrence in the first days of May. Your orders are to sail to this sea or coastal area, to attempt to make contact with them at the coastal point indicated, and thereafter to take them on board.'

In my capacity as second staff officer in the operations department of the C-in-C, I myself had set up this strictly secret operational plan and worked out the details. Besides time and place of the meeting, these included the relevant nautical and meteorological details, characteristics of the fairways, coast formations, navigational aids, etc., and, not least, the expected enemy counter-measures. The rest was left to Franke, who had a free hand.

The operation was not so far-fetched as it may sound. The coded information from the prisoners had reached us through a simple correspondence via a clandestine address. They were not being very closely guarded as an escape from Canada seemed in any case impossible — and no one reckoned on a German U-boat surfacing at the front door. Rather, the difficulties lay in the ice prevalent at that time of year. The spring ice would impede a passage into the Gulf of St. Lawrence through the Cabot Strait between Newfoundland and Nova Scotia. Nevertheless every attempt was to be made and the timetable adhered to.

And this was what happened. Franke and U 262 had a lot of trouble but he made it. First they met thin ice layers which changed into large fields of drift ice and finally they stuck in limitless expanses of ice. They therefore decided to run submerged under the ice barrier off the Cabot Strait, risky for a U-boat of that time. Surfacing again and breaking through the ice cover over their heads only succeeded after several attempts, during which the net cutter was torn, the AA armament damaged and the bow caps of three torpedo tubes were bent and would no longer open. Not a ship was to be seen inside the Gulf of St. Lawrence, but three planes were circling over the area Franke was aiming for. He waited for darkness to fall.

At the agreed rendezvous there was open water, a mirror-calm sea and good visibility. The line of the coast could be clearly seen and Franke went in close until the brilliant light of the beacon at North Point caught the boat. The escapers would probably make contact with light signals. But despite strong hopes and a long wait there was no sign of them. As Franke wrote, 'efforts to make contact were carried out through several days and nights, but without success. Finally the search was broken off according to orders.'

The return journey passed less dramatically, the open Atlantic was reached without a hitch. All involved had done their best, boat and crew had fully proved themselves. A pity it was not to be. Why not? For a long time we puzzled over this, and it was learnt only after the war that the break-out from the camp had not taken place because surveillance had been tightened up after a previous unsuccessful escape attempt by another group. So that was the story of U 262.

My own boat fared no better. U 333 had carried out a winter patrol, its fifth, without me. It had lasted 48 days and during the whole seven weeks nothing of importance had happened.

The sea had been suspiciously empty, not a ship far and wide. What had happened to the convoys? Had they been redirected? The ocean was large and the battle there was still like looking for a needle in a haystack. Was the enemy pausing for breath, or were new developments involved? U 333's very next patrol gave us food for thought.

On 3 March, 1943, Werner Schwaff sailed again in U 333. On the evening of the next day, at 2131 in the middle of the Bay, the boat was suddenly lit up by a searchlight from a low-flying twin-engined land-based aircraft. The machine just jumped out of the darkness. Immediate defensive fire with incendiary ammunition set the left wing alight and, as the plane skimmed over the boat, it was already burning furiously. It dropped four bombs, then plunged into the sea. The first bomb crashed below the conning tower on a level with the galley hatch, causing only superficial damage, and flew overboard. The other three bombs all fell astern, or so it was assumed, and did not affect the boat. But when U 333 was able to proceed for a longer period on the surface the men heard a noise aft, rolling in the rhythm of the sea, and when an examination was made a bomb was discovered; it had dug into the stern casing and burst open without exploding. The fuse was cautiously removed and later given to the weapons experts.

Immediately after the fight, U 333 had reported shooting down the enemy aircraft, in a brief radio signal. Thirty-six hours later, on 6 March, Schwaff sent off a second signal which, according to Roskill, the author of the official British history of the war at sea, 'was to have important consequences.' In this, Schwaff dealt in detail with the peculiar circumstances of the attack. For one thing, the searchlight claimed his attention, but then he reported most importantly that his set, which should have indicated the radiation of the airborne radar, had remained silent. The warning set in question was the Metox Receiver 600. As successor to the so-called Biscay Cross, it had been used on all U-boats since the autumn of 1942. On surfacing, the cumbersome aerial on the conning tower had to be turned every time through 360 degrees and, before diving, taken down into the control room. On a crash dive it was a hindrance. On the other hand the set registered all radar impulses of attacking aircraft at up to 100 kilometres, on the usual wavelength, that is, of 1.4 to 1.8 metres. Had our opponent now changed his frequency so that our sets no longer picked him up?

(above) *18. The crippled* U 570 *forced to the surface prior to its capture off Iceland – and* commissioning *into the Royal Navy as HMS* Graph. (below) *19. USS* Core, *one of the aircraft carriers deployed to close the mid-Atlantic gap.* U 333 *was attacked by an aircraft from this carrier.*

(above) *20. U-boats receive a punishing from long-range land-based aircraft . . .*
(below) *21. . . . . like this Mosquito. (The first photograph shows a depth charge falling, centre, and two sailors by the conning tower.)*

This was the opinion, subsequently proved correct, which had been held at Dönitz's headquarters. His war diary contains the following passage: 'U 333 is approached at night by a hitherto undetected enemy aircraft in square BF 5879. The enemy is working on carrier frequencies which lie outside the frequency of our (present) radio-locating receiver. An enemy machine shot down over Holland which apparently had a D/F set with a 9.7 centimetre frequency on board is at present the only evidence of this possibility.'

And this was in fact the case. On 2 February, 1943, a British Stirling bomber was shot down by a night fighter near Rotterdam. From the wreckage experts from the *Luftwaffe* and electrical manufacturers discovered that its direction-finding set worked on a wavelength of 9.7 centimetres, something we had never thought possible. It was given the name 'Rotterdam apparatus' and was one of the great surprises of the Second World War. It must be remembered: the German Metox receiver had usually reacted to the predecessor of this D/F set built for wavelengths of 1.4 to 1.8 metres. To the new centimetre set it did not respond at all. This sensitive new British apparatus, representing a further development and called ASV Mark III, specially made for aircraft, located convoys at 40 miles and, what directly concerned us, surfaced U-boats at 12 miles.

After we had caught up, much too quickly for our opponents, with the secret of the centimetre radar which had just been put into service, the British did not doubt that within a few months we would develop a counter-measure. And they were not entirely wrong, seeing that our scientists had already achieved some success in this field. But since the end of the French campaign in 1940 there was a large gap, namely an order from Hitler which forbade any development of new appliances and systems which could not be completed within a year. At that time Hitler saw victory within his grasp and considered new weapons, etc., superfluous. In addition a number of well known experts had left Germany for political or racial reasons — to be welcomed with open arms by those in foreign research. Such omissions, errors and false appreciations could not be made good from one day to the next. We now had to pay the price.

Incidentally, the former radar search-receiver of the U-boat arm was not a purely German invention but, ironically enough, the product of Franco–British cooperation. It was one of those secrets which fell into our hands in the course of the 1940 *blitzkrieg*, or was handed to us at the highest level after the armistice. Thereafter it was no longer made for its original clients but for simplicity's sake built for the German *Kriegsmarine* by the manufacturing firm in Paris: the Metox radar warning set.

Today we know that the machine shot down by U 333 was a Wellington Mark III of 172 Squadron. It had taken off on 4 March from the airfield at Chivenor, Devon, for an anti-U-boat patrol. These patrols over the Bay usually lasted nine and a half hours. This Wellington had not returned, the crew of six had lost their lives. Everything had happened so quickly, they did not even have time to make a radio signal.

Biscay patrols had always been flown, similarly reconnaissance flights along the approach routes between Scotland and Iceland. Our opponent systematically watched from the air over a net covering these areas like a spider's web and leaving nothing out of account. But in March, 1943, the Biscay patrols were intensified and 172 Squadron of Wellingtons was the first to be equipped with the new centimetre radar ASV Mark III. In addition, all the machines were given searchlights and the two combined were well able to track a surfaced U-boat with accuracy even at night.

The searchlight did not come as a complete surprise. Already on 5 July, 1942, one had picked up U 502, a week later U 159: the first trials of a new weapon. It bore the name Leigh Light after its inventor. At his desk a light had dawned, as it were, on Squadron Leader Humphrey Leigh, an old airman of the First World War. But the idea raised certain practical problems: questions of the light source, its dimensions, its mobility, the air stream. Would the reflection blind the pilot, would the arc lamps disturb the radar? Finally recourse was had to a naval searchlight of 61 centimetres diameter such as destroyers carried and therewith, after long trials, a usable appliance was perfected. So much was clear: when the new ASV Mark III was deployed in combination with the Leigh Light, surfaced U-boats would no longer be safe from air attack even at night.

In a British Monthly Report of this period the following relevant paragraphs appear:

'The change of tactics which became apparent in November (1942) was forced upon the enemy by a predominant and urgent need to avoid or repel attack by aircraft. To complete his discomfiture it is necessary to concert measures which will deprive the U-boat of its time on the surface under cover of darkness and also of the assistance of long-range aircraft. The latter problem may be solved by CVEs [Carrier Vessel Escorts] carrying more fighter aircraft.

'The extension of our successful daylight measures to the hours of darkness is more difficult to achieve. A Liberator squadron has now been equipped with Leigh Lights and we now have five squadrons of Leigh-Light Wellingtons. The possession of bases in the Azores means that Gibraltar convoys remain within range of the type of aircraft . . . Western Approaches are trying out schemes of identification and certain tactical dispositions to help to increase the effectiveness of our night effort and thus obtain more kills.'

On 23 March, 1943, Dönitz noted that passage through the Bay was becoming even more dangerous. 'Since February the effect of air surveillance has increased alarmingly when many boats are returning from big convoy battles.' The number of reports speaking of surprise attacks, and that despite darkness or poor visibility, increased to such an extent that Dönitz, as mentioned earlier (p. 86), ordered boats in the Bay of Biscay to travel submerged at night. They were only allowed to surface by day to charge the batteries.

To use the enemy's words, he was indeed in process of concerting measures 'which will deprive the U-boat of its time on the surface under cover of darkness . . .'

As staff officer in Berlin I could also observe the concentration of front-line U-boats in groups of 6, 8, 15 and more with the intention of putting them together into a convoy battle. These 'pack tactics', so feared by our enemies, were the speciality of Dönitz and his chief of staff, Rear Admiral Godt.

Hitherto I myself had had only a vague conception of the mass deployment of the boats. For even in a pack, one boat knows next to nothing about the others unless the radio signals are analysed or the group concentrates to within visual distance, which seldom occurs. One imagines oneself alone in a wide space, a small dot in the endless Atlantic. But U 333 was always only one of the boats directed to a convoy by radio after the first sighting reports of someone else. Of course one knows that other colleagues with their boats have the same objective, but there is no overall picture. All the threads came together with Dönitz. Many of us out there at the front involved in pack operations may have thought: those up there at their office desks, it's fine for them to talk. From where I now sat, however, the situation looked a bit different; I could see what wide-ranging preparations and intensive evaluation of all intelligence were necessary to organise a convoy battle. This kind of war-from-a-desk calls for nerves. It is the unknown factors which create the strain.

In the comparatively narrow and calculable dimensions of land warfare the enemy deployment and direction of attack are known almost to the kilometre. Certainly there are surprises, but usually everything goes by laws which general staff officers have practised at war school or sand table. The rest is a matter of human reserves and material reinforcements. Weather factors can work favourably or unfavourably for one side or another.

At sea, bad weather at times makes fighting absolutely impossible. I myself was involved in a small convoy battle with U 333 when a hurricane came down on us. I saw the enemy destroyers and corvettes now high up, now deep down, and was myself thrown to and fro and up and down, so that the enemy could not drop depth charges nor I fire torpedoes. Here the weather simply stopped everything. Yet we and other boats had been in direct contact with the convoy, one of us having been the first to see it. For in contrast with land warfare that is the great art: to find the enemy.

The men in the higher regions perhaps learn that beyond the 'big pond' a convoy is forming up to bring valuable material to England. Its course can be roughly guessed. But the Atlantic has global dimensions, there are not so many U-boats to seal it off, and if such a convoy of 40 large freighters flanked by half a dozen warships deviates from its anticipated course by only a few degrees, within a few thousand sea miles it will be lost in the ocean expanses and escape. The ships observe radio silence, sail without lights, make their escape. And that was exactly what U 333 on its fifth patrol under Lieutenant Schwaff had experienced. Two whole groups, 'Falcon' and 'Mercenary', had moved forward to find nothing.

The group or pack tactics at least cover a sector, allow concentrated striking power and, in a combined attack, are able to confuse the enemy to the utmost: they were an invention of Dönitz. The impetus came from his experience in the First World War. In those days U-boats operated individually. But shortly before the end of the war, in September, 1918, Dönitz as commander of UB 68 together with Lieutenant-Commander Steinbauer in UB 48 had successfully attacked the centre of a British convoy in the Mediterranean on the night of a new moon. In the years of peace he had crystallised his thoughts. In 1935 the first orders for group tactics were drawn up, continually improved, tested at *Wehrmacht* manoeuvres in 1937 and later summarised in the *Handbook for U-boat Commanders*.

All that naturally presupposed a large number of U-boats. So long as these were not available in the first years of the war, there was no other choice than to allow the boats to attack singly. When the number of boats increased Dönitz was in a position to concentrate several in groups. He had waited long enough for this and when the 'wolf packs', as they were later called, appeared, this change of tactics took the enemy completely by surprise. The British naval historian Roskill speaks of a 'form of attack which we had neither foreseen nor against which we had prepared tactical or technical counter-measures'.

March, 1943, was again a black month for the Allies. The U-boats picked off from their convoys over 100 ships totalling nearly 650,000 GRT. At the same time the Atlantic occasionally showed its worst side. Surfaced U-boats were repeatedly smothered by the heavy seas and nearly foundered.

But the enemy counter-measures grew stronger month by month. In the same month the British–American–Canadian Atlantic Convoy Conference in Washington gave the anti-U-boat war the highest priority ('the defeat of the U-boat must remain a first charge on the resources of the Allies'). Against the U-boat packs Admiral Horton organised concerted action between hunter groups and aircraft carriers in cooperation with long-range aircraft. The convoys were provided with escort and support groups of destroyers and corvettes (which will be discussed later) and with hunter–killer groups from the other side of the Atlantic. And there was something else decisive: they were in process of closing the 36-hour gap in the Atlantic which lay between the absence of aircraft on the one side and the arrival of aircraft on the other. And in this they succeeded, with long-distance Liberators and aircraft carriers, according to the suggestions of Admiral

Horton. For the U-boats the days of quick booty came rapidly to an end. The hunters became the hunted.

My employment at headquarters gave me a good insight into British psychological warfare which was now intensified and aimed at our U-boat crews. The officer with us responsible for analysis of enemy propaganda was Commander (retd.) Dr. Gott-fried Teuffer. His actual task was to register sunk and missing U-boats, to find out the fate of the crews and to establish who had been lost or fallen into captivity. It was obvious that the British derived their propaganda, which they disseminated for instance over the 'short-wave Atlantic transmitter', in part from the state-ments of prisoners whom they persuaded by subtle methods to talk. That was clear and emerges from a 'Monthly Report' which dealt with the 'Rescue of Survivors from U-boats' by convoy vessels.

'After destroying a U-boat, a Commanding Officer may be in doubt as to whether to let survivors "swim for it" or not. The risk of attack by another U-boat or by aircraft, the need to rejoin a convoy passing through a danger area, the condition of his ship and the state of the weather must be set against the value of the prisoners taken.

'The Intelligence Division of the Naval Staff has built up an extremely efficient system of interrogation of prisoners of war and the interrogation officers have by their skill and patience obtained information of the greatest value. Some prisoners have an invin-cible security consciousness, others are merely bad-mannered or stupid, but the majority make a useful contribution to our intelligence.

'In the past year, prisoners taken from U-boats have provided information on the following subjects, among others: patrol lines and pack tactics, "Gnat" (acoustic) and "Curly" (independently course-changing) torpedoes, submarine bubble targets, radar decoy balloons, search-receiver listening gear, W/T organisation, diving depths, speeds and angles, and anti-aircraft armament and tactics.'

There it is in black and white, but at that time we did not know everything. Dr. Teuffer was given the task of analysing the psycho-logical warfare. We became friends and I often watched him at work. His area of responsibility grew appreciably and he had to appoint radio operators to write down the programmes of the ever more audacious British 'Atlantic transmitter'. To start with, we in the Steinplatz laughed at the primitive repertoire which was specifically aimed at the German U-boat men in home ports and our bases in Norway, in the Atlantic and Mediterranean and which, among other things, entertained the crews at sea with gossip. In the early weeks we were highly amused, but soon alarmed. Dönitz called this new weapon *Giftküche Atlantik* (poison kitchen Atlantic) and on several occasions told Hitler, who had always been interested in the enemy propaganda, about this transmitter.

On hearing 'Atlantic' for the first time as a layman one might have thought it was a radio station for U-boat men situated somewhere in occupied France or Norway. The men in the far north, on the Atlantic or in the Mediterranean base of Toulon or at sea knew very well that the enemy was at work here. Not only because listening to the 'Atlantic' station was forbidden and punished, but because it discussed matters one could not and ought not to know. For instance, jokes were made about the latest German measures in the field of radio location. New weapons were either praised or ridiculed. So the security continually preached in the bases seemed hardly to exist any more. If the enemy, who apparently possessed the latest and most secret information, trumpeted it into the ether, why should one not discuss it with friends and swap stories of one's experiences with weapons in St. Nazaire or in the cafés of Lorient?

That was exactly one of the objects which the British wished to achieve. They knew that German intelligence officers gave lectures once a month in the U-boat bases about the dangers of espionage and agents listening in to conversations, and the men paid attention because it was in itself quite an interesting subject. But in view of increasing loose talk these warning lectures were now given once a fortnight and in some bases even weekly. That was not only irksome, for it took place during the men's free time, but gradually it grew boring. Soon people no longer listened, and that could only suit the British, as Dönitz had to admit. From now on everything was done to warn the U-boat men about the interrogation methods of the British; for it had quickly become clear to us that the British specialists in the interrogation of prisoners were working very closely with the 'Atlantic transmitter' and tried to make captured U-boat men forthcoming and ready to talk.

Later, in November, 1943, the C-in-C's Standing Order No. 512

was to be read out to the men. This would stress that 'silence is golden', and that a prisoner's thoughtless remark could cost a sailor at sea his life. It would lay down precisely how a man was to conduct himself before the interrogation officers. 'Once on board the ship that picks up the German shipwrecked submariner it is necessary to pull oneself together. Also, do not discuss service matters amongst yourselves!

'Do not accept gifts from the interrogation officers. Refuse alcohol and do not smoke. There are hidden listening devices in almost every room. The British collect several prisoners in one cell. Do not discuss your experiences or service matters there, either. Be on your guard against traitors. Under the mask of comrade, German-speaking men will approach you, pretending to belong to the U-boat arm. Do not speak with them. Before the interrogation officer, only name, rank, date of birth and address may be given. Refuse to speak English, even when you can.

'Finally,' — so it was stated in Order No. 512 — 'do not let yourselves be bluffed. The British pretend to know a great deal. In reality that is only a bluff. Do not fall for it!'

Quite certainly many of our U-boat men doubted this last remark in particular; for the British were not bluffing. If the 'Atlantic transmitter' used very coarse language and vulgar expressions unheard of on the wireless but which were known as soldiers' German, then it was 'in'. If, for instance, it reported in detail how at a party in the officers' mess of the 9th Flotilla in Brest the senior officer had pushed handfuls of cigarettes into the *décolletées* of the ladies present (signalling staff and nurses in civilian clothes) and then invited his young officers to 'please help yourselves', that was no bluff but the truth. This had really happened, and some petty officers and C.P.O.'s who heard it may have said to themselves: if our superiors do such things, then why not . . .?

And again that helped the British; for any undisciplined behaviour makes for disintegration. The actual purpose of such reporting, though, was to show that the enemy heard and saw everything.

Finally, the *Atlantiksender* went over to giving the latest sporting news. That was easily done. The British already had their agents in the bases who, amongst other things, could observe the sporting activities of the flotillas, and from that the enemy could deduce which boats were still at base and which at the front. And if they managed as well to report to London the result of the game and individual names, then often on the same evening the transmitter could broadcast: 'This afternoon 3rd Flotilla La Rochelle played 12th Flotilla Bordeaux and won 5–3!' Then would follow the names of the goal scorers. Considering the general enthusiasm for sport in the navy, which was officially fostered, it was only too understandable that the men at sea wanted to know whether their flotilla had won or lost. On U 333 too, with its particularly enthusiastic sportsmen whom I had in fact selected, I noticed that out in the Atlantic my radio operators listened to at least the sports news on the enemy transmitter and whispered the results to their friends. To this I had to turn a deaf ear.

The news given on the *Atlantiksender* proved to us staff officers that despite all our warnings the enemy was very successful in the field of prisoner interrogation. After long discussion the naval command suggested making a kind of documentary film as an antidote. Actors in captured British uniforms imitated interrogation officers, others, captured German U-boat men. The supposed tricks of the British were shown and the right and wrong ways for a prisoner to react. The interrogation officer tempted with whisky and cigarettes, a naive German sailor gradually took the bait and imperceptibly became a traitor. In another scene threats were made. The U-boat man panicked and said out of fear what he never should have said. Then an example was shown of how a prisoner fared when he simply gave the few personal details required by international convention and added not another word. The interrogating officer gave up, left the man unmolested because he respected him.

The film was made but never shown. It was basically equivocal in its message. For its unintended message was that one could survive quite well and undisturbed in captivity as long as one behaved 'correctly'. If the film had been shown it would have played straight into British hands. The thought could have struck the audience: after all, captivity in the West is not so bad. And therewith the film would have begun to undermine morale.

The British department responsible for the interrogation of German U-boat prisoners and its assessment had the identifying letters NID 1/PW. As a result of experiences with the captured crew of U 570 it gained in importance and was extended. Another department was founded, NID 17z, from which the 'Short-wave

Atlantic transmitter' emerged. Its initiator was Commander R.N. (retd.) Ian Fleming, adjutant to the chief of the British Intelligence Service and counter-espionage. He had a brilliant, imaginative mind and after the war became world famous as the creator of James Bond. As assistant he had recruited Commander Donald McLachlan, later to become Editor of *The Sunday Telegraph*. They acquired the cooperation of other journalists, among them Sefton Delmer, the chief reporter of the *Daily Express*, who had lived for many years in Berlin. With such a team it was possible to make deliberate and dangerous propaganda which we could not counter in psychological warfare.

In addition, the British possessed an impressive knowledge of individuals. I myself was never in captivity but shortly after the war one of the chief officers of NID 1/PW showed me my index card. There, neatly registered in minute detail, was everything ever published in the German daily press and periodicals about me and my boat. The most important dates in my life, my career, my weakness for sport, down to my favourite drink, rum. If I had ever come before an interrogation officer, he would probably have poured me a rum, talked about boxing and asked after my French lady friend of whom they even knew the Christian name. This performance would have amused me but they would have achieved nothing by it.

But how different would be the case of a young torpedo petty officer fished up in the Bay who two days later is sitting before the interrogation officer and, to his amazement, is greeted with the words: 'Schmidt, my good fellow, what a lucky dog you are — saved on your wedding anniversary! That's your birthday now as well, in a manner of speaking.' The man will gape in astonishment that this British officer even knows his wedding day, and he but a minor sinew in the U-boat arm. If he is then asked whether it is correct that among the torpedoes carried in his boat there were only two of the acoustic type T 5, he will most probably answer with readiness: 'No, *Herr Kapitän*, we were carrying four' — and not feel a traitor, for clearly the Englishman knows everything.

At the same time it was easy for British Intelligence to come by such dates. Long before the war they had started a comprehensive card index on regular personnel of the *Kriegsmarine*. In the case of a sailor from Stuttgart announcing his engagement in the local paper, the paper would not only be read in London but the announcement of the engagement would be cut out and stuck onto his card. When later the local paper in Pillau, where the 2nd U-boat training division was stationed, announced the ordinary seaman's wedding, that would be added to the card with the note 'probably seconded to the U-boat arm'. If about nine months later the same man, meanwhile promoted, proudly announced in a Wesermünder newspaper the birth of his son, Uwe, that would also be registered, and it was now highly probable that he was attending the naval technical school in Wesermünde and had entered the engineering branch of the U-boat arm. Should he ever be taken prisoner, the officer questioning him could ask at an early stage after his little Uwe and so impress him as to loosen his tongue. If the officer then asked about a detail of the diesel exhaust he could count on a clear answer which he would not otherwise have received.

Unfortunately there were also U-boat men who, without being particularly infected by the enemy propaganda or tricks in captivity, became at once allies of the enemy, whether they were silent opponents of the regime or whether other personal grounds decided them. There is proof that such isolated cases did occur.

I return to the British memorandum 'Rescue of Survivors from U-boats' which, among the secrets revealed by German prisoners, mentions the 'submarine bubble target' called by us *Bold*. The story of *Bold* is curious and worth mentioning.

On 28 September, 1942, Hitler had a two-hour conference with senior naval officers in the Reich Chancellery. A record written down by Dönitz states, *inter alia*:

'In further discussions the *Führer* came to speak of the possibility of simulating the destruction of a U-boat to deceive the enemy. Here he referred to numerous reports of airmen according to which the sighting of a large patch of oil had led to the assumption and reporting of a U-boat kill. The *Führer* was thinking of a kind of torpedo which would burst on the surface of the water, eject oil, generate bubbles, etc. It was objected that the loss of an attack tube for such a torpedo would be regrettable. C-in-C U-boats suggested that instead the firing of such a device from the casing of the boat could be considered. It was declared that the matter would be pursued.'

It was pursued and so from Hitler's idea arose the so-called *Bold*, an abbreviation of *Kobold*, a deceiving spirit. It was a chemical means of deception expelled from U-boats through a special tube to mislead the enemy direction-finding. More exactly, when they were pursued, our U-boats threw out a container 15 centimetres in diameter filled with a chemical substance which dissolved in water to form a dense area of hydrogen gas of which the bubbles disturbed the ultra sound waves of the enemy locating sets and simulated the underwater presence of a U-boat which in reality was moving away. In fact *Bold* enjoyed a momentary success in confusing the Anglo–American U-boat hunters, corvettes and destroyers so that they plastered the chemical area underwater with a positive rain of depth charges while the U-boat they were pursuing had long since slipped away. On a later patrol I myself used *Bold* with success and to make the affair more credible shot out a couple of cleaning cloths and socks into the bargain, which made the enemy believe they had made a U-boat kill.

As far as prisoners' statements were concerned in this particular case, Commander Donald McLachlan of Section NID 17z writes in his book *Room 39*: 'One of the prisoners gave us an exact description of the "pill slinger" code-name *Bold*, which produces bubbles below water. We called this German weapon Submarine Bubble Target (SBT). The thing was annoying to us, but was never really dangerous; for our destroyer commanders were now informed about how this secret contraption worked.'

Moreover the British were in no way reticent about the fact that they knew our secret. On the contrary, hardly had the traitor spoken about *Bold* than the Atlantic transmitter began to mention it frequently, describing it as a useless rubbishy weapon — *Scheisswaffe*. That was typical and did not fail in effect, for while we were still whispering about *Bold* the enemy was publicly reporting on it without constraint.

After Dönitz, other branches of the navy now appointed officers responsible for countering enemy propaganda. In a talk to his commanding officers the Grand Admiral mentioned this new measure, saying: 'I consider it necessary that every office having contact with enemy propaganda or politics or similar matters should employ hard-bitten fighting men whose clear soldierly attitude and proven common sense renders them immune to the inevitable influences from the enemy side connected with their official occupations.'

Until then I myself had thought as little of propaganda as of advertisement. Since Dr. Goebbels, who had always struck us as somewhat frivolous, had built up a whole ministry of propaganda, the word had a bad taste. We officers believed him as little as we believed the enemy. Everything was dubious, for instance the leaflets dropped over Germany in which the U-boats were called 'floating coffins' and which contained the sentence, 'Insurance companies estimate the life expectancy of a German U-boat sailor at fifty days.' The young sailors concerned laughed at this and were proud to belong to so dangerous a branch of the service. But this leaflet may have put the parents of the young people and other outsiders in fear and trembling. And those, again, were the deeper effects intended.

The British were apparently in two minds about the success of their propaganda. Just after the end of the war Lt. Cmdr. Patrick Beesly visited the large special camp 'S' in Schleswig–Holstein where U-boat crews were held prisoner. Beesly, who was a well known secret-service man and also involved in breaking the German wireless code 'M', writes:

'For black naval propaganda the so-called "Atlantic transmitter" was responsible. The author is of the opinion that the influence of the transmissions on the morale of the German navy was small. During a two-month stay in Flensburg after the collapse I was impressed by the high morale and discipline of members of the *Kriegsmarine*.'

The morale of our crews was consistently excellent. But to set so little store by this black propaganda astonished me. At a meeting of German and British naval officers in Bonn in the autumn of 1979 I spoke to Beesly about this and he replied: 'I meant that the fighting morale of the men was not shaken by the transmitter. But the other aims of the so-called black propaganda and of that transmitter were achieved, and the successes were considerable.'

11
The hunters become the hunted

March 1943 opened promisingly for the U-boats. In the first twenty days we sank 105 ships totalling over half a million gross register tons, equivalent to half the new British construction for an entire year. These successes capped a period, July to December 1942, in which our U-boats had accounted for around 3 million GRT, against comparatively light losses: five U-boats in December 1942, six in January 1943, 19 in February, dropping to 15 this March.

The British supply situation seemed seriously threatened, and voices on the island warned that with such high losses supplies would only last for another two months — then that would be the end. At this time the enemy in all seriousness asked himself the question: did the convoy system still offer effective protection against the pack tactics? Moreover, according to Rear Admiral Edelsten, the British Intelligence Service had been unable since the beginning of March to decipher German radio signals and had to admit 'that for some time, perhaps for months we shall learn nothing more about the movements of U-boats.' Everything stood on the razor's edge and the British historian Roskill says in retrospect: 'In the spring of 1943 we narrowly escaped defeat in the Atlantic.'

Risky as it might be, now more than ever the convoys had to sail and try to get through. At this time a fast convoy (identification letters HX) started every six days eastbound from USA/Canada, and every six days another fast convoy (ON) of empty ships started westwards. And every eight days a slow convoy (SC) sailed eastwards, and a slow one (ONS) in ballast started westbound. Fast and slow are relative concepts, but when the British assert today that even their fast convoys seldom achieved more than 10 knots, that seems somewhat of an underestimate. At all events it was possible to keep on their heels. The fast convoys now comprised up to 60 ships, the slow ones 40. Four or five ships at a time sailed in line ahead. So a 60-ship convoy was about 6 sea miles broad and a good two miles deep. It moved forward on the broad front of the rectangle and at the sides offered a narrower surface to attack. The safety cordon round a convoy described a circle with a diameter of about 60 miles. That was a wide area. Later, a second, inner, ring was added to the outer one, which doubled our difficulties in attack. Of course with our U-boat packs we could form extensive stop lines, but neither the packs nor the convoys were always in the expected position.

At the beginning of 1943, 143 U-boats were employed in Atlantic operations of which, according to the triple division (in transit, in port and on combat duty) a bare third were in the operational area. In the North Sea, Mediterranean and Black Sea there were 21, 24 and 3 U-boats respectively. As the number of enemy escort vessels increased so the U-boats were spotted more frequently and in larger numbers, which naturally led to an over-estimate of those employed in attacks. There were really no more than stated and a much greater number of U-boats would have been required to achieve successes comparable with previous years. Here too British understatement had painted in the gloomiest colours. In reality their situation was by no means so bad. The turning point was just coming.

During these early months of 1943 I was still staff officer with Dönitz and experienced this change in the U-boat war from a central vantage point. In March there were several heavy convoy battles, amongst others with HX 228. Here for the first time an aircraft carrier appeared as escort, USS *Bogue*, which hampered the U-boats, inflicted losses on them and boded ill for the future. Then came convoys SC 122 and HX 229 which sailed without carrier protection. They were brought to bay through a deciphered radio signal (we could do that too), but were favoured by bad weather. More than 40 U-boats advanced against the two convoys. But now American long-distance Liberators (duration of flight 16 hours) were overflying the Atlantic from one side and Fortress bombers (11 hours) and Sunderlands (9 hours) from Northern Ireland on the other, and threatening us continually. Nevertheless on this occasion another 21 merchant ships totalling 141,000 tons were picked off. Later, two groups, 'Sea Devil' and 'Sea Wolf' with 32 boats, formed a long patrol line from the southern point of

Greenland south-eastwards. Again they were hampered by bad weather, lost contact with ON 1 pounding westwards and finally chased after SC 123 and HX 230 sailing towards England. Storms made life a misery for everyone and the success was not repeated. When they abated, the carrier *Bogue* was suddenly there again and stayed with the merchant ships for six days. Attacks against them were a clear failure. A pack of 30 U-boats only sank one straggler, and on top of that lost U 169 and U 469 in the process, both sunk by British aircraft. Returning commanders unanimously reported strong sea and air protection. Three quarters of the boats had suffered depth-charging.

One thing was obvious: what had been so long expected had now happened. Long-distance aircraft and carriers had finally closed the so-called 'Gap' in the Atlantic air surveillance. All ships on the big pond between England and America now received reconnaissance and protection from above. The scissors snapped shut to cut off the U-boats' lifeline.

Further, in addition to the Escort Groups, Admiral Sir Max Horton, Commander-in-Chief Western Approaches, attached to the convoys five independently operating Support Groups whose task it was to flush out, pursue and destroy the U-boats before they could attack. To these groups belonged capable leaders like Commander F. J. (Johnnie) Walker R. N. and the Canadian Commander J. D. Prentice. Beside the USS *Bogue, Biter, Dasher* and *Archer* appeared as further aircraft carriers. And as if that was not enough, suitable merchant ships were converted into carriers, called MAC's, Merchant Aircraft Carriers, like the 8,000-ton *Empire McAlpine*. And they all had only one aim: 'attack and kill.'

That was only the beginning. For now, after three and a half years of war, began the murderous battle with convoys which cost a U-boat for every merchant ship sunk. And as time went on, the proportion turned even more in the enemy's favour. In the middle of May, convoys ON 184 and HX 239 did not lose a single ship, while in each case a U-boat went to the depths: U 657 and U 752. When the convoy SC 130 was attacked by 19 U-boats, it too suffered no loss, but six U-boats were sunk. All were despatched in the middle of May, partly by surface craft, partly from the air.

April and May had brought a complete turning point. Not, as is suggested, because fewer ships were sailing or more U-boats were sunk, but because from now on the U-boats could no longer carry out their concentrated attacks on convoys even in favourable circumstances. They could hardly get near. According to Alfred Price, the Allies had more than 1,100 aircraft at their disposal, as well as various aircraft carriers. A new depth charge that could be set to shallow depths was in use, a new more accurate homing torpedo and an anti-submarine rocket. There were magnetic airborne locating devices, the ten-centimetre radar and, of course, Huff-Duff — although these last two were virtually unknown to us and could not be countered by anything of equal value on our side. Now, far from finding themselves forced to submerge, the U-boats were being compelled to surface, and were regularly finished off. The consequences were terrible. If the April losses remained at 15, in May they rose to 41, up to four boats on a single day (19 May).

At first the U-boat command believed that the lack of success was due only to the inexperience of the young commanders, but it soon learnt differently. In its present form the U-boat — a mere submersible with slow underwater speed and limited duration of dive — was no longer effective enough and was inferior to modern defensive techniques. A completely new type of submarine, the Walter U-boat, driven by turbines and achieving 28 knots underwater, was still under trial and not expected at the front before the end of 1944.

In May, Grand Admiral Dönitz faced the difficult question of either suspending the U-boat war with the existing types or of fighting on with them despite obvious inferiority. On the staff we discussed this at length, each one of us being free to express his opinion. It was in particular the weighty human consequences which preoccupied Dönitz. For one thing he had a very close relationship with his subordinates, (no one else in high command was so close to his men), and for another, he had suffered personally. Among the victims in May had been one of his two sons who as watch-keeping officer had gone down with U 954, while a year later he lost his other son with the E-boats. But outwardly, when he paced to and fro among the staff, Dönitz put on a hard expression and an almost unapproachable manner. On 24 May, under pressure of the appalling losses, he withdrew the U-boats from the North Atlantic and redeployed them to the area south of the Azores.

Admiral Horton saw himself within reach of the goal. The colossal sea and air defences of the two greatest sea powers in the

world had abruptly suppressed the U-boat war in the North Atlantic. On 26 May, 1943, he sent a message to the units under his
command in which he said: 'In the last two months the Battle of the
Atlantic has undergone a decisive change in our favour . . . All
escort groups, support groups, escort carriers and their machines
as well as the aircraft from the various air commands have contributed to this great success . . . The climax of the battle has been
surmounted . . .'

It was at this juncture, on the last day of May, that Dönitz
reported the situation to Hitler, who insisted that the U-boat war
be pursued regardless of losses — the conversation was recorded in
Chapter One, p. 1. Hitler's decision had to be seen in the context
of the total situation. On all fronts Germany found herself on the
defensive, and on the home front the Reich was exposed to heavy
air-raids. The Atlantic theatre of war tied down strong enemy sea
and air forces which could otherwise have been used against the
homeland or along the Norwegian coast. It was the westerly bas-
tion. Besides, the enemy was forced to maintain a considerable
material capacity and organisation for logistical support, and this
had to be withdrawn from elsewhere.

Dönitz had no doubt that the continuation of the battle would be
a veritable bed of nails. The only question was, would the ordinary
U-boat man see the necessity of a battle in which great successes
could no longer be achieved and only selfless commitment was
envisaged? The Grand Admiral spoke about this to the operational
flotillas on the Atlantic coast. The U-boat men — and this must be
said — backed their commanders in approving the decision to fight
on, and shared the responsibility. Even in times of the most
terrible defeat they preserved their cohesion and discipline. They
endured long patrols under most dangerous conditions and great
privations. They were always ready to fight on, even with the
heaviest losses. To the end of the war their spirit was unbroken.

Amid all our discussions about causes and effects the question kept
recurring whether our radio signals were safe against decoding.
Already in January 1943 convoys were often eluding the U-boats
despite detailed position reports; by June and July they were
invariably eluding interception. Were the positions of our
U-boats, which had to be reported from time to time, known to the
enemy and had he simply bypassed them? If yes, our code had once

again been broken — or treason was involved. At that time the word 'treason' was bandied about pretty freely and I have already described how Dönitz checked out his own staff. The attitude of the naval high command to code security was in principle very positive. The scientific preparation and production of codes was provided by the Berlin firm of Kurski & Krüger, the mathematical calculations by Heimsoht & Rinke. Working with them were the so-called 'Astronomers' who dealt with millions of possibilities. There were no intermediaries between the two firms and the naval high command.

Whole books have been written about 'cracking' the key or the secret codes. Despite all security measures it was practised with varying success by both sides. German radio research (cover name: *B-Dienst*) with about 1,100 staff supplied much useful information from the start. On the other hand it was only from 1941, when on boarding U-boats and weather ships in the far Atlantic they obtained a variety of cipher material, that the British managed to break into the German coding system. In contrast with the British navy, which still worked with code books in a substitution system, we used an enciphering machine. The German 'M' code (popularly known as Enigma) was a typewriter which by means of three, later four rotors and exchangeable plugs jumbled the clear text and resolved it again at the receiving end. Aware of these principles, the British built up in stages a gigantic organisation with thousands of helpers at Bletchley Park in Buckinghamshire, even developed a computer, and concerned themselves exclusively with the assessment of German radio signals. That lasted in each case from two to seven days, for though the method remained the same the code key changed and had to be identified.

Of equal importance to the cracking of a code is the attempt to conceal from the enemy that one can see his cards. This, in the long run, cannot be kept secret; when, for instance, on 12 January, 1943, the 'Milch Cow' U 459 (von Wilamowitz-Möllendorf) had met enemy destroyers instead of the expected U-boat at a remote rendezvous in mid-Atlantic, one could hardly speak of chance. All the signs indicated that our code had once again been broken.

So the breaking of secret codes varied from one side to the other. Periods with a mass of information alternated with black-outs. In March, 1943, the German *B-Dienst* deciphered 175 Allied radio signals in twenty days, of which ten could be used by Dönitz for very successful operations. At the beginning of March the deciphering of German radio signals took from three to seven days. The signal for the transfer of the U-boats to south of the Azores was only clearly readable after a week because the reference point on the squared chart had not been found. It can be seen from this that in itself a deciphered signal is not everything, but often requires additional material, confirmation and comparisons. Beesly writes: 'On the whole a delay of 24 hours was tolerable, and even after three days a decipher might succeed in starting counter-measures.' But from the beginning of March until June, 1943, the British Intelligence Service had a total black-out, which we did not know, while our *B-Dienst*, according to Vice-Admiral Peter Gretton, was reading the British messages like an open book.

Could the British at this time read the U-boat signals? Our chief of naval intelligence denied such a possibility. In his opinion the M-code was completely secure. To decipher it, he argued, if it was possible at all, would require a colossal technical investment and would be so time-consuming that the results would be out of date and worthless. And though doubts remained in Dönitz's staff, we could not prove him wrong.

Rear Admiral Stummel, head of the Second department of the naval staff (operations), having introduced the code system and ultimately been responsible for it, still stresses today that no hint of treason was connected with our code system and its method, and that, thanks to his staff's achievements, no assistance was given the enemy in decipherment by our men in the radio service. The turning point only came when the enemy had captured all the background material. From the start our own radio intelligence achieved valuable breaks particularly useful to the conduct of the U-boat war. Even a new, extraordinarily elaborate British code made only a brief interruption of these insights into the enemy's radio traffic. In conclusion the admiral remarks that, despite the enemy's discovery of the operating method, the Enigma procedure 'had an inhibiting effect on decipherment, for one must not forget that the key was changed daily.' By contrast, the British methods remained almost continually vulnerable, even without captured material.

In this connection Captain (retd.) Heinz Bonatz, former chief of the naval command's radio intelligence division, comments: 'The discomfiture of the British after the capitulation at their first discovery of the considerable German success in deciphering Allied coded material would certainly not have been so great if they or the USA had succeeded earlier in solving the much more difficult and therefore more secure M-code.'

Incidentally, German intelligence was able to crack not only the western Allies' codes but also those of the Russians, so obtaining information at first hand.

But though very useful to both sides, the intelligence services could not decide the war. They were one factor among several, and no Ultra guaranteed victory. Experience showed that an absolutely unbreakable system does not exist. Admiral Stummel himself only speaks of 'inhibiting'. Anything can be deciphered, it is only a question of time and circumstance. It is also not enough to be informed of the enemy's intentions, one must be able to counter them effectively, and that at the right place and time. There are other ways of detecting the presence of U-boats, and to hunt out a convoy is problematical enough when it preserves total radio silence.

U 333, the boat of the three little fishes, had once again been lucky. From 13 April to 2 June, 1943, during the whole of 'black May' when so many of us did not return, it lay in La Pallice, partly in the dockyard, partly fitting out. Lieutenant Schwaff had brought it safely back. On 18 April he took leave of the crew to hand over to me, and that was the last we saw of him. He took command of U 440 and was sunk only six weeks later by aerial bombs off the north Spanish coast by Cape Ortegal. The entire crew was lost. It was the last of the 41 boats destroyed in May.

I assumed that after the terrible losses the morale of the crews in the bases would have reached a low point, but apart from a few exceptions that was not the case, and in my flotilla not at all. While I was still on Dönitz's staff in Berlin the Grand Admiral had already spoken to them and found their spirit unbroken. Shortly afterwards I was sent to the front with Herbert Kuppisch and Friedrich Guggenberger to find out the cause of our heavy losses, as mentioned in Chapter 1 (p. 4), and I travelled via Paris to La Pallice.

Back on board U 333, I carefully scrutinised my men. There were a few strange faces among them, but we soon got a grip on our new crew members. Soon everything was running as before. The old petty officers grinned. They were glad that I had returned and said quite openly that they preferred an experienced commander; they had feared having to go on patrol under a young, inexperienced man, of whom there were already quite a few.

Before we sailed I drove to Mérimac. That was an airfield where our VFW 200's were based. I had a friend there, Major Kowalewski, from whom I wanted to discover what difficulties a large aircraft had to overcome when attacking a ship, taking into consideration wind and weather. I also wanted to learn about the instruments in the aircraft, in particular the altimeter. I hoped to profit from these details when defending myself against enemy aircraft. The fact that whole magazines simply bounced off their fuselage gave me a real headache. The enemy heavy bombers and flying boats were armoured on the underside and completely invulnerable to the smaller calibres. It took a lucky hit to bring one down.

On 2 June, when I left my hotel in the morning, a friend said to me on the steps: 'Well, good luck! You're sailing today, aren't you?'

I was very surprised. My friend did belong to the navy, but not to the U-boat arm, and I had always believed that our sailing dates were kept strictly secret. So I asked in my turn: 'Who told you that?' He replied seriously: 'The *Atlantiksender* spread it about last night: Cremer is sailing with U 333 on 2 June.'

I stared at him and had a strange feeling in the pit of my stomach. It was really not pleasant to discover that the enemy already had my number, and I resolved to be particularly on the alert in the Bay.

Curiously enough, nothing then happened. The air was so clear that we could move on the surface in brilliant daylight and only dived at night. In addition to ourselves, U 572 was also putting to sea.

Like all boats we still had the old Metox warning set on board and occasionally its 'magic eye' lit up to register contact with unidentified objects. In retrospect that meant that by no means all enemy aircraft were yet equipped with the new ten-centimetre radar, and so we could get warning of their approach. But apart from a machine which flew very low over us in fog on the fourth day and vanished again in the murk there was nothing to report, as an official communiqué might say. I radioed to Dönitz a report of our undisturbed movement by day. The signal was picked up and deciphered by the enemy. As a consequence all the U-boats which sailed after us and tried to do the same were suddenly exposed again to surprise daylight attacks. It was the terrible time of the Biscay crisis and tactics changed very rapidly.

The British described this with a certain satisfaction in 'We know all' — Annex to D/AHB (RAF): 'U 333 (on its seventh war cruise) and U 572 departed La Pallice. On 7 June they reported that the Bay of Biscay had been traversed successfully on the surface by day and underwater by night . . . Immediately thereafter, U-boats in groups 3 to 5 left Biscay on 7, 8, 9, 10, and 12 June . . .' Apparently the British Intelligence Service had been able to revert to the German radio code which had been lost at the beginning of March.

At the end of June the British reinforced the blockade round the Bay with specially organised U-hunting groups of sea and air formations. A force of about seven aircraft flew three times daily on a parallel course through two bordering areas which were given the names *Musketry* and *Seasluck*. On sighting a U-boat the aircraft maintained contact and called up the hunter groups which operated almost up to Spanish territorial waters, waiting for U-boats on the way home.

The seventh war patrol of U 333 (my fifth) to the middle Atlantic began under good auspices but was a total failure. The cruise lasted 90 days, so was very long and dragged on to the end of August. To me physically it was pretty exhausting. In volunteering for service again I had taken on too much. I was in no way as fit as I had tried to persuade myself and often, when I had to leave the boat for the bridge I hardly had the strength to dress without help.

In the summer of 1943 sinkings in the Atlantic were extraordinarily small, losses on the other hand once more high. From 17 boats in June they rose to 37 in July and 25 in August. With the exception of 'black May' the July losses were greater than in any other month during the war, and among its 37 victims were four 'Milch Cows' — a loss which could not be made good. In the Atlantic all hell was loose.

Meanwhile the Allies had marked out their battle zones. British and Canadians took on the New York, Halifax and England convoys. The USA set up the Tenth Fleet, a formation covering the entire range of anti-U-boat activities, and guarded the New York-Gibraltar route, the oil transports from Trinidad and the West of the

South Atlantic. They took such care of this that they smashed everything that stood in their way. Their CVE's (Carrier Vessel Escorts) consisted of aircraft carriers like *Bogue, Core, Santée, Card* and *Rock Island* and were surrounded by hunter–killer groups: destroyers, frigates and corvettes. Their crews were extremely well trained. The ships themselves possessed modern radar equipment and sensitive direction-finders with which they could trace in a moment the origin of a radio signal, even a short-code one, from its direction. That was Huff-Duff, previously mentioned, which I had already met once. We still had no idea of its existence and exposed ourselves to it with unavoidable signals. For close-quarters fighting they were equipped with new-type Asdic underwater sonar locating sets, with modern depth charges, with all those aids which made it almost impossible for a U-boat, once pin-pointed, to escape. In that one summer the Americans made up for almost two years of neglect.

The mid-Atlantic 'gap' no longer existed. Aircraft were humming about everywhere, seeking to kill us. Undisturbed supply areas where we could at last get some air after long underwater passages and for a short time brown our pale skins in the sun became few and far between. And gone, too, were those pauses for rest when we could splash in sea water and clean ourselves with sea-water soap, when we could turn our attention to nature, to marine life, the turtles, the giant oceanic jelly-fish and occasionally perhaps a shark. All that was past.

During those 90 days we were supplied three times: with fuel oil, spare parts, lubricating oil and food. The suppliers were regular fighting boats like ourselves, for there were hardly any 'Milch Cows' left. Our faithful von Wilamowitz-Möllendorf in U 459 was not met with again, either. All ten of these big U-tankers were lost, seven of them alone in that fateful summer of 1943. U 459 caught it on 24 July off the Bay in an unusually dramatic manner. The 'Milch Cow' was attacked by a Leigh-Light Wellington of the *Musketry* patrol, but was able to shoot down the machine. As it fell the bomber grazed the boat, tore away the guns and their crews and plunged in pieces into the sea. Amongst the wreckage left behind on deck the crew found two depth charges. The commander went to full speed and let the bombs roll into the water from the stern. Little did he suspect that they were no usual depth charges but Air Force bombs which exploded in only eight metres of water. One went up directly under the stern, destroyed the rudder, damaged machinery, caused a fire. When another plane appeared, the boat was unmanoeuvrable and defenceless. Von Wilamowitz-Möllendorf ordered his men to abandon ship. Then he laid a scuttling charge and went down with U 459. A British warship saved 45 survivors.

U 333 never got the chance of a shot. After withdrawal from the North Atlantic we lay in wait with a number of other U-boats in a line south of the Azores. There we were expecting the American convoys which were recently heading through the Mediterranean via Suez to the Persian Gulf with war material for Russia, or throwing men and materials into the Mediterranean for their landing on Sicily on 10 July, 1943. Yet though we stared the eyes out of our heads during this fine-weather period we caught none of the legendary convoys.

Nothing was stirring. The Atlantic spread in midsummer peace from horizon to horizon. We marked time, submerged, surfaced again, reported our position and practised patience. To be precise, something did happen from time to time, but when we chased after a mast-head and the whole ship gradually became visible it would be a neutral for sure, a Spaniard from Bilbao, a Portuguese or someone else whose wake disappeared once more from sight.

It was the period of long days. One evening in mid-June, the clock showing 2238, masts came in sight. Did I say masts? A whole forest of them — a convoy at last! We all hurried to battle stations as though electrified, the tubes were made ready. At top speed we dieseled in pursuit but, however hard we tried, could not close with the enemy. A night of full moon followed the vanishing daylight with very good visibility, but did not deceive us into thinking we could keep up. A torpedo I sent after the convoy missed and was lost in the blue. The convoy had not even noticed us and I do not know whether my sighting report gave other boats a chance.

And so it went on, surfacing, submerging, zig-zagging, waiting . . . We had already been four weeks at sea when in the early afternoon of 29 June, as though presented to us on a plate, a big, heavily laden convoy appeared, eastward-bound. I made a signal, then purposefully went after it. That is easily said, but — went to periscope depth, studied the ships, surfaced again, followed up. The convoy was moving in three lines of unequal length, with the fat morsels in the middle. I cautiously tried to come up on a bearing but soon saw that I would not be able to do so without being noticed through the security screen. This went on all afternoon, and so far quite well, until I had a big steamer within reach and in the cross-wires. Then the escorts located me and at once turned towards me. I stayed surfaced, took up a reciprocal course and with a slim silhouette in the growing twilight hoped to get away from them. They set after me, were quicker than I was with my 16 knots, and suddenly one of them slapped on a searchlight. I sent the bridge watch below and stayed alone on the conning tower. With a lead of only one mile, in the searchlight glare the whole thing was acquiring a horrid similarity with the *Crocus* onslaught off Freetown. It was high time to go down to the cellar before we got a licking. Crash dive!

Down we went, with two pursuers after us. Their Asdic failed to get a good contact, their depth charges were inaccurate. They lost track of us. The propeller noises grew fainter and fainter and finally ceased. When we came up again the convoy was a good bit further on and disappeared in darkness and rain showers.

Above us a depression was moving away. Low cloud cover, moderate visibility. Several neutral steamers passed and for a while, wasting fuel, we trundled after them. For us a fast convoy remained unreachable. For the sake of picking up something better I suggested moving to the coast of Africa. But before Dönitz's reply arrived, the boat's two air-compressors broke down.

Expressed in general terms, that meant that I had no compressed air to blow out the ballast tanks and bring the boat to the surface. It is roughly as though a fish lost the function of its air bladder and sank slowly to the bottom. One can indeed push the boat to the surface by means of the hydroplanes and motors, and, once there, blow out the tanks with the diesel exhaust. In times of peace that is no problem. But when the going is rough, with the possible addition of motor or engine damage, it can cost lives. And things seemed to be hotting up, for during the following weeks we continually heard short-code signals from other boats which were being attacked by aircraft. With their meagre anti-aircraft defences (two machine-guns and one two-centimetre gun), they were having difficulty in defending themselves.

Shortly after this I myself caught it in the neck, as reported by the aircraft carrier USS *Core*: two of her aircraft were involved on the afternoon of 13 July, 1943: 'At 1521 the gunner noticed a white wake about ten miles away . . .' (That was I, Cremer, with U 333.) 'Both machines turned to port when Lt. Williams, using cloud cover during his approach, noticed that a fully surfaced U-boat was causing the wake. Its speed was between 12 and 14 knots. Lt. Williams signalled Lt. Steiger (second aircraft) to begin a strafing run . . .

'. . . Steiger approached the boat from the starboard bow to attack it at low level . . . During his approach Williams noticed a man running in front on the conning tower as though he wanted to serve the gun. Williams dropped a loading of four depth charges (Mark 47) from a height of 250 feet and photographed the explosions through the rear gunner's turret. The first two grazed the bow 35 feet before the conning tower. Both machines climbed to 3,500 feet to observe the result of the attack. The boat described a right-handed circle and came to a stop. Escaping oil covered the whole area described by the circle. Meanwhile the crew had manned the gun and began to fire. The shots all lay too low and behind the turning machines . . .'

From my viewpoint the engagement passed somewhat differently. I had just surfaced when the first plane, a twin-engined machine came in sight. It kept contact and made radio signals. A second added its firepower and came towards us very low over the water. I reduced speed, had the two-centimetre manned and the new machine guns, FlaMG 38, and emptied a magazine in greeting. As though in reply the threatened machine opened its bomb doors. As it flew over us one could clearly see our rounds disappearing into the plane. The Flak 38 gave up after a short burst. Perhaps it was the ammunition, perhaps the gun was still too wet, I don't know.

The bomber pilot probably assumed that his bombs had hit the target. He circled round 4,000 metres away and made more signals. Now I manned my 88-millimetre gun and began to fire. The calculations, lateral and vertical, were easy and the shell, fitted with a delayed-action fuse, exploded just in front of his nose. With the second shot I corrected the distance. He lost pleasure in risk-taking and buzzed off.

The American report also stated that on a renewed approach the second machine (Lt. Steiger) 'suddenly swerved to the left. Its nose dropped and it plunged into the water . . . A thorough search carried out in the area later revealed no trace, either of the pilot or of the machine.' The kill, or whatever it was, was not noticed by us although the Americans maintained in all seriousness 'the submarine had gotten one of our planes'. We had other things to do and for the time being submerged.

Meanwhile reinforcements called up by radio were approaching, five more machines from *Core* and the destroyer *Barker*. On the way they came upon the 'Milch Cow' U 487, which this time did not escape. It was an unequal battle. The columns of water from the bombs lifted up the boat, it dipped at an angle of 45 degrees and in a very short time had disappeared. The destroyer saved 35 survivors who were drifting on floats. In all the hectic activity I had been lost sight of so that once more I could seek open water.

In an analysis of the battle report occurs the following passage: '. . . the fact that Williams' radar was functioning within seventeen miles of the U-boat's location may be of significance. As the U-boat was nevertheless surprised one may assume that it possessed no radar warning set, or if it did, a not very efficient one . . .'

Here they had hit the nail on the head. I have already said that we still went to sea with the obsolete Metox warning set which did not react to modern centimetre radar. This continued for a while until on 16 August the Metox was abandoned on orders from Dönitz because it allegedly radiated and, until the introduction of the new Naxos set, we had no warning set at all.

Once more U 333 had survived. Nevertheless, prospects were gloomy. Already we had been 42 days at sea again and had only recently tanked up with oil. Now food and fuel were again running short, and it was the same with other boats.

To explain this further: the U-boats withdrawn from the North Atlantic had been sent by headquarters to relatively distant operational areas. They were knocking around not only in mid-Atlantic but in the Trinidad area, off Brazil and Freetown, Africa. The large IX-D types, so-called Monsoon boats, were already operating off South Africa and in the Indian Ocean. To extend the radius of action of boats sailing out and returning it was intended to provide intermediate supply in the middle Atlantic where at agreed rendezvous they would find supply boats.

When in June, 1943, the first CVEs or Task Groups of the Tenth Fleet appeared with *Bogue, Core* and *Santée* in the middle Atlantic the U-boat command misunderstood their offensive character and assumed they would confine themselves as previously to the mere protection of convoys. But the Americans turned the tables, resolved on a big clean-up. From the radio traffic between Dönitz and his boats, which they deciphered with a two- to three-day delay, they could detect our supply organisation from the relevant operational movements. It was clear that if they succeeded in breaking the supply network the whole system would collapse. A catastrophe was impending.

As for me in U 333, besides our shortages I had to struggle with the wretched compressor damage. We tinkered with it and patched continually, discovering in the process that we were dealing with a veteran compressor which looked solid enough when freshly painted on land but, taken apart, proved thoroughly unsound. In mid-July I did receive some spare parts from U 618, and shortly afterwards further ones from U 600, but they only brought a temporary improvement. This went on for a full six weeks, accompanied by the constant anxiety: Heaven preserve us from accidents! In reply to my repeated requests for early delivery of a new Junkers compressor, 'Cremer advised that intended delivery impossible because no tanker available.' This is how the Americans formulated the exchange, which they followed attentively on the ether. 'He is to patch up a compressor as best he can by trading parts with another combat U-boat, U 571 (Lüssow).' And this did happen, but not until 5 August at night when the receipt of an E-compressor from Lüssow restored the longed-for air to blow out the tanks and therewith restore manoeuvrability.

This and similar events were logically interpreted by the Americans as 'instances of the collapsing supply system'. No U-tankers were available! Of ten U-tankers only two survived that summer, and according to the Americans the supply system received the most severe blow through the loss of the U-tanker U 487 on 13 July by the hunter-killers of *Core*. The next day the auxiliary tanker U 160 was lost. Both were on the way to a dozen other boats whose areas had now to be altered. The consequence was a chain reaction extending further and further, confounding Dönitz's short- and long-term plans.

Almost without exception the 'Milch Cows' were dead. Now

more than previously operational boats were transformed into auxiliary tankers to supply fuel and other necessities to boats in need.
The big Monsoon boats of Type IX-D, with a capacity for 500 tons
of diesel oil, were whistled back en route for the Indian Ocean and
down-graded to bunker boats in the middle Atlantic. Their
fighting task was abandoned and from Dönitz their protests
received only a laconic 'No other solution possible. Bunkering is to
be carried out.' Things became much worse. The Task Groups
destroyed auxiliary tankers and fighting boats in like manner and
by the end of August there was no more talk of continuing operations but simply of the necessity of saving what could be saved to
get the boats back 'home' with the last drop of oil. It was much as it
had been previously in the North Atlantic.

There was violent action everywhere. On 11 August Klemens
Schamong, my former I.W.O., now commander of U 468, caught
it off the West African coast. His boat was attacked by an RAF
machine. Caught by heavy defensive fire, the aircraft burst into
flames and crashed. The pilot, who in so doing lost his life, held on
to the last and laid a series of depth charges across U 468 which tore
open the pressure hull and destroyed the boat. Schamong and
seven of his men climbed into a float and were picked up three days
later by a British warship. Months later, as a result of statements by
the U-boat men, the dead pilot, Flying Officer L. Trigg, was posthumously awarded the highest British decoration for valour, the
Victoria Cross.

U 333 may have recovered her manoeuvrability but this did not
mean much. After chasing the Portuguese steamer *Maria Christina*
on 12 August, we too were down to our last drop of oil. The dream
was over! All U-boats which had to tank up for their return journey
were allotted a particular map square. Absolute radio silence was
ordered for a radius of 400 miles, tactical reports excluded.

Now we lay at sea anchor, a kind of bag of sail cloth on a long line
which kept the boat head-to-sea, and pitched in the swell. Just
imagine: a battle-worthy U-boat motionless in the ocean. Not only
that, a day later the food ran out and we had only hot coffee. The
men joked that meals were being replaced by soldierly fortitude.
There was nothing for us to do but await whatever came. Shortly
after us U 230 (Paul Siegmann) arrived in the same straitened
circumstances that we were in. How serious my situation was can
be judged by the fact that I had to borrow 1,500 litres of lubricating

oil in 15-litre bottles. Finally we were five boats dawdling away the time without fuel or food. The situation was not only grotesque, it was desperate, seeing that as a matter of principle every single boat had previously been supplied in an area of its own for security reasons and a concentration of boats had been avoided. And here we were, five of us confined in the narrowest space, a prey to anything that might happen.

It was not till four days later that Harpe came in sight with the auxiliary tanker U 129 and provided us with essentials. By then seven boats had turned up to be refuelled. The weather was good. In the long, lazy swell it was easy to pull the delivery hose across and so everything went fairly quickly. And afterwards we could again eat our fill — on rice and sausages, tinned loaves and spread.

When the order to return came we set off home separately. On 22 August U 333 passed the island of Santa Maria in the Azores. By day aircraft from the British island base kept us submerged. And then we neared the most dangerous part of the journey, the passage through the Bay of Biscay.

To the British, the Bay had always been a thorn in the flesh. From 1941 onwards, when most of the German Luftwaffe were drawn off to the east, they had made life difficult for the U-boats on passage in and out. This summer of 1943, with reinforced sea and air power, they prepared an onslaught which brought them the desired success. From the end of April to the beginning of August, in a period of 97 days, their aircraft sank 26 U-boats in the Bay and damaged 17, which were forced to turn back. The German navy had tried to counter these attacks with U-boats heavily armed as 'flak traps', but had abandoned the scheme. After all, it was not the task of U-boats to shoot down aircraft, but to avoid them. At the beginning of August the peak of the offensive seemed to have passed. Instead, the enemy naval forces took to sealing the ring round the Bay. Dönitz repeatedly urged extreme caution.

In any case, so far as I was concerned I had no desire, after 90 useless days, to come to an equally useless end. As far as possible I would avoid all complications and look for a 'private route', if need be somewhat outside legality, but inside safer waters. Nobody was to blame me for that. The weather was summery with a light wind, sea slight, visibility clear to a great distance. On the night of 28 August, even before we reached the Spanish coast at Cape Finisterre, we received a foretaste of what awaited us and heard rumbling far off to the north. There a British support group was zealously at work, scattering its depth charges. The explosions rang in my ears for a long time and were repeated the nearer we came. Alternately surfaced and submerged, we crept on from Cape to Cape: Finisterre, Villāno, Prior, Punta de la Estaca, Peñas. Off Villāno matters deteriorated. Depth charges, fast-churning propellers: the destroyers and corvettes were giving someone a pasting. Indeed they were blasting at everything and nothing, even if it turned out in the end to be merely an existing wreck.

I slipped away as best I could and kept as close to land as possible. Rather rub off a neutral corner than be rubbed out oneself. I infiltrated myself among merchant steamers and Spanish fishing vessels; on my right hand as a good background the high coast, close enough to be touched, and I had only one thought: if they knock us off now we can at least swim to land. And today I still think that is a healthy notion.

In the early morning, just off our French base, we heard the propeller noises of a foreign submarine. Surfaced, but saw nothing. We made a wide circle and placed ourselves astern of the sounds. Not till later did we see one another, just in time to refrain from shooting. Friend or foe? It was a Japanese. One of those boats bringing raw materials from the Far East for the German armament industry, wolfram in particular. Among ourselves we called the Japanese U-boats 'cherry blossoms'. (After a time we learnt that the Japanese were not sinking any Anglo–American freighters in the Pacific if it looked as though they were taking war materials to the Soviet Union. At all costs the Japanese were determined not to be involved in war with Russia.)

When we tied up in La Pallice/La Rochelle on 30 August, 1943, Adalbert Schnee, at that time staff officer with Dönitz, received me. 'Thank God, you at least are back. For the last three days there is no news at all of Kuppisch, and Guggenberger caught it in July . . .'

Friedrich Guggenberger with U 513 had succumbed to an aircraft off the Brazilian coast, but he had been saved. My friend Herbert Kuppisch, who latterly had commanded the auxiliary tanker U 847, had been lost in the middle Atlantic to an aircraft off USS *Core*. Of course one normally learns that sort of thing after long uncertainty; in the first moment of home-coming it left me speechless.

(above) *22. The U-boat's 2-cm anti-aircraft battery . . .*
(below) *23. . . . is exposed to the weather . . .*

(above) 24. . . . *and to enemy fire.* (below) 25. *Freighters travelling in convoy, whose protective screens the U-boats ultimately found it hard to penetrate.*

Crew of U 333 during the attack of the frigate HMS Exe off Gibraltar (see pp. 155 ff).
(above) 26. Waiting for the explosion.
(below) 27, 28. Thirty seconds to dive to sixty feet. (overleaf) (above) 29. Valves slacked off (below left) 30. The explosions shake the diesel loose from its housing; it is shored up with beams. (below right) 31. After the Exe's attack U 333's periscope is bent. It still proudly displays two stripes for two downed aircraft.

32. *In the last stage of the U-boat war, the Schnorchel allows boats to remain submerged and provides air to their diesels.* 33. *The new Type XXI boats are prefabricated in sections inland and assembled at the dockyard.*

34,35. U 2519 *heading for sea trials. These Type XXI boats might have revolutionised the U-boat war, but came too late.*

So of the three of us who had been sent out a few months back to discover 'What is going on out there' only I had returned. What was going on no longer needed clarification, the news had got around. Only about the 'how' were there still any doubts. Otherwise the facts spoke for themselves — in the North Atlantic, in the Bay and the middle Atlantic. In the three months, June through August, we had sunk barely 60 freighters — for a loss of 79 U-boats. That spoke volumes for the superiority of the enemy. Now we were fighting with our backs to the wall.

Strangely, on that long patrol I discovered once and for all what courage is. A fighting man will allow matters to come to the crunch and accept the risks — and is usually buoyed by the feeling: it won't happen to me. But once he has been marked as I had (and possesses wound badges in black and silver) and, barely recovered, returns to the fight, then things look different: he has experienced wounds and pain and knows that he can suffer the experience again at any moment. He knows that imminent death is not merely possible but indeed probable. To carry on regardless requires real courage. I am not applying this particularly to myself. It is assumed as a matter of course that a professional fighting man is ready to sacrifice himself. At any rate that was the case in those days, and especially among officers.

At least Guggenberger had been able to sink five ships. I came back empty-handed and it almost sounds as though Admiral Godt was trying to comfort me when he concluded his comments with the words: 'The long patrol, unsuccessful through no fault of his, was unfortunately a disappointment for the experienced commander.'

Meanwhile, I was still alive — we were all alive. My crew were grateful to me. For the second boat, U 572 (Heinz Kummetat), in whose company we had started the passage through the Bay, had found a watery grave with its entire crew in an air attack off Trinidad.

12
Collision with a frigate

After every lengthy patrol it was customary to exchange up to three members of the crew. Old and experienced ones were sent to new boats and their places were taken by beginners, of whom there was no lack. They were eager to come to U 333. 'Ali' — as I was called — 'Ali is as good as life insurance.'

There was no real reason for such optimism, although we had been given new apparatus which seemed to offer a better chance of success and survival. Metox had been replaced by the Naxos Radar Warning Receiver, built by the Kiel firm of Hagenuk, which covered the Allies' ten-centimetre wavelength. In addition the U-boats had been given an increased anti-aircraft armament with quadruple 20-millimetre guns with a high rate of fire, and a semi-automatic 3.7, besides strengthened bridge armour. More crucially, every boat was equipped with four *Zaunkönig* torpedoes ('Wren' but better known to the Allies as the 'Gnat').

The Gnat possessed an acoustical tracking head which reacted to the wash and propeller sounds of a ship, as described on page 28. Marvellous things were told of this torpedo. It was a weapon to rely on, a 'destroyer cracker'. Thus in the second half of September, 1943, spurred on by a signal from Dönitz, 'The Führer is following every phase of your battle. Attack! Go to it! Sink them!', the U-boat group *Leuthen* claimed to have sunk 6 merchant ships and 12 escort vessels out of two Atlantic convoys (ON 202 and ONS 18) with 24 Gnats. So here was one of the promised new wonder-weapons to raise our morale, and we too were to have surprising experiences with it.

It began in mid-October when we had slipped out again and were operating with the *Schill* group west of the Bay. The political horizon was darkening. In September Italy had concluded an armistice with the Allies and on 13 October its new government under Marshal Badoglio declared war on Germany. The Axis was broken, the Allies had the free run of the Mediterranean and their sea traffic intensified.

With a barrier of eight U-boats we awaited a convoy from Sierra Leone and another from Gibraltar which had combined on 24 October into the convoy SL 138/MKS 28 heading north. Reconnaissance by our Air Command Atlantic had observed the mass of the ships, which were protected by seven vessels of the British Escort Group B1. In the further course of the passage they were lost from sight, but rediscovered at noon on 30 October. A mass attack by the U-boats, planned for the following night, was postponed. The alerted convoy had reduced speed and was holding back. When star-shells rose in the distance and U262 (Heinz Franke) gave early warning of the first ships, dawn was already breaking. There was a faint breeze, the air was clear.

By the time it was light I could see the convoy. Then a one-funnel destroyer came up. I held her in the periscope sights, had a Gnat made ready for firing and gave my orders in a loud voice so that the crew heard whom I was attacking. The destroyer was coming towards me in the ideal zero-angle position, moving quite slowly. Following her came an escort dropping depth charges, intended presumably for another U-boat. The destroyer came closer still, 3,500 metres, now — ! 'Tube five — Fire!'

After the shot I went at once to 30 metres so that the torpedo, with its sensitivity to sound, should not turn and take us as a target (as the weapon had been known to do during its trials). Now it was to show what it could do. The wait seemed interminable, but after four full minutes and twenty seconds there was a bang big enough to shake the U-boat. Hurrah — hit!

At 0832 the last in the second column of ships, the Norwegian steamer *Hallfried* (2,968 GRT) had been struck on the port side at very close range by one torpedo and had sunk in about 30 seconds.

When I raised the periscope again, in place of the sunken merchant ship the sea was covered with debris. Of the destroyer there was nothing to be seen, it too had gone. The escort vessel was still dropping depth charges, another put a boat out and saved three survivors from the *Hallfried*. Two more came over from the opposite, starboard, side and took part in hunting the U-boat, making at least 12 depth-charge attacks. The last depth charge exploded and 75 seconds later a stream of air bubbles rose to the surface for a considerable length of time. But evidence of a U-boat destruction was not found. No wonder, for the air bubbles came from me. I had foxed my pursuers with a *Bold* and been able to get away. At 1450 another object was attacked but proved to be 'non-sub'. But staying behind in the wake of two other warships, *Whitehall* and *Geranium*, was the bombed and sinking U 306 with Claus von Trotha and all his men. For a while the pursuers curved to and fro until the last one broke off the search and turned behind the convoy which had continued its journey without pause.

The charges which we had been made to feel this time had been louder and more powerful. Some belonged to a new type, the Hedgehog. These did not react to water pressure but exploded only on striking an object. And they were not thrown astern but ahead, several at a time — somewhat like the five fingers of an out-stretched hand, groping for a U-boat.

My first acoustic torpedo had proved itself. The destroyer had disappeared and was credited to me. The mood of my crew rose up, the 'old man' was again in fine form. We thought that to knock out a destroyer was something very special. And rightly so.

The convoy came under increasing air protection and although we stayed on its tail we could not catch up even after dark and on the surface. The engagement, during which we had lost one U-boat against one merchant ship, had been a failure and was broken off. We returned to a waiting position and looked forward to the next engagement. In the late afternoon of the following day, as we were submerged, the hydrophone operators once more reported the high-pitched sound of fast-revolving propellers. Went to periscope depth and again found a destroyer before us in a favourable position. Still affected by the previous day's success, I fired the next Gnat from tube 3. What I should have done was to have made quite certain, reducing the range to 3,000 metres at the most: in fact our target was at least 4,000 metres off. But conditions seemed to promise success, I was bursting with impatience and self-confidence, and took the chance — and scored no hit. Now two of the acoustic torpedoes had gone.

We broke off our pursuit of the convoy and returned to a fresh patrol line in the same area of the grid as before.

On the night of 4 November we were submerged when weak sounds were heard in the narrow listening spectrum. On surfacing we found thick, all-dissolving fog. The world was silent and empty, and we heard the echo of our own words. And yet there was something in the air. There — for a moment a light appeared, was swallowed in the fog, then reappeared. Probably the masthead-light of a neutral steamer coming from the Azores, soundlessly lost again in the fog bank underlining the dreamlike quality of the scene. Here and there the lanterns of fishing vessels threw dull reflections on the water.

This silent hovering between illusion and reality continued, confusing the senses and seducing our thoughts. How long, I do not know. Suddenly, we could not believe our eyes, the scene changed abruptly as on a stage. The imagined steamer turned into the vague shadow of a warship. Distorted by the shifting veil of the fog, disjointed and growing to a gigantic size, hulls, masts and funnels came into view. As though behind an intervening curtain, instead of peaceable trawlers a cavalcade of great ships went gliding past, muffled as in cotton wool by the fog and as silent as ghosts.

There was no time for reflection, everything had to be done on the spur of the moment. Target range and reference points were missing in this swirling mist. Purely on impulse I advanced at random between two shadows into the emptiness . . . and was at once spotted and attacked by a destroyer. This one too came to-wards me in the zero-angle position, so running directly onto the knife.

An ideal firing position which I could not resist, although every-thing happened helter-skelter and I had to guess the firing data. No matter. The third Gnat was quickly sent off and . . . in the bad visibility we were now so close to one another that after firing I had to stop to avoid a collision and the crazy question occurred to me, just who was running onto whose knife? So I turned and made off.

While behind me the mass of the convoy melted again in the fog, the destroyer did not let me go. I stayed as last man on the bridge, perhaps a fraction too long. From below the O.O.W. was urging: 'We must dive, Sir — we must dive!' Confident in my torpedo — and in victory — I shouted back: 'Not yet, jitter-bug. The des-troyer will go up at any moment, just you watch!'

But nothing of the kind happened. Only when the chief quartermaster put his head through the hatch and started swearing and the destroyer turned its searchlight on us did I have to admit that once more something had failed to function. Now the third Gnat had gone.

We escaped by a hair's breadth. We had not yet dropped to 100 metres when the first depth charges came down. Thank God, they were set shallow. At 180 metres we levelled out and from 0718 were exposed to a rain of depth charges until the enemy himself tired. U 333 moved away with insignificant damage, leaving behind a faint trail of oil. Sceptical now about the new wonder-weapon, I noted in the log 'The stern Gnat must be retained as a last resort.'

On 13 November the sailing was reported of a convoy with ships from Gibraltar and North African ports which next day joined up with a Sierra Leone convoy about 100 miles south of Cape St. Vincent and now consisted of 66 freighters: SL 139/MKS 30. To start with it was accompanied by 40th Escort Group, but during the passage to Britain 7th and 5th Escort Groups were fetched from other convoys and the 4th from Belfast, so that the 66 merchant ships were gradually surrounded by 28 escort vessels: frigates, corvettes, destroyers and the Canadian anti-aircraft cruiser HMCS *Prince Robert* which had come from Plymouth — the Luftwaffe now had only a fitful presence over the ocean, but reconnaissance aircraft and even bomber formations were occasionally spotted. RAF Wellingtons from 171 Squadron in Gibraltar provided air protection, reinforced by Mosquitos and Beaufighters off Cape Ortegal. Direct convoy protection was then to be assumed by aircraft from Cornwall (RCAF 422 Squadron and RAF Liberators from 453 Squadron).

Against this doubly and trebly screened convoy we had the *Schill* Groups I, II and III in three stop lines about a day's sailing apart. Air Command Atlantic was involved with 25 long-distance bombers of type HE 177. This time the convoy battle promised to be both vast and varied.

On 16 November the convoy was first sighted by a German aircraft, and thereafter there were several sightings. In the morning hours of 18 November the ships sailing up from the south came into action against the U-boats on watch in the north. The scene was roughly midway between the Azores and the Portuguese coast. This was a grey November morning after a clear moonlit night. The sickle stayed for a long time in the sky before it was properly light. Small clouds came up. A slight wind was blowing from the north-east, and when the sun shone in the course of the morning it showed a sea stirred into a slight swell by the winds of recent days. U 333 was moving underwater and when I occasionally raised the periscope, spray splashed against the lens. The empty horizon was a sharp dividing line which in the rhythm of the sea rose up, then disappeared behind the wave-tops. The clock showed 1130.

It was relatively quiet in the boat. Amid the gurgle and wash of the water came other sounds, weak at first, then growing stronger. The operators signalled ships' propellers from the south. I let things start gently and hung on the periscope. After a while the silhouette of a great many freighters appeared. Fourteen rows of ships were coming in their full width with foaming bow waves directly towards me. It was a unique sight: the expected convoy SL 139/MKS 30. Chance would have it that U 333 was the first boat to intercept the enemy.

In front sailed two escort vessels, clearly destroyers. U 333 lay roughly in the middle between them, in an attack position which would probably not recur. I only needed to let myself drop into the convoy and attack like a pike in a carp pond. All tubes were ready for an underwater shot, flooded and with bow caps open. All I had to do was lie still, let the enemy draw closer and then: at him with a roar! But everything turned out quite differently.

The destroyers were signalling to one another. The right-hand one was zig-zagging continually while the left kept to a straight course. I had my periscope up again, hoping it would not be noticeable in the light motion of the sea, when suddenly I saw an aircraft flit past my lens barely 30 metres above the water. At the same moment the locating signals of the enemy Asdic struck the U-boat's side with their horrible ping-ping-ping-ping, so loud I might have sent them out myself. We had been discovered. Involuntarily everyone held his breath.

The left escort, it turned out to be the frigate *Exe*, was already turning towards us and in a moment was so close I could distinguish details on deck. I intended to fire a spreading salvo of three into the convoy and had already ordered 'salvo ready', meaning after previous misses to be on the safe side and let the ships come closer, despite the menacing frigate whose sailors I could now see running to and fro. I was still staring obstinately through the periscope when a pattern of ten depth charges exploded with a deafening roar round the boat. We had got into the middle of a carpet.

The effect was terrible and is hard to describe. Suddenly everything went black and everything stopped, even the motors. In the

155

whirl of the shock waves the rudderless boat was seized like a cork and thrust upwards. There was a cracking and creaking noise, the world seemed to have come to an end, then crashes and thuds as the boat was thrown onto its side and everything loose came adrift. I managed to grab the steel strop on the periscope, then my legs were pulled from under me. We had collided with the frigate's bottom which was now thrusting away above us, steel against steel. Certainly the British were no less shaken than we, seeing that 'just before the first charge exploded, the ratings on watch in the boiler room heard the periscope scrape down the side' (Precis of Attack by HMS *Exe*. Reference A.U.D. 861/43).

Seconds later, the periscope broke off. The swaying boat reared up, struck the hull of the *Exe* with its conning tower and the control room and listening compartment immediately flooded. The water quickly rose above the floor plates. The light of a torch lying on the chart table showed a picture of devastation. All the indicator gear was hanging loose, the glass was splintered, light bulbs had burst. Cable ends spread in bundles through the control room, the emergency lighting accumulators had torn free. Before I even got to the depth-keeping controls the boat was again shaken by the heaviest depth charges. Like a stone we slipped backwards towards the ocean bed which here lay 5,000 metres below.

From the engine room the hydrostatic external pressure, indicating depth, was passed on from mouth to mouth and the fall of the boat stopped by blowing the tanks with compressed air. It rose slowly, then faster and faster until it had to be flooded again so as not to shoot out of the water like an arrow. Beams from the torches flicked over the walls glistening with moisture. It trickled and poured. As none of the pumps was working the water that had come in was transferred in buckets from hand to hand from the lower lying stern — where it was already above the coaming of the alleyway hatch — into the central bilge. Gradually the boat swung back from the slanting position to the horizontal.

Fortunately the switchboard was still dry, there was no short-circuit. We could put back the knife switches which had fallen out and in feverish haste got the electric motors working. Though the noise of the port propeller shaft showed that damage had been caused, its turning again was music in our ears.

My log says: 'Decide to hold the boat by all possible means and slowly go deeper. Damage very great and cannot yet be assessed.'

From the British viewpoint we were 'in the centre of the (first) pattern when it exploded' and 'the first attack must certainly have damaged the U-boat so severely that it was unable to surface.' When an oil patch was sighted at 1156 and a sample was collected it was believed we had sunk.

But in fact we had let ourselves drop from 60 to 140 metres. Meanwhile the entire convoy in its whole length went thumping past us overhead. In such a situation that is about the safest place for a stricken U-boat, particular as any hydrophone contact is lost in propeller wash. Nothing can touch one, unless perhaps a ship is torpedoed and falls on one's head.

But hardly was the mass of the ships past than we were overwhelmed with a drum-fire such as I had never yet experienced. And that is saying a lot. It began at mid-day and went on till 2055 like a continuous thunder storm, now close, now further away, the heavy-sounding depth charges and the lighter Hedgehogs. And each time we thought, 'Now there'll be a direct hit,' but in fact the explosions detonated further away, we had to wipe the cold sweat from our faces. So-called heroism has not much to do with it. And when finally the torture ended and the great silence began we refused to believe it, but stood there wide-eyed, gasping and struggling for breath, waiting for the next series.

Luckily we had little time for reflection. There was too much to do. The worst damage had to be repaired. Damage to instruments (speed and trim indicators, water and pressure gauges, depth recorder) belonged to the lesser evils. Broken telephones and radio could be accepted. Even a destroyed fire-control panel lost significance for survival, particularly as the heads of all the torpedoes in the tubes had been dented, not to mention the plastic cap of my acoustic torpedo which I had thought so important. From the seepage of water in the boat runnels were formed which could be pumped out more or less.

But the starboard diesel had been thrust sideways and fallen from its base, and this was more than problematical. Now by the sweat of our brow we had to wedge and support it with beams. And hardly less serious was the port propeller shaft, which had been bent and was hammering loudly. To complete our misfortune, the radio installation was so badly damaged that despite trying three times I was only able to send a short mutilated signal.

Air was running out. Our bodily exertions had used it up

quicker than usual and it had to be improved with potash cart-ridges and oxygen. There was a stink of battery gas — the ventila-tion lines had been broken — and of watery oil. Eventually the fug became chokingly thick, and compressed air was getting short. After nine hours of depth charging which had thoroughly shaken the boat and had necessitated our repeatedly blowing the tanks to maintain station, there was hardly any compressed air left. The boat was tending to lose depth again and could be kept trimmed only with difficulty. I had to go up regardless, and so, one hour after the last charge had exploded and the great, perhaps deceptive silence had fallen, I brought U 333 to the surface.

Up above it was dark. Sea state 5 to 6 with heavy swell, the slim outline of the boat hiding in the troughs. Somewhere there was a destroyer, but she spotted nothing. The watch came up and we inspected the scope of the exterior damage. The forward net-cutter was broken, the bridge cowling bent forward. Both periscopes were useless, the attack periscope bent, the night-sighting peri-scope broken. Radio direction-finder and anti-aircraft guns had gone, as though shaven off. The lurching boat had a list. It was only just floating above water, and I had another shock, in so far as one was capable of more, to see air bubbles surging from both sides. Apparently all the ballast tanks had cracks. U 333 could float only to a limited extent.

The diesels would not start. Despite repeated blowing, the boat would not stay on the surface but slowly sank downwards by the stern. We had to submerge again so as not to drown on the bridge. Last man down as always, I shut the conning-tower hatch — or tried to. This time it stuck. Meanwhile the boat was submerging completely and streams of water poured through the opening. I clung to the wheel until I fell into the control room. We blew the last of the compressed air into the tanks and the hatch slowly emerged from the swirling water. I had swallowed a great deal, was soaking wet and numbed, but with the help of the 2W.O., was clear-headed enough to find the curious cause of the defect: part of a blade knocked off from the propeller of the frigate *Exe* had slipped and blocked the hatch.

Things were against us — as though a renewed attempt was being made to do away with us. After many experiments we finally got the port diesel going — it began to function 'slow ahead' — and eventually the starboard diesel started as well. The ballast tanks were no longer airtight, but with the exhaust gases we blew into them we could roughly keep a balance with the water coming in. But the boat was still more or less unstable and threatened to drop away under our feet. And somewhere water was continually dribbling inboard where we struggled with the damaged pumps. We had no alternative but to move 'dynamically' and gently get away.

Next day already on the way home I wrote in the log: 'Surfacing goes better', and the day after, 'considerably better, which means I have got accustomed to the condition of slowly sinking.' Though that speaks volumes, it says nothing about our wet feet. Yes indeed, we had been given a pasting. My people patched everything possible with what lay to hand. That was very little. And so we went hobbling home with a wreck. And with all the iron around us, navigated with the magnetic needle alone, for the gyro compass too was broken.

Let us return to the scene of action. What was the result of this convoy battle SL 139/MKS 30? More than meagre, much ado about nothing. In an encounter lasting from 18 to 21 November, 1943, in which 23 U-boats and 25 long-distance bombers operated against 28 escort vessels and various aircraft, only a single steamer was sunk out of a mass of 66 merchant ships (the *Marsa*, 4,405 GRT from London) and one damaged (the *Delius*, 6,065 GRT from Liverpool). In addition the corvette *Winchelsea* suffered damage. All this from German aircraft which dropped glider bombs in the last hours of the three-day battle. One U-boat, U 515 (Henke), fired an acoustic torpedo at the corvette *Chanticler*, putting out of action both engines and the rudder. A salvage vessel came to her help.

We lost three boats: U 211 to a Wellington, U 536 was forced to surface and destroyed by the corvettes *Nene*, *Snowberry* and *Calgary*. Hammered by *Foley* and *Crane*, U 538 stayed down for good. U-boats shot down a Sunderland and a Liberator. Two German aircraft were lost and two had to turn back.

Of the 23 German U-boats only one got near the merchant ships: U 333. All the others were forced away.

Admiral Horton notes in a résumé of 23 December, 1943: 'It seems that at least two, possibly three U-boats were sunk by escort vessels. Only one U-boat succeeded in reaching the inner screen. It was attacked by HMS *Exe*, Commander G. V. Legassick, before it could attack the convoy. A lack of determination to come in contact with the Support Forces was noticeable on the part of the U-boats.'

Well, he could talk! After all, this was not 1914 or 1941. Yet the statement was somehow correct. A too rapid training of U-boat commanders was showing up mistakes. They had to take the place of the fallen as quickly as possible and were not prepared thoroughly enough. 'Shot through too quickly', as we old hands called it. The short time they spent in the *AGRU-Front* or Training Group gave them no real idea of the actual conditions. And the complicated defence techniques of the enemy sometimes exceeded their comprehension. Again, the enemy defence forces had not only increased numerically. The crews had learnt a lot during the long war, were carried on a wave of success and were sharper than ever before.

The RAF Coastal Command also concerned itself with my boat and wrote: 'U 333 encountered the outer surface screen and was so severely damaged by depth charges that she barely managed to reach port on 1 December after a nightmare journey.' Indeed it was a nightmare, with a boat — as I noted in the log of 24.11 — 'that can only be kept with great difficulty above water. Both diesels took it in turn to fail. Surface travel ever more difficult owing to sea state.'

Slight amusement was caused by the Biscay weather report which prophesied 'some occasional drizzle' while according to the log we on the bridge were getting seas full in the face. On 27 I wrote: 'No astronomical reckoning, no R.D.F., no sounding lead and thick fog, a fine navigation.' The fog had its good side, as it concealed us, but, relying heavily as we were on identifying coastal features, it was a mixed blessing. On 1 December I closed up with the escort that was to bring us into La Pallice. Moving dynamically I could not stop U 333 and to the horror of the escort commander, who already saw me in the mine fields, I had to turn in a circle, otherwise the boat would have sunk. In the lock they came running with compressed air bottles and with high pressure drove the water out of the leaking ballast tanks, otherwise at the pier itself we would have laid ourselves on the bottom. Then the heap of scrap was docked. The race between air and water was at an end.

I was scarcely ashore when I learnt that Kasch in U 540 had got involved with aircraft somewhere between Iceland and Greenland.

There were no survivors. He was the Lieutenant Kasch whom v. Wilamowitz-Möllendorf had lent me after the *Crocus* engagement so that in my wounded condition he could give me support on the way home; now he too had gone. The old hands were diminishing. But among the other ranks the saying went the rounds more than ever: 'Ali Cremer is as good as life insurance.'

While we were still heading for base, 15 boats from the *Schill* Group had been formed into a new Group, *Weddigen*, and sent against another big convoy in the same area, SL 140/MKS 31, which was just as strongly protected by the 4th and 2nd Hunter Groups under the well known Commander Walker R. N., if not more strongly after USS *Bogue* and four destroyers had joined. Powerful forces of night-flying aircraft led the Hunter Groups to the U-boats. Four U-boats had to be written off: U 86, U 542, U 600 and U 648 — and all the merchant ships continued their journey unhindered.

That was enough. On 7 December, 1943, the *Weddigen* Group was dispersed and attacks on convoys were abandoned.

After the heavy collision with the frigate *Exe*, which had also been damaged and had to go into dock, U 333 underwent repairs for almost two and a half months. I gave lectures in the different bases on underwater tactics, dealing with depth-charge damage and similar subjects. For the first time in the war the crew could spend Christmas and New Year in harbour and in part with their families. After the hardships of the last, hair-raising patrol on which the utmost was demanded of each of us, they could now recover. And as a recognised success, from 31 October we had a destroyer in the bag . . . but here was the snag. Very much later it was discovered that my proud Gnat had been a so-called near-detonator which had exploded like a soap bubble immediately astern of the destroyer and merely shaken it. That I had lost the ship in the periscope must have been due to the sea state.

I was not alone in this experience; for the uncontrollable behaviour of the acoustic torpedo developed into a disaster approaching the failure of the G 7e torpedo in the first year of the war. The latter's electro-magnetic fuse had frequently failed at the critical moment and gave the aces of that time the feeling that they were 'fighting with a wooden gun'. The Gnat with its sensitivity to sound was equally temperamental and unpredictable. Thus the

161

alleged successes of the *Leuthen* Group, which claimed 12 destroyers sunk and a further three probably damaged with 24 Gnat shots, were a catastrophic overestimate made in the heat of the moment. In reality they had sunk six merchant ships and three escorts and damaged one. There had indeed been plenty of bangs, but no less than 14 acoustic torpedoes had been detonated by the noise made by the wake of enemy ships, or exploded too late. For good reason the enemy said nothing and encouraged our faith in the wonder weapon.

Study of log books and other material by the well known German naval expert Professor Jürgen Rohwer showed that of 610 Gnats fired, at the most one third found their target.

As regards the method of operation: A moving ship emits underwater sound waves in a broad frequency band, depending on its speed and construction. In the sphere of ultrasonic frequency the radiation is concentrated on the ship's propellers. The acoustic torpedo was set to a mean value in the frequency of about 24.5 kilohertz and the British outmanoeuvred the frequency of the Gnat by a simple alteration of speed. A churning wake or wave motion at times diverted the Gnat and triggered its sensitive firing pistol too soon or too late. Explosions in the wake of ships simulated hits and sinkings. Delays in the automatic steering could alter the radius and also send the torpedo past the target. It could double back and theoretically home in on the propeller noises of its own vessel. All in all, complicated physical processes are involved which have to be simplified for easier understanding. I received very interesting and instructive explanations about the Gnat from men who at that time were responsible for its construction.

But the actual reason for this torpedo's failure was probably that it had been put into service too soon. We U-boat commanders were repeatedly insisting on a modern torpedo to 'crack' the convoy escorts. Whereupon we had been given this excellent instrument which had indeed been tested but not yet ranged in. Everything had to happen swiftly, as with our recruits, so this weapon was thrust into our hands before it was ready for operations. If one had waited a few months and carried out further tests, everything would have looked different. By the end of 1943 the optimism of the U-boat Command over the Gnat had faded and it was not till the end of 1944 that it was able to achieve a large number of hits.

On 15 July, 1981, in reply to a question on this subject, the

British Ministry of Defence, Naval Historical Branch, supplied the author of this book with the following instructive information about the Gnat.

'From the beginning of the war it was appreciated that the Germans might introduce an acoustic homing torpedo. In 1942 a German soldier under interrogation described details of trials which indicated the development of such a weapon and early in 1943 survivors from U-boats spoke of a new torpedo that was soon to come into use, while in August other survivors spoke of its introduction as being imminent.

'It was first employed in September against convoys ON 202 and ONS 18. At that time we assessed that it had a maximum speed of 25 knots and a homing radius of 500 yards. In the early hours of 20 September, HMS *Lagan* was torpedoed while hunting a U-boat near ON 202 but was able to reach harbour. As a result it was assessed that the torpedo was fired from the stern tubes of the U-boat at the escort chasing it and after running straight for a set range would circle until the escort was detected. It was considered that the torpedo could be angled and would usually be fired from the surface at night and from periscope depth by day. Countermeasures were based on the assumption that the torpedo would be used defensively and were divided into tactical and material. As regards the former, "Step Aside", "Slow Safe Speed" and "High Safe Speed" were formulated . . .'

The British very quickly recognised the Gnat's method of operation and, by deliberately making their escorts increase or reduce speed, stayed outside the acoustic frequency which brought it into action.

At the end of 1943, urged on by the progress of technology, by contradictory advice, and by setbacks, Grand Admiral Dönitz ordered the formation of a scientific naval operational staff in Berlin. Already before 1942 he had demanded a closer connection between current operational experience and technical research, following the example of the British, who were holding regular and very effective anti-U-boat seminars at which operational chiefs, front-line officers and technicians took part. They had taken up the idea very much sooner of drawing scientists into Operational Research Groups for consultation and using their methods to analyse operations and develop new procedures. But all similar suggestions from Dönitz had been turned down by the then C-in-C Navy, Grand Admiral Raeder. In the opinion of Professor Rohwer, 'a good and experienced high-frequency technician as observer on Dönitz's staff would have recognised many developments much earlier from direct contact with the U-boat leadership and with returning U-boat men than did the officers who were necessarily functioning as amateurs in this field.'

Now Grand Admiral Dönitz tried to make this direct connection between front-line and research, and called on Professor Küpfmüller to be head of the Scientific Operations Staff, 'in order to make good our technical inferiority and restore the fighting capability of the U-boat which the enemy has taken from us, not by superior tactics or strategy but through his superiority in the technical field.'

Things had indeed reached a stage where the new German Naxos radar warning set, which picked up the Allied ten-centimetre radar, was to be outstripped by the very latest radar set on the yet shorter three-centimetre wavelength, and had to be modified. In addition, the Allies already possessed a defence against the Gnat and also a homing torpedo of their own which they affectionately called Fido. This was a deadly accurate weapon, technically called Mark 24 Mine, which was carried in the bomb chute of aircraft and to which a number of U-boats had already fallen victim. It was kept so secret that to the end of the war we learnt nothing whatever about it. So in a number of respects the situation was even worse than we imagined. And as for the Scientific Operations Staff, Professor Rohwer considers that it had no practical effect until after the U-boat war was already decided.

Whereas in the first half of 1943 German U-boats had sunk about 1,700,000 tons, in the second half the tally was only 500,000 tons, not even quite as much as in March of this year. Hitler totally failed to grasp the situation; in his New Year's address, January, 1944, he said: 'The apparent stagnation in the U-boat war is to be ascribed to a single technical invention of the enemy. We are working to neutralise it and are convinced that this will happen in quite a short time.'

Grand Admiral Dönitz, for his part, stated on 20 January, 1944: 'The day will come when I will offer Churchill a first-class U-boat war. The U-boat arm has not been broken by the reverses of the year 1943. On the contrary, it has become stronger.'

13
The French resistance

In Paris on the way through to Germany I had a chance to exchange experiences with Lieutenant-Commander Werner Henke of U 515. It was Henke who in the big convoy battle of November had put the corvette *Chanticler* out of action with an acoustic torpedo. We met at the Hotel Claridge and talked of what concerned us most: the depth-charge pursuits of the Gibraltar convoy.

On that subject there was a lot to be said. Finally we agreed that 200 metres' depth of water and more, hitherto apparently safe from depth charges, in the latest circumstances represented a risk as soon as the enemy had located a U-boat. For he had meanwhile learnt to determine not only the location but the exact submerged depth of the boat and shoot himself in on it. He no longer dropped his depth charges with a tolerance of 20 to 40 metres but landed them directly level with the boat and spread them over a whole area. Now, at a depth of 200 metres, hitherto so secure, a small gash, the smallest hole no thicker than a thumb, would suffice to shoot a stream of water into the boat with twenty atmospheres' pressure, something which no plugs or other measures could stop. The boat would have to surface.

For this reason we aimed in future to carry out evasive manoeuvres which the enemy would be slow to keep up with, so making him lag behind. That meant steering for a series of rapidly changing depths and frequently altering course. Also we intended to release *Bold*, the submarine bubble target derided in enemy propaganda but doubtless taken seriously, and cover the surface of the water with air bubbles, scraps of uniform, cleaning cloths and such like in order to simulate a hit. Werner Henke had little opportunity to practise such tactics, however. A few months after we parted, his boat was sunk on the Gibraltar route by the Support Group USS *Guadalcanal*. He himself was taken prisoner and was shot by a guard when attempting to escape. We had been the last two commanders to have fought since 1941 in the Atlantic from western France and now I was the one and only survivor.

The Claridge was, and still is today, an elegant hostelry in the Champs Elysées, reserved in those days for generals and holders of the Knight's Cross. We decorated U-boat commanders were in the habit of putting up there. When a boat had returned from patrol we had just enough time to catch up on sleep and visit the barber. While at base the crew cleared out the boat completely and handed over the empty hull to the dockyard for repair, we were already on the train bound for Germany to make our verbal report to Dönitz. In Paris we were granted one day's respite to change trains from the Gare Montparnasse to the Gare du Nord, and it was here for the first time that we really came to ourselves and, through the mere contrast alone, succumbed to the magic of this unique city.

The Paris of 1944 was no longer the Paris of after the French campaign. But we did not notice the dirt or the shortages, nor the traces of inevitable decay after four years of war. After murderous battles in monastic confinement we climbed out of a damp abyss where, apart from the bridge watch, no one saw the sun or breathed fresh air, let alone smoked a cigarette. Here we found ourselves suddenly removed from all danger over night, in a world still intact and with all its people. We had pale faces, almost green, and deep rings under our eyes, so that the Claridge receptionists eyed us thoughtfully.

The contrast was overwhelming. Just the luxury of lying in a broad bed without the necessity of remaining in a half-sleep, continually alert for suspicious noises; free of the constriction of U 333, where not everyone even had a bunk to himself and the off-duty watch crept into the still-warm bunks of the watchkeepers, bedded down on the floor plates or crouched in a corner. Once again to be able to bathe at leisure, with a freshwater shower and a squirt of Eau d'Orsay instead of a hurried wash with sea-water soap which had taken on the penetrating smell of fuel oil. Sauna and sports equipment in Claridge's basement helped to loosen up our bodies unused to movement. And who did not enjoy French cooking, still cultivated even in those days? On board, fresh food would have been eaten up within the first week, and from then on everything would come from a tin, enriched with so-called *Bratlingspulver*, a sort of soy flavouring notable only for its blandness, enough to make one sick.

After the much too short interlude in Paris, the Berlin train took me back to the harsh reality of destroyed railway stations and pulverised German cities. The people who lived there had other cares. After my report to the Grand Admiral there was a modest one-course meal with the staff. Dönitz insisted that only the prescribed rations should be served.

On this occasion I met Professor Küpfmüller, a middle-aged Professor of Physics who, as head of the Scientific Operations Staff, was brought into every situation conference and sought a direct dialogue with the fighting men, which had a positive effect.

At that time we could not explain how the enemy more and more frequently located us on the surface without our improved Naxos set giving any warning of radar impulses. The set did, after all, react on all wavelengths in use. As we had still heard nothing of Huff-Duff locating sets we looked for plausible explanations and finally decided to credit the enemy with infra-red procedures. This field, which was new at that time, offers two alternatives. In the active method an invisible infra-red ray is emitted. As soon as the passage of a person or object (e.g. a ship) interrupts this ray it is recorded by reflection. Now it is also true that, contrariwise, every object emits infra-red energy. Its quantity and spectral distribution depends on the material and its temperature. The object itself, its movement and direction are recorded on a receiver. This so-called passive method offers good possibilities for military exploitation, particularly as the object or the person concerned does not react to being located. Unlike radar location, the infra-red method cannot be picked up by warning sets. It has a surprise effect.

Today infra-red light circuits are common, with light-beam telephony and light barriers such as door-openers, surveillance installations and alarm triggers. Unfortunately at that time we did not have sufficient manpower, resources and materials to produce more than a few experimental sets for military use. Some of these infra-red sets were installed on the Channel, serving to survey the shipping along the English coast. With them it was possible to establish the number of ships, their speed and direction by the passive method, whether in broad daylight, blackest night or in fog. The infra-red eye saw through virtually everything.

The German long-range batteries used it; with unexpected accuracy searchlights bathed aircraft in brilliant light, and artillery hit the target even in the dark. At that time Germany was a world-leader in infra-red research without even knowing it! It was assumed the enemy would be in tune with developments and possess similar knowledge, but the deduction was false: compared with us the Allies knew extremely little. (Accordingly, one of their first steps after the collapse of Germany was an attempt to catch up by obtaining all available research material and getting hold of scientists working in this field, headed by Dr. Edgar Kutzscher. This was some while after they had captured an infra-red apparatus together with a crew on the Channel coast, with the aid of a motor torpedo boat, and slipped a Dutch spy into Dr. Kutzscher's laboratory.)

There was a poster commonly seen in those days, showing a man eavesdropping in black silhouette with the warning: 'Pst! The enemy is listening!' The presence of many foreign workers in the Reich and their employment in the armament industry had enormously extended the possibilities for spying and sabotage. This was particularly true in occupied France, where initial resignation had long since changed into resistance, and millions of pairs of eyes watched all we did. And where eavesdroppers were not necessarily dark haired but blonde.

After their rapid defeat in 1940 any resistance had seemed pointless to the French and they had tried to adjust themselves. This went as far as open collaboration, as for example in the production of the Metox radar warning set in Paris, and this occurred from the highest level down to assistants working in German offices. There was even close cooperation with German counter-espionage or later with the Gestapo, which was not averse to recruiting members of the underworld for its purposes. And there were agents who worked for both sides.

But as the war dragged on and German successes diminished the French resistance grew, awakened and encouraged by General De Gaulle's National Committee of the Free French in London. Psychological warfare was initiated from beyond the Channel, in the ether and with leaflets. One of the General's first fellow warriors was 'Rémy' who in 1940 went with him to England, and there began by broadcasting a call to resistance. Returning via Portugal and Spain, he started to build up a network in France and send information to England. The British parachuted radio sets into France and at times there was even a direct connection with the Scilly Isles by means of fishing vessels. Gradually the resistance was formed as an expression of the popular will, aided by the patriotic attitude of the Church which declared for the resistance from the beginning. A variety of groups arose, were broken up and formed again. The place was seething with agents so that from the autumn of 1943 the German *Abwehr* with its limited personnel could no longer cope.

From the beginning, spying activity was naturally concentrated on our U-boat bases. Rémy's organisation grew so large that hardly anything happened in the Atlantic ports that was not reported to England. In Bordeaux alone an engineer employed in a U-boat base employed a group of 30 informers. There was no need to take part in such a violent undertaking as the British raid on St. Nazaire or to attack a fuel container. From many small and often at first glance insignificant fragments which were transmitted to him, the enemy was able to obtain an overall picture. A harbour pilot in Bordeaux might register the comings and goings of our units; a street sweeper at the railway station of St. Jean might report train movements to Germany; construction workers in Brest might report that they were ramming in great posts for mooring German battleships (a report which would unleash on them a rain of British bombs); a spy might ferret out the thickness of walls in our U-boat bunkers: everything was enciphered and sent off to England. For this a former radio expert from the French navy was responsible in Angers. When the RAF was hampered in its attacks on U-boat bases by artificial fog, the chemical formula of the gas was sent over as requested from the French factory—which was also collaborating with us. And when a former engineer officer succeeded, during a meal break, in removing from a safe and photographing plans of the bases at Brest, Lorient, St. Nazaire, La Pallice and Bordeaux, these microfilms also found their way across the Channel. Compared with such ventures the reporting of naval football match results, broadcast by the Atlantic transmitter, was child's play.

In the middle of February 1944, when I started my seventh patrol with U 333, the enemy received warnings of that too and noted on 20 February: 'U 333 was detected in the Bay of Biscay outward bound to the North Channel for inshore reconnaissance patrol.' That said everything.

The North Channel is the passage between the northern point of Ireland and Scotland. Here the wide Atlantic becomes a relatively shallow stretch of water flanked by cliffs and islands and at the narrowest point only ten miles broad. As the northern gateway to the Irish Sea and the ports in western Britain it was used by convoys avoiding the southern entrance which was nearer to the enemy. Here before the lion's den they could be intercepted or even now be taught to fear. Inshore reconnaissance meant observation of the sea traffic and possible attack under a coastline which did not belong to neutral Ireland, was guarded by British naval forces from nearby Londonderry, and sealed off with mine fields. Nobody could know what awaited us in this area, recent experience was lacking.

It did not look as though we were destined to earn ourselves any bouquets this time. In any case none of us would have indulged that kind of thought any more, even without our false start; a strong trail of oil forced us to turn back for repairs, while in the 'council of elders', composed of captain, chief engineer and chief mechanic, we assured ourselves that everything would be made good in time. Then off to a fresh start! But hardly had we put our nose up than aircraft warnings from our new Naxos set drove us down again, sometimes at intervals of only a few minutes. It was like being in an elevator: up—down, up—down! Only in the process our enthusiasm gradually dwindled — as did the supply of air for blowing out the tanks. This finally compelled me to push through to the south by a roundabout route. Ireland and Scotland were still a long way off.

We slipped through the Bay, got to the west, were allotted to a newly formed *Preussen* Group, and were ordered to selected areas for attack, at given depths. We missed convoys, heard depth charges, were variously shaken up by variable spring weather, and in the first fortnight were rather distracted from our original assignment than encouraged. Eventually, in the night of 6–7 March, 1944, the expected signal arrived which set us free: 'Cremer to leave *Preussen* Group. Free manoeuvre as planned.'

Though we picked no quarrel with inanimate objects, they again showed their malice in the following days. The 3.7 A A gun went on strike, the Naxos set gave out, and because of our heavy pounding the attack periscope could only be turned with effort. The log read like a repair list. We proceeded more below than above water and at economical speed advanced only slowly, but despite the compass going crazy we reached map squares AL and AM in the north and the buffer zone of the North Channel.

Bright moonlight was followed by dark nights, just what I needed to be able to surface at night occasionally. Accompanied by slight phosphorescence and the first Northern Lights we were cautiously approaching the mine field at the entrance to the North Channel when in the morning hours of 21 March the surfaced boat was located by an aircraft. The plane was only a forerunner and our presence a stab in the wasps' nest.

Ten days before, the 2nd Support Group under Captain John Walker had left Londonderry and was then in the North Atlantic with the aircraft carrier HMS *Vindex*, where it sank U 653 (Hans-Albrecht Kandler). Johnnie Walker, with fourteen acknowledged sinkings, the most successful U-boat killer in the Royal Navy, had developed tactics which required many hours and the greatest perseverance but which finally, almost without exception, produced results. While in the early stages of the Atlantic battle a handful of escorts could make only brief counter-attacks against attacking U-boats and then had to hurry back to the convoy, with Walker the situation was reversed. Several escorts advanced in a coordinated attack against the U-boat and did not let go of it. They followed its evasive manoeuvres until finally, like hunters with their quarry, they had encircled it and brought it down. U 653 had fought the most ferocious engagements on the surface with Walker's boat; the U-boat had been worsted and hardly a man had survived. Shortly after its destruction Walker's Support Group had been directed to Scapa Flow, arriving there on 24 March: HMS *Starling, Magpie, Whimbrel, Wild Goose* and *Wren*.

In English opinion 'the move could well have taken the Group across the path of U 333', to which I can only say 'it certainly did', for our courses definitely crossed. After the reconnaissance plane had observed and reported me in the early morning of 21 March, at about 1100 strong propeller noises were heard approaching in a broad spectrum extending from west to south. I tried to outmanoeuvre the enemy and break through to the south-west but it was a hopeless enterprise. The weather itself was bad. A long Atlantic swell was running which even at 40 metres depth made itself unpleasantly felt and swung the boat to and fro.

This Group came at U 333 from two sides in the attack formation preferred by Walker. In broad line abreast the ships dropped depth charges at very short intervals. As prelude numerous samples were dropped in a few minutes, their explosions merging with one another so that it was impossible to count them. Their pressure waves were so enormous that the conning-tower hatch began to shudder and we were all thrown about. Then it became suspiciously quiet until the odious ping — ping — ping of a searching ship was first heard thinly, then louder. Then that, too, broke off and there was another pause, explained perhaps by the fact that the enemy did not succeed in locating us with certainty. It may be that the weather was responsible. At any rate it was a situation of 'no reports being made since their contact was not firm enough.'

This probably saved our lives, for suddenly all hell was let loose again. But now they were throwing them without aim, on suspicion. Escaping was not to be thought of. The ocean was too shallow here and the slightest of our machinery noises would have betrayed us. It was best to play 'possum and let nothing be heard of us — come what might. So I laid the boat on the bottom where it bedded itself softly in sand and mud. I ordered the crew to rest and as far as possible not to think of depth charges, though it was impossible not to hear them. I thought: whoever throws so many will soon have none left. Meanwhile the hands of our clock kept moving, the search dragged on and lasted into the night.

It was deathly still in the boat, if that does not sound macabre. As distinct from in films and many a book, the U-boat men controlled themselves in precarious situations and only seldom lost their nerve. There were neither cries nor groans and even orders were passed in a whisper from mouth to mouth. Pst! The enemy is listening! Water is an uncanny conductor. I myself crouched in the control room, knees and stomach wrapped in soft catskins. It was cold and old wounds were hurting.

The propeller noises of the destroyers sounded muffled, then clearer. They came closer, moved further off, sometimes singly, sometimes several together. Time passed. The air was used up, the potash cartridges were nearly expended and I had to supply oxygen. Everyone was breathing in short, heavy gasps. After ten hours (but what hours!) I was forced to go up. All hands — Action stations — Surface! At once they were wide awake.

'Blow tanks!' A high-pitched hissing noise. That was all — nothing else. The boat would not budge, an invisible hand was holding it down. This was something quite new. Again, the same manoeuvre. 'Blow tanks!'

Nothing moved. The boat stuck to the sea-bed as though part of it.

Heavens! I suddenly thought. I had not taken into account the tide range and the strong current on this coast, and now quicksand and mud had covered the boat like a flounder. With every minute the natural forces were continuing their work and if we did not somehow succeed in driving U 333 upwards they would end by burying us alive in the iron coffin. That was not at all improbable – a gentle death by suffocation. One goes to sleep and drifts away. Moving on, my thoughts turned to escape apparatus. One puts on the inflatable lifejacket, uses the mouthpiece and the nose clip, opens the hatch and climbs upwards with the still escaping air into captivity. Assuming, of course, that the hatch can be opened and, further, that one is lucky enough to be found. All this was prompted by the initial fright.

Was there really no prospect of shifting the boat? Perhaps it would be possible by inclining manoeuvres, quickly shifting the weight, to give the boat a nudge. Ten men would have to run through the boat from bow to stern and back again — from the bow torpedo compartment through the C.P.O.'s and officers' mess, through the control room, the petty officers' accommodation, through the galley, past the diesel engines to the stern torpedo compartment and the electric motors. Through four steel bulkheads, watertight doors and circular access hatches with high sills on which one could break one's legs. In itself this called for acrobatics, even more so when it had to be done quickly, with a swing. Anxiety gave my people wings and they made it in record time.

U 333 dipped a little forward, backward somewhat more. Once again . . . and again. The boat actually started to move, like a see-saw. Now, extra pressure in the tanks! At the third or fourth attempt we felt under our feet that the boat was reluctantly releasing itself from the sea-bed and throwing off its restraints. Thereafter, with a jerk, it rose upwards so quickly that the motors were only just able to start in time and I opened up the conning-tower hatch like a madman. The fresh air was not a little welcome.

Fortunately for us the weather above was really execrable. Choppy sea breaking over the conning tower. Pitch black night, drizzle, about 300 metres' visibility. I myself was literally on top again and wrote grandiloquently in the log '. . . one has the impression off the North Channel that whole school classes are fitted out with boats and given free U-hunting.'

After we had been discovered and everyone warned of our presence, to stay on near the coast seemed to me unpromising. I decided to head westwards as far as longitude 15 and then south to get at the Gibraltar convoys. There at least there was more water under the keel and freedom of movement. But wherever we came, escorts and hunter groups were at work everywhere, everywhere there were rumblings, crashes and bangs. There could hardly be so many U-boats left and on 22 March, 1944, the British themselves summarised: 'Many Type VII boats have been lost in the Atlantic, with only 18 still operational, including U 333 in the North Channel.'

The U-boat war had broken up into smaller engagements and individual actions whose object it was to tie down the colossal Allied defence forces and keep the U-boat arm itself in being until the big types became operational. These new boats were being completed at home despite all setbacks. Meanwhile we were trying to pretend to the enemy that we had a larger number of operational U-boats than were actually available. The mere presence of a single boat could upset an entire region. Among our deception schemes was 'lively radio traffic' in which we threw out completely senseless communications, difficult to decipher, like: 'Today 4.4.44, is the 444th patrol day of U 333 and we are in square 4711 . . .'

We had absolutely no chance to attack, nothing came before our sights the whole time. In the slight hope of being able to do something all the same I considered a delayed return 'until fighting power used up. As sufficient fuel available, will stretch the food.' Dönitz, however, categorically ordered us home: 'Cremer return without loss of time. No dawdling.'

So we achieved no sinkings. Instead we had troubles enough. The conning-tower hatch stuck; fire when a switchboard for the electric motors began to smoulder; then the gyro compass started sticking because the ball had developed a crack through the heavy battering we had received. One night little flames began to dance on the Naxos aerial, pale blue and ghostly, St. Elmo's fire, disturbing radio location.

No sinkings, but instead a novelty. After securing alongside at base on 20 April I could tell the flotilla commander and his staff of strange noises heard during a destroyer attack in the Atlantic. The pounding of the ship's propellers was drowned by a loud buzzing noise, changing sometimes to the howl of a circular saw, then dropping to the monotonous hum of an insect. A new type of whistle buoy had to be involved which the destroyers trailed behind them. My exact description of a hitherto unknown enemy gadget gave it the temporary name of 'Cremer's bumble-bee'.

This British invention, later revealed as the 'Foxer', did not come quite unexpectedly. It was a measure against our acoustic torpedoes, to keep them away from the ship's hull and detonate them in the wake. To attract a Gnat 'bite', the sound of the Foxer had to be louder than the ship's propellers. The device consisted of two parallel steel tubes which, dragged behind, vibrated in the boil of the wake and drowned everything else. In fact they created a hellish noise. The Foxer also had disadvantages in that it impaired underwater acoustic position-finding, so reducing the offensive capability of the destroyers. But when our problematical Gnats became more reliable, as against *Chanticler* in the great convoy battle, caution outweighed aggressive spirit. The Foxer was introduced and we in U 333 were the first who got to hear of it.

In order to outmanoeuvre the Foxer we, in our turn, developed a new improved acoustic torpedo which steered for the Foxer and ran beneath it. That is, it 'shut its ears' for a time until it had overtaken the Foxer. Then it switched on again, unaffected now from behind, could react to the propeller noises and head straight for its real target. Human ingenuity is inexhaustible when it comes to killing one another.

Spring 1944. The situation had become more tense and the Invasion ahead was casting its shadow. All resistance movements had united, much as they differed in their ultimate political aims, united against the common enemy who had stuck for four years on French soil and whose supremacy on the fronts was now visibly fading.

In the bases it was not the same as formerly. Relationships with the civil population acquired a different tone. Trades people, if they had not slipped away, became noticeably reserved. Instead of responding to our greetings with a smile as formerly, they preferred to look away. Our civilian help in camps, canteens and messes gave notice or simply stayed away, many went to ground in the course of partial evacuations. The attitude of French people in the street became more self-confident, if not actually provocative. It was no longer advisable to go alone into town, but only in pairs and armed. When on the way to Germany I visited my relations in Metz, they no longer dared to show themselves with me in public and we ate at home.

Swinging between fear and hope, the population avoided every appearance of agreement with the Germans. Everyone listened to the Resistance which had sworn bloody vengeance on all collaborators. And as is known, all accounts were settled after our retreat, and political opponents were done away with under the guise of patriotism. But that is a chapter by itself which does not belong in this book.

With the Allied landings in June, 1944, the Resistance received a still greater boost in the areas still occupied by us. There was open resistance, though the armed assaults by extreme groups remained only isolated actions. In retrospect everyone tried to prove they had been in the Resistance or had at least rejected the occupiers, to save their skins or even their hair, which was cut off in the case of those women who had had dealings with the Germans. Of course all patriots were opposed to us.

Perhaps in the depth of their hearts the young girls were as well, whatever their names, and whether they went on the beat, worked for a German office or hung about in bars. As for instance in the 'Schéhérazade' which was far from the fighting and was supervised, tolerated, perhaps for obvious reasons even encouraged, and had no adequate counterpart for us commanders on the coast.

On the coast there were other possibilities. After the war, when I got to know the mysterious 'Rémy' personally, I asked him among other things: 'How did you actually get to know the exact dates when my boat returned from and sailed for patrol, which the British then trumpeted to all the world?'

He laughed. 'We got the tip from the laundry.'

'From the laundry? How was that possible?'

'Look,' Rémy continued. 'One of our women agents worked there and kept her eye on you. From your boat's bed linen which you brought to be washed and fetched only when about to sail she could tell exactly when you had returned and that you were intending to go out again on a long patrol. Then she reported to us simply "Helga is ready again" and we were in the picture.'

Did I not say, everyone was in the Resistance!

14
My transfer to an Electro-boat

Summer 1944. Amongst our allies, Bulgaria had asked the Western Allies for an armistice, Roumania was negotiating a separate peace with the Soviets. The Russians began their summer offensive. In Italy the Allies had entered Rome. Two days later, in the early hours of 6 June, 1944, British, Americans and Canadians landed on the Normandy coast.

After the Allies had long and carefully planned the opening of this second front, and Adolf Hitler, with confidence in his Atlantic Wall, had once again opened his mouth wide to invite a duel on French soil, promising to sweep the invaders into the sea, D-Day had finally dawned. After airborne divisions had landed behind the German front an immense armada of transports and landing craft approached, protected by carpet bombing from thousands of aircraft and an artillery box laid down by largest calibre naval guns. It was surrounded by 700 warships, among them six battleships, 22 cruisers, numerous destroyers and smaller vessels down to motor torpedo boats. The exact figures seem to vary according to time, place and viewpoint of the chroniclers who have written a whole library about the Invasion. All are agreed that once the industrial and military potential of the enemy was fully harnessed, a war machine of gigantic proportions was brought into action to effect the greatest landing operation of all time.

Operation Overlord proceeded with clockwork precision. Our defences were suppressed, counter-attacks were smashed, the Atlantic Wall began to crumble. By the time we recovered, the Allies had established themselves in France — at the mouth of the Orne, on the Calvados coast and on the Cotentin peninsula. For us the Invasion did not come from a cloudless sky. As early as May, British Intelligence noted 'a certain nervousness' in all German headquarters about an invasion in France and Norway.

A fortnight before the landing they deciphered a signal from Dönitz to the Admiral (Western France). In essence:

1. 37 to 40 U-boats were to combine into a group;
2. All U-boats were to sail on the day of the Invasion, at the latest on the day after. A few boats were to patrol between the Scilly Isles, Cornwall and the French coast. A second wave from Brest was to take up positions for an attack in the Channel, while the majority were to station themselves in the centre and south of the Bay of Biscay to forestall an invasion in the Bordeaux area.

The British had no need to decipher this signal to confirm the obvious. As the eastern entry to the Channel with its shallow depths was blocked by mines, any U-boat attack had to be expected from the west. To prevent these boats even reaching the invasion area, the British transferred four extra Support Groups to Plymouth at the western exit from the Channel, where they joined up with six other flotillas. In addition three escort carriers were cruising off Land's End: *Tracker*, *Activity* and *Vindex*. In the air the entire region between the south coast of Ireland and the north-west coast of France up to the Cherbourg peninsula was covered by aircraft of all types from the reinforced Coastal Command. From the start the enemy had the advantage. Admittedly, he too had only water to cook with, but he had a larger pot.

As emerged from the above signal, the boats in the Atlantic bases had for some time been formed into a group — called *Landwirt* (farmer) — for counter-attack. In the flotillas there was much talk by commanders down to the youngest sailor about the coming Invasion. Its possible date was dependent on moon and tide conditions and could to some extent be forecast. When our leave was stopped rumour intensified. From 4 May on, all U-boats in the Atlantic bases were at six hours' notice. They had received from Grand Admiral Dönitz an order of the day:

'Every enemy vessel which serves the landing, even if it ferries only half a hundred soldiers or a tank, is a target demanding the full commitment of the boat. It is to be attacked even if one's own boat is put at risk. When it is a matter of getting at the enemy landing fleet, no thought must be given to the danger of shallow water or possible mine barriers or any other consideration. Every man and every weapon of the enemy destroyed before the landing reduces the enemy's chance of success. But the U-boat which inflicts losses on the enemy at the landing has fulfilled its highest task and justified its existence, even though it stays there.'

By 'stays', of course, was meant 'is destroyed'. As can be imagined, this call was discussed by the crews. More than once I heard, 'Now we are to sacrifice ourselves.' No amount of empty words or undisciplined bearing was going to suppress this view, which sprang from a certain fatalism. But in any case I heard little of it in U 333.

However, as the saying goes, nothing is eaten as hot as it is cooked. What else was a C-in-C to say in those days — what was expected of him? Besides, one had to know how to read between the lines. To hazard a U-boat against a tank or handful of soldiers would be to underestimate the size of the invasion, and the investment would be out of all proportion to the reward. This led one to question how seriously the order was intended, seeing that as many men as possible had to survive to man the new submarines already announced.

The previous U-boat types had been improved by an apparatus which enabled them to stay underwater much longer than previously. This was the *Schnorchel* (anglicised as the snorkel or snort), an air mast which could be raised above water at periscope depth to let fresh air into the boat. It was now possible to keep the diesel engines running at periscope depth and charge the batteries without having to surface. In the head of the snorkel was a float valve which, on dipping, automatically shut in the sea's motion and opened again in air. This process involved changes of pressure unpleasant for the ear drums, but these had to be accepted. The *Schnorchel* was a transitional measure to help us a little on our way. But as with so many things, the air-raids on Germany had damaged production sites and communications with the result that only 9 of the 36 boats in the *Landwirt* Group were fitted with the apparatus. This helps to explain later events. One of the boats which had to do without this apparatus was U 333.

Because of the continual air attacks on the capital, Dönitz's headquarters in the Hotel am Steinplatz had been evacuated to the suburb of Bernau, where he spent the night of 5–6 June, 1944. At that time over 5,000 Anglo–American vessels were crossing on a fairly narrow front from British harbours to Normandy, in the midst of them the immeasurable mass of landing craft crammed with soldiers and war material. Initial doubts as to whether or not this was the expected invasion soon vanished.

In the early hours of the morning Dönitz received a call from Admiral Krancke, the naval commander of Group West. Dönitz woke Rear Admiral Godt and Captain Hessler who were sleeping on camp beds in the next room. The code word for the alarm went out. All three believed they had issued the necessary orders for the U-boats. Now they could only wait, fearing the worst. The German navy no longer had sufficient striking power. We had no heavy surface units in that sea area, merely some destroyers, torpedo boats and other small craft, and former fishing vessels used as patrol and mine-sweeping flotillas. From the start it was a hopeless undertaking — but perhaps the U-boats might manage . . .

At 0535 on 6 June the U-boats were ordered to sail. In all, 36 boats left the Atlantic bases: 17 from Brest, 14 from St. Nazaire, 4 from La Pallice and 1 from Lorient. As U 333 had been kept back and loaded with ammunition for Cherbourg—which she never reached, incidentally—my departure was delayed until the afternoon. Initially we were allocated to those 19 boats intended to take up a waiting position in the Bay of Biscay. When it became clear that the Allies would not land there but on the Channel coast, new dispositions were made and all boats were sent to the Channel. Listening to our signals, the enemy summarised his observations precisely. Commander Roger Winn: 'The reaction of the C-in-C U-boats to the Invasion is prompt and energetic, but confused. The disposition of the boats now deviates in numerous points from the plan originally laid down for the U-boats. In several cases issued orders have been countermanded. But all boats have been instructed to attack ruthlessly.'

Of the 36 U-boats only 9, as we have said, were fitted with *Schnorchels* so most found themselves forced to surface in order to charge the batteries and were exposed to the air attacks of 19 Group Coastal Command. In realistic large-scale exercises the British had tested their anti-U-boat defences with their 'Musketry' patrols. They controlled an area of 20,000 square miles. A surfaced U-boat passed from one radar screen to another — and on average it could stay surfaced for only about 13 minutes, a period insufficient to charge the batteries or to top up the high-pressure air. The enemy's calculations proved correct. After the first two days it was already apparent that owing to the overwhelming air superiority the non-snorting boats would not even reach the invasion area. In the night of 6–7 June alone the Allies sighted German U-boats 22 times.

The air was full of the hum of engines. Even in the inner Bay we had to keep off low-flying Mosquito bombers with the combined fire-power of several boats. After all, those birds were armed with 75-millimetre cannon. In the night of 7–8 June, in very good visibility, with a bright full moon over the silver sea which sharply defined our silhouette, there were several bombing attacks. It was the period of the short summer nights and soon the dawn light revealed us completely to enemy eyes. Since, in the circumstances, an approach to the operational area on the surface was out of the question, Dönitz ordered all non-snorters to surface only to charge batteries. In addition, *Landwirt* was reformed. The snorkel boats pressed on ahead but did not achieve much either. And while big things were taking place in the invasion area we merely crept along. On the first day 76 sea miles; on the second only 50, of which 27 were submerged, i.e. about four kilometres an hour. Before we reached the goal matters would have been decided.

In fact for U 333 it was all over in seven days. We scarcely set foot on deck the whole time and were fully stretched fighting off aircraft. No trace of enemy surface forces. The only vessels we sighted were neutral fishing boats fully illuminated.

The continual tension was further underlined by a couple of remarkable episodes. 10 June dawned in a lively enough fashion. Repeated and loud detection, from closest proximity, made us disappear again and again in the early hours. Crash dive — according to the log 'after 4 minutes, 3 minutes, after 1 minute — after 1 minute'. Then the inevitable happened: the repeated ups and downs had so reduced the compressed air in the bottles and drained the batteries that I was forced to surface in daylight to replenish. It was 0910 and hardly had we opened the hatch than we were approached by a Sunderland from astern. Like a hawk it plunged steeply down on us from about 200 metres and, as sometimes in tense situations the smallest impressions implant themselves with lightning speed, now in the glazed cockpit of the heavy flying boat I believed I saw the distorted faces of the crew. We escaped a collision by less than 30 metres, then it was all over. Relics of what I called an 'imposing' burst of fire were various bullet holes in conning tower and hull, the thunder of water fountains thrown up by depth charges which had missed their target, and the fading howl of engines. We had been totally unable to defend ourselves. The 3.7-centimetre AA gun had jammed after the very first shot.

The pilot had levelled up the machine and maintained contact some way off. I lulled him into security, then suddenly opened fire with the 2-centimetre which drove him away. While the Sunderland was still turning I let U 333 dive quickly and laid the boat on the bottom in 150 metres.

I had to reflect on this flying boat which was not exactly suited to a Kamikaze dive and ask myself what could have taken place on board. What was the point of those aerial acrobatics which brought little advantage anyway? Years afterwards the circumstances emerged from a Ministry of Defence report D/AHB (RAF) 8/13 of 20 February, 1981, which stated: 'On 10 June, 1944, Sunderland "Y" of 10 Squadron, captained by Flight Lieutenant H. A. McGregor, RAAF, was on anti-U-boat patrol. At 0915 hours the aircraft sighted a U-boat surfacing. In attempting an immediate attack, the aircraft descended rapidly in a steep turn. This action was so severe that it caused the armourer, who was lowering the port bomb door, to lose his balance and cause the door to jam. The same manoeuvre caused the nose gunner some delay in getting to his position, but as soon as possible he opened fire with the forward-firing guns. The aircraft was held on a steady course to enable continuous fire on the submarine's conning tower. As the deflection path of the aircraft would not provide an optimum target, the pilot made an "S" manoeuvre to regain his original flight path. Depth charges were set "shallow" and were released at 75 feet above the sea, but three of the six charges failed to drop free. The closest of the three depth charges exploded about 30 yards astern of the U-boat and 10 yards beyond. It was estimated that about two thirds of the 460 rounds of machine gun fire hit in the vicinity of the U-boat's conning tower.

'After the attack the aircraft continued to circle while an attempt was made to repair the release mechanism of the remaining depth charges. During that time the U-boat fired about 20 rounds of flak, accurate for range and height. Meanwhile the U-boat steered an evasive course after the attack, and after approximately five minutes submerged on its original course. Assessment: Miss astern, no damage claimed.'

So that was it. An over-hasty dive. On board the heavy machine everything had been thrown about, and there were breakdowns. Hence the startled faces, as it seemed to me, which stared at me from the cockpit, almost close enough to be touched. If the thing had not been so serious one could have laughed.

Creeping cautiously, we moved forward. In the dark I tried to deceive the enemy with 'Aphrodite' — hydrogen balloons of one meter diameter attached to a float with strips of aluminium foil hanging from them. They were intended to confuse radar location and mislead the aircraft. But the pilots, reminded of their own tricks, became more curious than ever and the opposite occurred. They flew at us. I put U 333 on a snaking course, but was twice brought to bay and attacked. My heavy defensive fire warded off the enemy, who withdrew into the protection of the clouds. We no longer saw him but could still hear his continual hum, loud or soft. There was not much point in 'Aphrodite', added to which the lines often caught up in our net-cutters and we had a lot of trouble clearing them.

The following midnight things got tough again. Once more the batteries forced us to surface. Caught by radar, I stayed up all the same, ready for defence with everything we had. The aircraft did not keep us waiting long. As though drawn by a thread, it came straight towards us out of the darkness at a height of about 70 metres, and directly into the fire of our 2-centimetre guns. With a single burst our gunner hit one engine of the aircraft, which at once burst into flames and crashed. While it was going down we were still being fired at by the rear gunner. Then the fire roared up hissing behind us in the night-darkened water. On impact the bombs exploded in blazing columns. For a while the wreck stayed afloat, the flames lighting up the surrounding sea and U 333 as well, while behind in the darkness other planes were already circling, not daring to come closer. I thought I saw a survivor jump out of the burning aircraft, a crew member insisted there were two. They must have got into a rubber boat for we heard weak signals from a small emergency transmitter.

One point to me. On the other hand we had not emerged unscathed. The loss of our radar set and the 3.7-centimetre AA gun considerably reduced our fighting power. In addition, the many bombs exploding nearby had made the boat spring a leak again. U 333 was trailing an oil slick particularly noticeable in moonlight. Tanks and conning tower were holed.

In those days U-boats at the entrance to the Channel were given a free choice of returning to base if the enemy defence was too strong, but almost all of them had already been sunk. With equal tenacity pilots of the Coastal Command intercepted the five U-boats north of the British Isles which began their movement to the invasion area from Norway. They did not get far. On 12 June all non-snorting U-boats that still survived were recalled — among them U 333. The last of them reached harbour by the evening of 15 June.

The battles I have described are typical and are among those which ended fairly well for us. There were not many of them. All non-snorting U-boats were destined to be either sunk or severely damaged by British aircraft. Of some 30 *Schnorchel* boats in operation 20 were lost between the start of the invasion and the end of August. In this period we lost altogether 82 U-boats in all seas (*United States, Submarine Losses World War II*, Washington 1963). One could extend the list of battle reports to any length, but one way or another the end would always be the same — and those that came off worse can no longer speak.

Our U-boats could do little against the Invasion. Up to 26 August they only sank five escort vessels, 12 ships totalling 56,845 tons, and four landing craft of 8,400 tons. One escort, three landing craft and five ships totalling 36,800 tons were torpedoed. But here again there were failures among the 'Gnat' acoustic torpedoes which were not operationally ready. Three enemy ships were lost to mines. On the other hand, thousands of transports and landing craft reached their destination.

In the first six months of 1944 on all oceans German U-boats sank altogether 387,250 gross register tons of enemy shipping.

Naturally we in the navy did not understand so much about land warfare and we could not survey the overall situation. But one thing was clear to us, namely that the Anglo-Americans were not standing still in their bridgeheads in Normandy, they were slowly but surely in process of realising their strategic intentions and occupying the whole of France. On 18 June the American First Army succeeded in breaking through on the Cotentin peninsula and cutting off Cherbourg, which capitulated twelve days later. While the Allies gained ground in central France, at the beginning of August the Americans took Rennes in Brittany. On 4 August the invasion army broke through at Avranches and then pushed forward in the direction of the Atlantic bases. We had discussed this possibility in the messes and thought of the fate of our flotillas. It would not be long before all our bases, with their defences facing seawards in the 'Atlantic Wall', were bypassed and cut off from behind, whether or not the High Command had designated them as fortresses. Where was reinforcement, fuel, ammunition, to come from? The inevitable occurred: from 24 to 26 August, 1944, the Biscay ports were evacuated by the flotillas and the U-boats still present transferred westwards round Ireland and Scotland to Norway.

I myself was not affected by these changes. In early July I was called to Captain Hans Rösing. He too wore the Knight's Cross and commanded *Unterseeboot West*. He received me with a smile and said: 'Ali Cremer, old friend, you're a lucky fellow.'

'That I represent something like life insurance, my people have always maintained,' I replied, 'but one should not trust too much to luck.'

'No, that's not it,' continued Rösing. 'You're getting one of the new Type XXI boats. It's already waiting at home for you.'

I was speechless. I was indeed one of the 'Old Guard' and the only one to have survived on that coast since 1941 and experienced the Invasion, but I had not reckoned with such proof of confidence. It was a real distinction to be entrusted with such a boat. For what had been created at home, despite all wartime difficulties, were the first genuine submarines we had waited so long for. In contrast to our previous U-boat types, or rather submersibles with a limited period of dive, whether or not they were improved with the *Schnorchel* as an expedient, with this new type one could remain perpetually underwater. Moreover, its speed made escape from pursuers easy.

In conversation with Rösing I sought permission to take with me as many as possible of my old U 333 crew. We were all keen to stay together, not only for technical reasons; as a team we had experienced and shared a lot. After some discussion I was allowed to keep more than half my people; after all, U 333 could not be stripped completely of its regular crew. Rösing had remarked incidentally: 'Your old boat is going to Fiedler.'

Lieutenant-Commander Hans Fiedler was younger than I and belonged to another crew. After failing to achieve anything with his first boat, U 120, he was given U 564. That was the successful boat of the famous Reinhard 'Teddy' Suhren, who had won the Oak Leaves with Swords and was now in command of *Unterseeboot Nord* in Norway. But Fiedler was ill-starred. Hardly had he taken over the boat than in June, 1943, he was so heavily damaged by a Sunderland in the Bay that, despite shooting down the aircraft, all he could do was to try to reach harbour accompanied by another boat — which he failed to do. Next day U 564 was again attacked from the air and sunk. Fiedler and some of the crew escaped. Soon afterwards he was given U 998, a continually ailing boat always up to tricks. There are craft like that, springing one technical fault after another on its skipper. For this reason U 998 was decommissioned on 27 June, 1944, in the Norwegian base of Bergen. From there Fiedler came with some of his crew to La Pallice and took over U 333.

Everything went quickly. There lay my boat in the bunker. Daylight fell through the wide entrance while electric lamps were mirrored in the water. Work was being done on the boat, the blue flames of the welders hissed, the pounding of pneumatic hammers echoed from the concrete walls. For the period of the transfer ceremony the dockyard workers stopped and stepped aside. The new crew formed up on the iron deck, in blue with leather packs as was the custom. As the ones who were leaving, we stood ready for departure on the pier. A few short words and orders, then my commander's pennant was struck and Fiedler's raised.

U 333 tugged lightly on the lines. A steel tube which had carried us who knows how far and to many places — the North Atlantic, the Florida coast, Sierra Leone, creeping through the Bay of Biscay, down to the Tropic of Cancer and up to the North Channel. Tested in many attacks, a little battered, a little patched, slightly rusty. The boat was no longer young, and it was a piece of our life, of my life . . . But we were given no time for rumination. Wartime routine and the pressure of events kept us on our toes. My new boat — U 2519 — lay at Hamburg and, besides greater safety and fighting power in the future, for the present it spelt for some of my people a longish reunion with their families. Happy anticipation outweighed the farewell mood. Only our comrades who were staying behind felt bad, as though sensing misfortune.

So, after a last look at U 333 with its three little fishes on the conning tower, we boarded the bus which was to take us out of the town to the railway. The countryside around the U-boat bases was already occupied by armed Resistance fighters. We passed without interference and were spared also by low-flying aircraft. The railway too had its dangers as the Resistance and enemy bombers had destroyed several bridges. But it was still possible to get through to Germany, though by diversions.

To conclude the story of U 333: Fiedler was ill-starred. He had taken over U 333 on 10 July, 1944, and thereafter sailed for the boat's eleventh patrol, in the direction of the Channel. No one ever saw it again. Three weeks later, on 31 July, contact was lost.

On that day four ships of the 2nd Escort Group, among them the sloop *Starling* and the frigate *Loch Killin*, were near the Scilly Isles. It was the Group, already mentioned, of the most successful British U-boat killer, the much decorated Captain F. J. Walker, RN who, with his flagship *Starling* or in combination with others, had sunk the most German U-boats, namely 20. Shortly before sailing, Walker, 48 years old, had died suddenly of a stroke, and, robbed of its leader, the Group was in a depressed mood. Who could replace the man who had carried them from victory to victory? But the task remained: hunt the U-boats!

The *Loch Killin* was equipped with a new anti-U-boat weapon, the 'Squid', a kind of mortar similar to the Hedgehog, which could hurl depth charges about 800 metres forward. Each charge weighed 350 pounds. But the Squid was twice as fast as the Hedgehog, and if the Hedgehog was a hand probing for the U-boat with five fingers, the Squid was a paw which struck and crushed everything.

At 1700 on 31 July, the listening room in *Loch Killin* reported the Asdic echo of a U-boat. The group leader in *Starling* was informed and with *Loch Killin* began a systematic search. At 1727 *Loch Killin* fired a Squid salvo. The depth charges were set for 40 metres. When *Starling* passed over the site of the attack, oil was seen everywhere on the surface. The U-boat had probably been hit. Twenty minutes later it was again attacked with Squid, whereupon wreckage and oil came up. The ships waited patiently.

At 1806 *Starling* threw a series of ten heavy depth charges set to depths of 80 to 130 metres. They were heard to explode. Then there was silence.

Just when it was thought to be all over, there was an unusually heavy explosion in the depths. More oil kept coming up.

Starling and *Loch Killin* continued to throw depth charges and Squid projectiles until the whole surface of the sea was covered with wreckage and objects of all kinds. But the U-boat stayed down.

It was the fifteenth boat *Starling* had helped to sink, and the 538th German U-boat which the British Admiralty claimed as destroyed. It was U 333, the boat of the 'three little fishes'.

The British Ministry of Defence records: 'This was the first successful sinking achieved by the use of "Squid" projectiles, the forward-firing depth charges.' And the Atlantic transmitter commented: 'It was a Type VII-C boat, probably under Lieutenant-Commander Fiedler. Before him Lieutenant-Commander Cremer had commanded this boat.'

I brooded on it for a long time.

15

A new generation of U-boats

Abandoned by luck, U 333 succumbed west of the Scillies and took with it to the depths the men we had handed over — something we learnt only very much later. I, with those remaining to me, had meanwhile arrived at Plön in Holstein. There, at the 1st U-boat training depot, the crew for U 2519 was expanded to about sixty men. Thereafter we were all sent for a fortnight to Bad Wiessee to make us fit again for active service. Here, near the picturesque Tegernsee, a U-boat rest home had been set up and a similar home for fighter pilots.

We naval people had a few sailing dinghies at our disposal and of course spent much of the day on the water. To get round the strict regulations which required everyone to be back in the home by 10 p.m. my crew adapted a cellar window through which they entered late at night — like climbing through a conning-tower hatch! To their great amusement they noticed that the skipper also used this method of entry.

The reason for my late nights was mainly the fighter pilots' home. We had indeed the better dinghies, but the pilots had plenty of cognac and champagne. At this time Captain Erich Hartmann, decorated with Oak Leaves, Swords and Brilliants, and called 'the most successful fighter pilot in the world', arrived in Bad Wiessee after a reception in Hitler's headquarters. This gave rise to the right sort of mood for a lively exchange of experience between Navy and Air Force. Our conversations were much taken up with comparisons between weapons and tactics of previous years. By and large the pilots were in the same situation as the U-boat arm. Today we were facing very tough and well trained enemies and superior weapons. We were agreed that technical superiority could only be partly compensated for by personal bravery. At the end of the day, technology would prove the deciding factor.

Of course a lot was drunk, but all our merriment was

overshadowed by the heavy air raids on our cities and the defensive battles of the U-boat men in the Atlantic who, as Churchill wrote in *The Second World War*, 'by stupendous efforts and in spite of all losses remained in action until almost the end . . . they carried the undying hope of a stalemate at sea.'

The battle was still raging on the invasion front. On 25 August De Gaulle had entered liberated Paris. Fighter pilots and U-boat men were clear that their present stay was only a brief interlude to catch their breath and that they were urgently awaited at the front with new weapon systems and energies restored. Not even Hartmann's stories from headquarters, which cautiously suggested that even Adolf Hitler himself probably considered the military situation hopeless and was banking on political differences between the Allies, could alter that. We soldiers were the last small spark of hope for the homeland, that the impending defeat might be concluded without disaster. Perhaps we still had a few trumps up our sleeve after all.

In the meantime the *Schnorchel* boats, now operating from Norway, had made a name for themselves, alarmed the enemy, and more or less been able to escape detection from the air. This applied to the wide, stormy waters in the north, where snorting was in any case difficult to locate, as it did to British coastal waters. A typical example was U 482 under Lieutenant-Commander Graf Matuschka, who had sailed for his first patrol in a *Schnorchel* boat in the late summer of 1944 and been able to register some success. On 29 September, 1944, he wrote in a letter:

'. . . After our first patrol we have returned in good shape to the north. Our task had led us to the west coast of England and given us quite unusual success. On 30.8. the boat sank the American turbine tanker *Jacksonville*, on 1.9. the corvette *Hurst Castle* and on 8.9. the motor ship *Pinto* as well as the British steamer *Empire Heritage* . . .'

But this beginner's luck engendered a false security. In the long run no good could come of it, particularly in such problematical waters as the North Channel. After Matuschka had sunk the Norwegian tanker *Spinanger* on his next patrol and had the luck as well to have the British aircraft carrier *Thane* come into his sights, the famous 2nd Support Group (Capt. Walker's) was sent after the boat: the sloops *Starling, Peacock* and *Hart*, the corvette *Amethyst* and the frigate *Loch Craggie*. They did not rest until by tested methods they had flushed out the tiresome U-boat. And that was the end of U 482 and its crew . . .

The 'Electro-boat', as the Type XXI was called, to which U 2519 belonged, had been preceded by developments in the Walter U-boat and these must be mentioned. After several years' experiment, the Kiel Professor Helmuth Walter had invented a power unit depending on the breakdown of high percent hydrogen peroxide (H_2O_2). The peroxide or superoxide was split by means of a catalyst in a decomposer and the resulting mixture of oxygen and water used as a propulsion jet in rockets or as the power source for a turbine: the Walter turbine.

Walter had the idea of incorporating this turbine, for which the steam could be generated by means of hydrogen peroxide, in U-boats. The result was a submarine independent of fresh air. The boat could no longer be located by radar because it could stay permanently underwater. The expelled residual CO_2 gases combined with the sea water and left no bubble track. The sound they made neutralised the engine noises and also made the boat immune from Asdic underwater location. The Walter turbine with an altered hull profile (in cross-section oval like a fish) produced high underwater speeds. At the end of 1942, 28 knots were achieved. All in all the Walter boat seemed to be the ideal submarine.

But for the time being its value was judged to be only experimental, particularly as its method of propulsion was not yet perfected. The fuel consumption was also extraordinarily high, and the system comported a danger of explosion which called for suitable precautions. Meanwhile there were only a very few experimental boats. Then, to gather experience, in 1942 Dönitz ordered a series of small Walter U-boats, Type XXVII, to be built for use in coastal waters, and a larger Walter U-boat, the later Type XXVI, to be planned for Atlantic operations.

But all experiments with the Walter U-boat remained dreams for the future, though according to Walter, 'all rocket engines and main propulsion units for fighter aircraft emerged as byproducts from the work with units for U-boats.' The search for 'the submarine of tomorrow' happened during a period when no real necessity for it existed, for the conventional Type VII-C was still dominating the seas and achieving great success. As a consequence its development was delayed, and the 'total submarine' was not yet available at a time when it was suddenly and urgently required: after 'black May', 1943.

Now the catastrophic situation in the U-boat war demanded quick decisions and it became necessary to create an intermediate type as a transition between the existing, greatly endangered Type VII-C and the Walter U-boat still in development. A first step in this direction was the *Schnorchel*, also developed by Walter from a Dutch idea. A further step was the attempt to combine the projected shape of the fast Walter boat with the established method of propulsion. If the space problem could be solved, leaving the diesel engine as it was, but supplied with fresh air by the *Schnorchel*, and the battery capacity trebled, then the 'conventional' U-boat would come very close to the total submarine. And so the later Type XXI arose — a boat in size, shape and above all in battery capacity far superior to the Type VII-C, the 'Electro-boat'. Not quite as fast as the Walter boat, but nonetheless difficult to locate and fast enough to escape its pursuers underwater. On 13 August, 1943, Dönitz ordered the dockyards to concentrate on Electro-boats. Three hundred were ordered, with a limited Walter-programme running parallel. All this took time and meanwhile the war continued.

At the beginning of October, 1944, we travelled with the whole crew to Hamburg for constructional training at the shipyard of Blohm & Voss where our Electro-boat 2519 was supposed to lie. But when Captain Rösing in La Pallice had aroused our expectations with his remark about the boat 'waiting' for us, he was greatly exaggerating. U 2519 was not to be launched till 18 October.

These new boats were 'shot through', meaning 'hurried through'. We coined the term earlier in reference to the short training of new commanders. Applied to the new XXI boats this meant new and rapid (or rather, ultra-rapid) construction methods. The boats were built in whole sections. Today sectional construction is a commonplace, particularly with large ships. At that time the Americans were building their well known Liberty and Victory ships in the same way. For us this method was unfamiliar, although in the First World War small U-boats had been brought in sections by rail to the Mediterranean and there assembled. Now Type XXI boats were prefabricated with highest priority in eight sections. Over thirty inland factories as far as Silesia were occupied with prefabricating the sections. Then the crude sections, which were so heavy they could only be moved on waterways, were brought to the coast and equipped in a dozen armament factories with pipe systems, cables, auxiliary machinery and the rest. In big final assembly yards in Hamburg, Bremen and Danzig the sections were welded together — and the boat was finished.

All this went on at conveyor-belt speed. In the summer of 1944 from keel-laying of the crude sections to delivery took 80 days, and attempts were made to reduce this to 71 days. Fifty days were earmarked for construction and equipping, four days for welding the sections together on the slipway up to the launch of the finished boat. A further six days were for final installations at the wharf. After a good week of testing at the dockyard the boat was handed over to the Navy. Only a few hours after a boat had been launched the sections of the next boat would be laid in the empty building space, as it were in the still-warm bed.

So it went on without pause, day and night, week by week, month after month, at the rate of about eight new boats monthly. Such activity did not stay hidden from the enemy, his air reconnaissance worked well. There were air-raids on production centres and communications, canals were breached, deadlines could not always be met. Despite repeated raids on Hamburg, damage at the shipyard of Blohm & Voss never held up the programme seriously. When the last boat, U 2552, was put into service there on 25 April, 1945, the Allies had already reached Bremen and Stade on the lower Elbe.

So here our new boat was in the making, U 2519. With a length of 76.7 metres and 8.0 metres width, the Type XXI was ten metres longer and two metres broader than the VII-C boat and, with a surfaced displacement of 1,621 tons, weighed more than twice our old U 333. The Type XXI contained two diesel engines totalling 4,000 h.p. But what gave it the name of Electro-boat were six electric motors equivalent in power to the diesels, namely 4,200 h.p. There were two double motors, two further double motors for slow speed, one double for high and a single motor for slow speed. The extensive fuel tanks in the smaller Walter boat were here taken up to the last inch with batteries. As we have said, the *Schnorchel* made the Electro-boat almost independent of the surface even with the diesels. But once on the surface it was intended to crash-dive in only 28 seconds. The specifications gave a diving depth of 250 metres — there was even talk of 400 metres.

The boat had the oval, fish-like cross-section of the Walter boat with a relatively narrow, round back, and without the previous broad cat-walk. The bridge was streamlined and offered more protection than in previous types. In principle this form has been continued up to the present atomic submarines. Experienced captains were to make two cruises with the Electro-boat and then transfer to the coming fast submarines with the Walter turbine, which was being improved. The Electro-boats were to go into service before the end of 1944, but circumstances delayed everything.

The few weeks which we shared between the depot ship *Veendam*, a 16,000-ton passenger steamer of the Holland–America line, and the new boat with the construction number 733, we were kept constantly busy — our duties only interrupted when the crew helped with fire-fighting after an air-raid on the residential areas of Hamburg–Wilhelmsburg. So much was new and unfamiliar and explained to us only in the 'constructional training'. The new boat won the crew's total approval, particularly as its larger dimensions gave them greater freedom of movement than the former 'greater German diving tubes' as Matuschka had called them. There were two living and sleeping spaces with a bunk for everyone, and a washroom with showers. And, most important, there were three toilets instead of the former primitive lavatory which frequently had to serve as food store as well, where one had trouble pumping out the contents by hand against the prevailing water pressure — a subject on which no words have been wasted in this book although it could claim a whole chapter to itself.

All our activities culminated in final instruction and test runs in which the technical personnel particularly had their hands full. Moving in, which continued till midnight, was followed next day by the commissioning of U 2519. It was 15 November, 1944.

Long weeks of trials followed. We passed through the Northeast Canal to the Baltic and from one harbour to another. Hand in hand with general drill went trials with new components: test run with the diesels in Kiel, checking the radio installation in Sonderburg. On a trip from Swinemünde to Danzig, we kept up 'full speed' for six hours and touched 17.5 knots underwater, exceeding our intended underwater speed of 16.8 knots. (That was something different from the 7.6 knots of old U 333.)

At a cruising speed of 10 knots the Electro-boat would have had a radius of action of 16,000 sea miles. That corresponds to a distance from the Channel to Cape Horn and back, or a round trip to Cape Town with a stay in that area lasting several weeks. Christmas was spent between firing torpedoes, snorting and crash diving in the deep Gulf of Danzig, the U-boat training ground. On one occasion (it was now mid-January, 1945) we spent three days on end underwater.

I carried out every imaginable test with U 2519. In its technology and armament, and especially in its handling, it was a splendid boat. It was designed to carry up to 24 torpedoes which could be fired in rapid succession. By means of a new sound-locating device we could have aimed at and hit a target blindfold without optical vision, and would have escaped all pursuers underwater.

All very fine in theory, but in practice . . .

On 24 January, 1945, as we were heading for Pillau for the last time, the Russian winter offensive was rolling forward, Königsberg was evacuated, the whole of East Prussia was encircled by the Soviets and could only be evacuated by sea.

While the U-boat training programme went on undeterred, literally over our heads the last merchant steamers and warships were leaving the east German harbours for the west, filled to overflowing with refugees and wounded. An unbroken procession for more than three months, the last 115 days of the war, westwards where the Allies had crossed the frontiers of the German Reich and were flattening everything in terrible air-raids.

In view of the depressing situation in the crumbling Reich, sailors inevitably had their own thoughts. These men, who had fought for years from the Atlantic bases, now cut off and surrounded, saw clearly enough the changes that had occurred at home. The overcrowded harbours, the bombed cities, the misery of the refugees, of the many wounded from the tottering eastern front, of the freezing, the care-worn, the tired dockyard workers — all this made them wonder how it would end. They felt that the end was approaching and were certainly thinking of survival.

On the other hand we saw new boats still being made and launched, though the waterways and canals bombed by the enemy occasionally held up delivery of the XXI sections at the appointed time. For the enemy knew exactly what was at stake.

At the beginning of the year the British First Sea Lord had painted an alarming picture in a memorandum. In February or March, 1945, he feared there would be a new big offensive on convoys and in coastal waters with new U-boats. He said the losses could possibly exceed those of spring, 1943, and affect all military operations. On the basis of this warning 300 allied escort vessels intended for the Far East were retained in England.

On our side Grand Admiral Dönitz made concrete statements. On 15 February: 'In the next few months the number of boats on operations will increase considerably. At the moment 237 boats are being made ready for operations (111 of the old type, 84 of Type XXI, 42 of Type XXIII). Every month approximately 60 boats will become operational. The present total number of U-boats is the highest that Germany has ever possessed.'

And Churchill wrote in retrospect: 'The first of these [new U-boat types] were already under trial. Real success for Germany depended on their early arrival on service in large numbers. Their high submerged speed threatened us with new problems and would indeed, as Dönitz predicted, have revolutionised U-boat warfare.'

At this time about 5,000 personnel and a staff of 300 engineers, some at the top of their profession, were working on the creation of the Walter turbine boat which was to go into mass production. The first three were expected to be operational at the beginning of May. The first eight of the smaller 234-ton Electro-boats of Type XXIII, intended for short range, had been sent to the English coast to gather experience. The commanders were unanimous in their praise of this new type. 'Ideal boat for short operations close to the coast. Fast, manoeuvrable, simple depth-keeping, offering small surface for location or attack. The enemy senses that a boat is there rather than obtaining clear proof and determining its position.'

And to round off the picture: as a 'small battle unit' there were new-type one- and two-man mini-U-boats, the 'Beaver' and the 'Seal', carrying torpedoes for attack at close quarters.

But while we were gathering our remaining strength to force the issue in the U-boat war, the 'Big Three' (Stalin, Roosevelt and Churchill) were meeting at Yalta in the Crimea to coordinate their further military measures and agree on policies after the war: division of Germany into occupation zones, formation of an Allied

Control Commission, fixing of the future Polish–Soviet western frontiers and other matters. Nevertheless and despite every confidence in victory the final communiqué stated: 'The possibility that German U-boats might again represent a serious danger to our shipping in the North Atlantic arouses our concern.'

Meanwhile, out in the Atlantic the U-boat war, with and without *Schnorchel*, was continuing and claiming victims on both sides. In January 1945, when Matuschka vanished, 14 German U-boats were lost, 21 in February and 33 in March, including 13 destroyed by the US Army Air Force in a single day in harbours and dockyards.

On 22 February, 1945, Fritz Hein caught it with U 300, sunk off the Straits of Gibraltar after torpedoing two ships. Lieutenant Fritz Hein had been with us on the long patrols in U 333. The reason for his bad luck was a torpedo failure. Trusting in an acoustic Gnat, he had risked coming too close and when his torpedo failed him he was overwhelmed by the enemy. A few months previously Hellmuth Kandzior had been sunk with U 743 west of the North Channel and almost at the same time Lieutenant-Commander Dietrich von der Esch had lost his life with U 863 eleven degrees south of the Equator — he had been with me in the little U 152. Now none of my former watch-keeping officers was still at sea, except for one. Only he and I had survived.

The great distances in the world's oceans, their far removal from the scenes of land warfare should not obscure the fact that the war at sea did not live a life of its own but was dependent on supply bases. When, according to the official communiqué, the navy and in particular the U-boats sank 62 enemy ships in March, 1945, one could nevertheless calculate that we were left with only a few weeks' respite. It was a race between time and success. Our supplies were dwindling, fuel oil and other fuels were getting short. And while the land war was encroaching more and more on German soil, the Soviets were aiming at the Oder, the western Allies were crossing the Rhine and the refugee ships were plying to and fro in the Baltic, we were instructed to feel ourselves responsible on our test runs for every drop of diesel oil.

U 2519 had to return to Blohm & Voss and go into dock. On 5 April bombs again fell on the dockyard area. The supports broke which held the boat upright in dry dock, the boat tipped over, denting the port ballast and fuel tanks and bending the periscope so that it was no longer usable.

The situation was desperate. In the east the Soviets were advancing towards Mecklenburg. The Americans had taken Essen and Hannover, the French had reached Stuttgart. The last German resistance was concentrating in an ever smaller area. On 20 April Grand Admiral Dönitz had received territorial command over the North (isolated from the South) including North Lower Saxony, Hamburg, Bremen, Lübeck and Schleswig–Holstein. Field Marshal Kesselring commanded in the South while Adolf Hitler had stayed in Berlin. The Reich was already divided before the Americans and Russians joined hands on 25 April at Torgau on the Elbe.

Before the ring closed round Berlin the Grand Admiral had left his former naval headquarters 'Koralle', a hutted camp near Bernau, and evacuated to Plön in Holstein. In his new sphere of command he at once blocked Hitler's mad 'scorched earth' order which envisaged amongst other things the destruction of sea ports and similar installations. Nothing of that kind was to take place without Dönitz's approval, which was never given. Actions on private initiative had to stop. He was particularly concerned for Hamburg. Bridges over the Elbe must not be destroyed. Delaying battles were to give time for possible negotiations with the enemy. Detailed military operations were not under his orders but were a matter for the respective commanders.

On 25 April, 1945, a High Command communiqué, after mentioning heavy battles south-east of Bremen and in Berlin, reported that 'an anti-tank unit of the Navy, led by Commander Cremer and consisting of volunteers from a U-boat base, had destroyed 24 tanks in a few days.' A report also appeared in the few remaining daily papers under the headline 'U-boat Commander as Tank-Hunter', stating that we had fought on the outskirts of Hamburg against British forces advancing through Lüneburg Heath from the south.

In the course of the defensive battles the Grand Admiral had put naval personnel at the disposal of the Commandant of Hamburg, Major General Voltz. And while my first lieutenant with part of the crew brought U 2519 out of Hamburg to Kiel (the boat was never again fit for operations), we had been formed into a 'naval anti-tank battalion' under my command. Dönitz commented: 'Though I knew the fighting courage of the U-boat men I was full of concern whether they would measure up to the unaccustomed land battle.'

My engine room petty officer wrote in his notebook: 'A single day's training has made an infantryman out of a U-boat man. On the following day I was made acquainted with the *Panzerfaust* (bazooka). A primitive gadget like a stove pipe with a rocket-style shell that actually could knock out tanks. On the third day, pistol shooting. On Friday 13 April, of all days, we take up position. We are dumped hither and thither. On 17 April, at 1030 the first attack by fifteen tanks of the Tommies. One of my comrades is severely wounded. On 19 our commander and the 2.W.O. fight beside us. "Ali" gives us new courage. We withdraw slowly towards Hamburg–Harburg.'

We were surrounded three times by tank units and reached the tank ditch with only 16 men. The ditch had been evacuated by the retreating *Volkssturm* (English equivalent, 'Home Guard') and we were to hold up the enemy spearheads. But the English broke through with their armoured cars and, without cover against tanks, we had only our bazookas and rapid-fire guns to force back the spearhead. What moved me most in those days was that the company which held up that attack with me consisted of 16- and 17-year-old Hitler youths, briefly trained in ground warfare and in field grey. Many of them seemed confused by their quick deployment and the reality of the battle, but others were of fanatical determination. But all were ready to defend their shattered home city.

Fortunately the British gave themselves time. Victory, and with it Hamburg, 'the gateway to the world', was already in their pocket. As soon as their armoured spearheads encountered resistance they stopped and left the field to the bombers before they moved on again.

Our service on the Hamburg front was ended by an order from the Grand Admiral's HQ: 'Commander Cremer and his men at once to Plön.' There Admiral Meisel, the Chief of Naval Operations, explained to me that from now on we were the 'Guard Battalion Cremer', responsible for the security of the headquarters and the person of the Grand Admiral. He ended with a remark typical of those days: 'We can't go on leaving the Grand Admiral protected only by his sheep dog.'

The petty officer wrote further in his notebook: 'We must hand in our U-boat gear and wear field grey.' Basically that went against the grain with us old U-boat men, but practicality had precedence. Not least the grey uniform was easier to keep clean in the terrain than the easily marked navy blue, and the so-called Guard Battalion was supposed to make a proper impression even in those hectic last days. At headquarters a lively coming and going of senior officers and state officials prevailed and my men had continually to stand to and do the honours: 'Watch — Fall in!' Actually they had deserved better.

Although the U-boat war no longer held the same significance in naval operations and all remaining forces were directed to the evacuation of the Baltic and the rescue of people from the Soviet sphere, the U-boat danger to the western Allies had in no way passed. On the contrary, on 18 April neutral press correspondents had reported from Berne:

'The North American Navy Minister Forrestal referred in significant terms to the actions of German U-boats in the Atlantic. He declared in Washington that the U-boat danger in the waters around England was very serious. The U-boats were trying to interrupt supply lines to the Continent. The boats were much improved and their destruction was a difficult matter. The Canadian Navy Minister McDonald expressed himself in similar terms, stating that German U-boats had even risked entering the Gulf of St. Lawrence, where they had shown no large-scale activity since 1942.'

By the much improved U-boats operating in the waters around England were apparently meant those first eight smaller Electroboats of Type XXIII whose presence could be sensed though not located. Whatever the intention behind such angled news items, genuine concern comes through about the battle in this final stage, seeing that in April 22 ships were destroyed by German U-boats in the Atlantic and the North Sea. Churchill wrote: 'Allied air attacks . . . destroyed many U-boats at their berths. Nevertheless when Dönitz ordered the U-boats to surrender, no fewer than 49 were still at sea . . . Such was the persistence of Germany's effort and the fortitude of the U-boat service.'

At home lack of fuel had brought U-boat manoeuvres to a halt. Many boats lay in harbour waiting for oil which never came. On the last day of April the first Type XXI Electro-boat left the Norwegian base of Bergen for operations. The boat carried the number U 2511, under Commander Schnee. It had been launched at

Blohm & Voss on 2 September, 1944, and delivered on 29 September. After trials lasting seven months U 2511 sailed for its first patrol. How would it shape? Adalbert Schnee reported:

'On the way out, first enemy contact with U-hunting group in North Sea. Establish that these hunting groups can no longer touch the boat with our high underwater speed. Escaped underwater with slight 30 degree change of course . . . Few hours later, met English cruiser with several destroyers. Started underwater attack, pushed into the escort and reached cruiser at 500 metres range. All unnoticed . . . My experience: boat was excellent in attack and defence, something quite new for U-boat men.'

The day seemed to have come of which Dönitz prophesied that he would offer Churchill a new, first-class U-boat war. But the day came too late. With the cruiser close before him, Schnee could not fire. Weapons fell silent. The U-boats, those that still had fuel, were advancing into a void. The war at sea was effectively at an end, and Schnee was already on the way back to Norway: since 4 May all U-boats had been ordered to hold their fire — the Dönitz government had entered into negotiations for an armistice, and unconditional surrender followed on the night of 8/9 May, 1945. Three hundred big Electro-boats were on order, but to no further purpose.

16
The last days

Three signals had thoroughly altered the situation and opened the way to an immediate end of the war. On the evening of 30 April at 1807 there arrived in Plön a brief communication signed by Bormann in Berlin whereby Adolf Hitler appointed Grand Admiral Dönitz his successor in place of Reichsmarschall Göring. Dönitz was forthwith to take all measures arising from the current situation. That sounded very much like a testament, which indeed it was; for before we in the staff quarters had recovered from the surprise, another radio signal followed next morning, despatched at 0740. It was received in Plön at 1053 and read: 'Testament in force. I will come to you as quickly as possible. Until then postpone publication.'

How Hitler's adviser and Head of the Party Chancellery intended to do that, he did not convey. Berlin was in the grip of the Soviets. Instead, at 1518 of the same day Dönitz received the last signal drafted half an hour previously in the Reich Chancellery and stating in part that Hitler 'expired at 1530 yesterday. Testament of 29.4. confers on you the office of President. Testament brought out of Berlin as ordered, for you, for Field Marshal Schörner and for safe-keeping for the public. Form and time of publication to troops and public are left to you.'

The precipitate course of events and the confusion in times surprised us greatly; in particular we puzzled over the word 'expired'. By all that had gone before we judged it right to assume that Hitler had sought and found death at the head of his troops. Therefore an announcement to that effect was broadcast from Hamburg at 2230 on 1 May. The German people heard of Hitler's suicide only much later.

Once again the mantle of history had fallen on the Grand Admiral's shoulders. Full of dark forebodings, he himself commented: 'One day I shall be seen as a tragic figure. At the moment when I became Commander-in-Chief of the Navy the U-boat war was lost and now, when I am Head of State, the war has already been decided.'

What moved Hitler to confer the problematical succession on Dönitz can only be guessed. Reichsminister Speer advised him to do so and as so often Hitler, believing himself betrayed and abandoned by his close followers, reacted intuitively. He chose the outsider. Dönitz came from Potsdam, from the old Prussia which had denied its officials and military men the right to vote. Politically they were isolated. A saying in the Third Reich spoke significantly of a People's Army, a National-Socialist Air Force and an Imperial Navy. In the First World War the Grand Admiral was one of the Kaiser's men. Perhaps Hitler, aware that his own cause was lost, clung to that very fact.

Among the enemy powers the Grand Admiral was still credited with being a fair opponent. They would talk with him. In any case he was only left with the role of liquidator of the bankrupt estate, in all ages and among all peoples a thankless task, for the people love only the victor. Dönitz did not evade this task, which necessarily began with putting an end to the war as quickly and tolerably as possible. That the negotiations degenerated into an unconditional surrender was to make things more difficult. Unconditional surrender had last been practised eighty years before in the American Civil War, and the southern states of the Union affected by it had only slowly recovered.

In an order of the day to the troops Dönitz had stated that chaos and collapse could only be avoided by unqualified execution of his orders. The armed forces in the east were flooding back. By sea the Navy and Merchant Navy were rescuing what already amounted to nearly two million refugees, wounded men and soldiers from as far away as Courland in Latvia. On 2 May the British thrust forward to Lübeck from their bridgehead near Lauenberg. All day long the headquarters at Plön were under air attack from Allied fighter bombers. It was high time to take avoiding action and in the night of 2/3 May the Grand Admiral moved with his staff and associated departments to Flensburg–Mürwik. I myself had to cover the withdrawal and followed the cavalcade with a self-propelled gun. We had to interrupt the journey repeatedly and take cover as the enemy aircraft lit up the roads with searchlights and shot at everything that moved.

We all arrived towards 0200. As Dönitz himself says, 'the rest of the night passed with a short sleep, and decision on questions from military commanders who, in that intermediate state between war and peace, were rightly uncertain how they should behave.' The staff quarters of the Grand Admiral and the Armed Forces High Command was a physical training school belonging to the naval school and separated from it by a small wood. The naval high command, the naval operations division, the high commands of the Army and Air Force came to Glücksburg. We, the guard battalion, occupied barracks opposite the P.T. school. The harbour at Flensburg was full of ships of all kinds, and the town swamped with refugees.

The war with the West had lost its meaning. In the very night of our arrival Dönitz discussed with Admiral von Friedeburg the possibility of a partial capitulation in the whole of North-west Germany. From their remarks it emerged that in a partial capitulation the withdrawal of our soldiers from the east by sea and land and the flood of refugees ought not to be held up. Dönitz did not operate like the Reichsführer SS Himmler who, as early as 24 April, had offered capitulation to the Western powers through the Swedish Count Bernadotte. No one would negotiate with Himmler. The Grand Admiral chose the direct approach and sent a delegation under von Friedeburg, the new C-in-C Navy, to Montgomery's headquarters on Lüneburg Heath. Through the Commandant of Hamburg, General Voltz, already mentioned, this meeting was arranged at the British 21st Army Group.

During von Friedeburg's absence there were continual discussions between Dönitz, who was trying to form a specialist cabinet, and experts like Count Schwerin von Krosigk and Albert Speer. The Grand Admiral recognised clearly that the days of an independent German government of whatever kind were numbered and he hastened to exploit the favourable moment. It was a race against time. As far as I as an outsider could glean, the chief subject of all discussions was how the expected chaos could be avoided.

When von Friedeburg returned from his mission, he stressed that his reception and treatment by the British had been correct. The conditions demanded by Field Marshal Montgomery corresponded basically to our own ideas. But as all movements were to stop and all ships be surrendered there had to be tough argument about the continuation of refugee transports and the withdrawal of troops. Von Friedeburg mentioned in my presence that after some discussion Montgomery had finally said, if German soldiers crossed the Soviet–British demarcation line merely to fall into British hands and if the refugee transports continued westwards by sea, very well — 'I'm not a monster, after all.' That was a tacit agreement, but which Monty could not give in writing. Therewith the agreement was concluded. So on 5 May, at 0800 German summer time, the armistice came into force in North-west Germany, the Netherlands, France, the West and East Frisian Islands including Heligoland, in Schleswig–Holstein and Denmark.

Von Friedeburg's next journey, to the headquarters of General Eisenhower, the Supreme Commander, Allied Forces in Europe, at Rheims passed less favourably. Eisenhower insisted on a simultaneous capitulation on all fronts, including the Russian — and unconditionally! Every soldier was to lay down his arms wherever he happened to be, no refugee was to move further and every ship had to steer for the nearest Allied harbour, including those occupied by the Soviets. I spoke with von Friedeburg after his return from Rheims. He was deeply depressed.

As there was no alternative, at 0241 on 7 May in Eisenhower's headquarters, Colonel General Jodl signed the unconditional surrender of the German forces on land, at sea and in the air. It came into force at midnight, central European time, on 8/9 May, 1945. All the same, between the partial capitulation and the general ceasefire on all fronts a respite of four days had been obtained during which the withdrawals from the east continued without interruption and refugees, wounded men and soldiers had been able to stream back into what was to become the British occupation zone. Among them were the remains of Busse's army from Silesia, of General Wenk's from Brandenburg and Heinrici's army group from the Pomeranian area. Large parts of Army Group Centre (Schörner) and South (Rendulic) fought their way through to the west. They all escaped Russian captivity. That was the dot on the 'i'; for in the last three months of the war about two million people had been able to save themselves by sea to the west. This figure can be proved, but in fact there were very many more.

On 4 May, 1945, as a preliminary gesture as it were to the offer of capitulation, the Grand Admiral had terminated the U-boat war.

His last order of the day to his very own arm of the service, in which, as always, he addressed his men in the familiar second person, ended with the words: 'Comrades! Preserve your brave U-boat spirit, with which you have fought through the long years bravely, toughly and unflinchingly; preserve it for the future, to the benefit of our Fatherland. Long live Germany! Your Grand Admiral.'

The agreements stipulated amongst other things 'that in a partial capitulation warships are to be surrendered and are not to be scuttled.' Accordingly an order of the Grand Admiral stated: '. . . movements of naval transports at sea are to continue. Nothing to be destroyed, no ships to be sunk, no demonstrations.' That touched us U-boat men to the quick, seeing that we would have to hand over our boats to the Anglo–Americans without a fight, whether they were at sea, in Norwegian harbours or in home bases.

The commanders in home bases discussed the matter. It seemed to them to be asking rather too much that they should hand over without more ado the boats they had become so involved with. The question was voiced whether this could be reconciled with the self-respect of a navy, particularly as a previous instruction from Naval Operations had visualised scuttling under the code name 'Rainbow'.

It was clear that the Grand Admiral had only ordered the total surrender of ships under the pressure of negotiations for capitulation. We U-boat commanders spontaneously decided to act in anticipation. When my first lieutenant rang me from Kiel to ask how he should respond, for I was still commander of U 2519, I told him: 'Ali Cremer does not show a white flag and does not surrender his boat — so scuttle it!'

And all the other commanders in the home ports did the same, so that, as far as could be ascertained, 15 U-boats sank in Wilhelmshaven in the first week in May, 1945, in Hamburg 10, in Travemünde 31, in Kiel 26 and in Flensburg 56. That was a total of 138 boats, among them my tested XXI-boat U 2519. With opened main vents and hatches they simply sank as the air bubbled out of them. This was done at the commanders' own risk, and on their own authority, without the Grand Admiral's knowledge.

When these incidents were reported to him, I was personally present. The Grand Admiral looked very surprised and at first disapproving, then a slight smile crossed his face. And we commanders also got away with it, for the Allied reprisals which we had expected did not occur.

The U-boats still at sea had been ordered to surface and head for certain harbours. About the same numbers as those mentioned above did as ordered and up to the end of June surrendered to the Allies from Narvik to Portsmouth, New Hampshire. One or two stragglers surfaced in mid-August at La Plata, Argentina. The boats which had survived the war and not been sunk were transferred to England with German skeleton crews. After the capitulation over 100 of these were taken out into the Atlantic and sunk in the so-called 'Operation Deadlight'. A few were kept and distributed among the Allied navies — for better and sometimes for worse: when the Royal Navy later tried to set a captured XXVI Walter U-boat in motion, the hydrogen peroxide propulsion exploded.

In a salt mine in the Harz the Americans had found the 1:1 wooden model of the same Type XXVI boat. It was the large Walter U-boat intended for the Atlantic. As they could apparently find no use for it, on withdrawing from Thuringia they left it to the Russians, who could probably get nothing more from it than the measurements. On the other hand at the Schichau shipyard at Danzig the Soviets captured five type XXI Electro-boats and later they developed their standard 'Whiskey' boat after this German pattern.

With the capitulation of Germany all hostilities had ceased except those in the Far East. The Second World War was nearly at an end. From no branch of the Services had it demanded such heavy sacrifices as from the U-boat arm. The statistics vary slightly according to the point of view. Of roughly 820 fighting U-boats 718 did not return; of about 39,000 U-boat men, 32,000 lost their lives.

Summarising, the British commented: 'Grand Admiral Dönitz had an almost fatherly attitude to his men, and his men repaid him with an unshakable loyalty such as is given to few military leaders. No fewer than 32,000 out of 39,000 German seamen were lost, only 5,000 fell into captivity. Such a high rate of loss in a large and excellently trained body of men in a long-drawn-out war is probably unique in the history of warfare. But, faced with overwhelming superiority, the U-boat crews fought stubbornly to the bitter end — which speaks highly for the leadership of Dönitz and the esprit de corps in his Service.'

THE LAST DAYS

So this is how the balance-sheet looked. Before the enemy had got its grip on the situation, German U-boats had sunk more than 2,500 Allied merchant ships totalling 14 million tons. Churchill said the only thing he had really feared in the war had been the German U-boats. They had destroyed 65 per cent of the British pre-war tonnage. Even when the U-boats could no longer strike heavy blows and to outsiders the U-boat war had become pointless, in the last eighteen months of the war they had been able to tie down immensely strong enemy defence forces.

The Western Approaches Command, headed by Dönitz's opposite number, Admiral Sir Max Horton, had proved an effective instrument in fighting the U-boats. More than 1,000 escort vessels had passed through its training centres. Even in the last year of the war on average 300 escorts were in the North Atlantic manned by 4,000 officers and 40,000 men. The whole command embraced 100 maritime and some other installations very far from the front with a total service personnel of 121,500, including 18,000 'Wrens'. Subordinate to Horton were seven other admirals in the main British ports, the Commodore Western Isles, Commodore Londonderry and the commanders of flotillas.

The list of dead of the Western Approaches Command contains 6,081 names 'of gallant men'. It is kept in Liverpool Cathedral. On 9 August, 1945, a service of thanksgiving was held in this cathedral in honour of the Western Approaches Command. A few days later, on 15 August, 1945, Admiral Horton left the Service at the age of 62 to make way for younger men. His admiral's flag was hauled down at sunset. His task had been fulfilled. On the previous day the Japanese government had accepted the conditions for capitulation. The Second World War was finally at an end.

So much for the U-boat war. What of this U-boat skipper? Back to Flensburg, the seat of the last German Reich and the armed forces headquarters. The harbour was filled with ships of every kind and the town overflowing with refugees. Since 10 May there had been an Allied Control Commission on the *Patria*, a 17,000-ton passenger ship of the Hamburg–America line. It was headed by Major General Rooks (USA) and Brigadier Foord (GB); it issued instructions concerning the demobilisation of the German forces and checked that the capitulation conditions were observed. Relations between the heads of the Commission and the Germans remained correct.

Dönitz and his advisers conferred continually, for the most part on the adjustment from war to peacetime conditions. They debated how they might direct the transition and its ramifications, given their own resources and within the freedom of action left to them by the Allies. People had to be brought back, accommodation had to be created, a food catastrophe avoided, medical help had to be provided, the misery of the refugees relieved, and more. The Allies had made it clear that collapse in any form was to be prevented and order maintained at all costs, if necessary by force of arms. Communications by radio and other means with Norway, with commanding generals and admirals were still intact.

The area of the naval school, the seat of the Dönitz government, was treated as an enclave and recognised as sovereign territory. The guard battalion stood under arms and was respected by the Control Commission. On Allied orders the war flag had to be hauled down. In place of the Hitler greeting the Grand Admiral had reintroduced the old military salute. There were no pictures of the Führer and no party emblems any more.

They were hectic days. Reich Protectors, Gauleiters, military commanders, civil service chiefs, brownshirts with arm bands, SS men and party functionaries of every colour, having quickly decamped after the capitulation, now turned up and stood around helplessly. Gaunt, sleepless, laconic, the Grand Admiral rebuffed them all. In the hospital of the naval school, for instance, was Alfred Rosenberg, one of the National-Socialist ideologues and author of *Myth of the 20th Century*, a book which was derided even by his fellows. He repeatedly tried to get through to Dönitz. Of necessity I had to announce him but the Grand Admiral's only reaction was: 'Keep Rosenberg away from me.'

For I was still in command of the guard battalion. The war was over and for us this meant a ceremonial with clean uniforms and polished shoes, the least that could be expected of a staff guard. Each day, at the request of the Control Commission, we had to enter our names, one and all, in a list so that no one should run away. I watched this for a few days and then gave up entering my name as it seemed to me too stupid and bureaucratic. But in the matter of bureaucracy we still had something to learn from the Allies, particularly the Americans. To be sure, the absence of my signature was to have consequences for me.

As already mentioned, the seat of the Dönitz government was

the former P.T. school. It was separated from the naval school, which housed soldiers as well as a hospital, by a small wood. In this wood there were nightly shootings, short bursts from a machine gun, and hand grenades were occasionally thrown — every kind of dangerous mischief was practised. A quantity of armed soldiers had collected in the neighbourhood of Flensburg–Mürwik. To give the Allies with their concern for safety no grounds for intervention, the garrison commandant and commander of the naval school, Captain Wolfgang Lüth, had the area guarded by sentries. Unfortunately he himself fell victim to this measure. Walking between the P.T. school and naval school after dark, Lüth was hit by a warning shot fired from the hip by a sentry. He was killed instantly. With Oak Leaves, Swords and Brilliants, Lüth was the most highly decorated officer in the U-boat arm. At the end he was commanding one of the large 'Monsoon' boats. His death, coming after the war had actually ended, gave us all a shock. The court martial immediately assigned to examine the case (which was still allowed under Allied supervision) acquitted the sentry. It had been a tragic misunderstanding, an accident, but an accident which could not be made good. On 16 May in a moving funeral ceremony Wolfgang Lüth was buried with due formality in the presence of those still available among the admirals and generals. The guard battalion lined the route. Three salvos rang out.

In retrospect it can be said that with this last great display the Reich and the Navy were symbolically carried to the grave. Shortly afterwards, on 23 May, 1945, the Grand Admiral and his cabinet were arrested.

At least in British calculations the Grand Admiral had played a definite role. If they had expected excesses and political radicalisation to arise from the collapse of the Third Reich, they could confront chaos with this figure who stood firm as a rock amid the confusion of events. After all, he was not the first admiral in recent European history to conduct state business. However, when the expected revolt did not occur and the exhausted people persisted in their apathy, Dönitz was no longer needed.

Nevertheless the Grand Admiral's critics must grant that in the moment of collapse even a defeated Germany leaned to the Western Powers and did not go over with flying colours to the Russians.

On the day after the burial of Wolfgang Lüth the staff of the Soviet Control Commission arrived, led by Major General Truskow. The Russians treated their German opposite numbers with marked courtesy. But now the break-up started. On the morning of 23 May, 1945, Grand Admiral Dönitz, Colonel General Jodl and Admiral von Friedeburg were summoned to the *Patria*. Dönitz guessed what that meant. On board they were received by Major General Rooks who told them that he had been ordered by Allied headquarters to disband the German Reich Government in power and the Supreme Command of the armed forces. The gentlemen were to consider themselves prisoners.

The 11th British armoured division surrounded the whole enclave. A considerable show of tanks, infantry and military police encircled us. The guard battalion was formally requested to parade and lay down its arms. A British officer then got out a list, and everyone had to fall in as his name was called. As each group of one hundred men was collected they were marched through a gateway flanked with barbed wire. They were escorted to a village in the neighbourhood of Heide/Holstein where there was a prison camp reserved for U-boat men.

The group got smaller and smaller until only I remained, surrounded by tanks and soldiers armed to the teeth with tommy-guns and hand grenades. When nothing further happened, I went up to the officer who had read out the names and asked: 'Well, what about me?'

He looked in vain for my name in his papers and asked back: 'Are you on the list?'

When I said no, he shook his head. 'Get out. Camp is full.'

I quickly went back to the barracks and was packing my belongings when another officer came in excitedly and said I was to report to the *Patria* at once. I must have made a pitiful impression because on the way a Soviet officer spoke to me in good German and offered words of comfort, implying that it would not be long now before things got better.

On board the *Patria* I was taken to Captain G. H. Roberts of the Royal Navy. He had been sent by Admiral Horton. Horton had made a point of personally attending the surrender of eight German U-boats in Londonderry, and had interviewed the commanders in a very fair manner: 'I do not wish any officer to answer a question that he objects to.' As the war with Japan had not yet ended he tried to learn as much as possible about our U-boat arm and had sent an inspection team for this purpose to Germany. Apart from Captain Roberts, a Captain Gretton of the Royal Navy and Group Captain Gates of Coastal Command were members. After their return Horton asked them only one question: 'Did you discover anything I did not already know?' Their answer was brief and to the point: 'No, Sir.'

When I entered Captain Roberts' cabin he stood up and unexpectedly gave me his hand. He began our conversation with the remark that he felt appreciation and respect for me and the U-boat men in general. We had a long discussion about various things, including techniques and the training of British submarine officers. And though on return to Horton he stated he had learnt nothing new from us, in the course of our talk I learnt a whole lot from him. For the first time I heard something of Huff-Duff, of 'Fido', their target-seeking torpedo and other matters which, being top secret, till then had been unknown to us. He asked pointed questions about my career, which they had followed very closely, and about U 333. There was indeed a secret list of the most successful German U-boat commanders at the British Admiralty with names, ranks, decorations and dates, but how they had come on me at this point is a mystery to me even today. As Roberts wrote to me years afterwards, he summarised his impressions at that time in a private diary: 'This fellow has a sense of honour, otherwise he would not have done all this with his body so full of bullets.'

In conclusion he asked: 'Have you a particular wish?' I saw my chance and replied: 'Certainly, Sir, after all those years filled with battle and death, I should not like to become a prisoner of war.' He nodded understandingly. 'I shall see what can be done.'

When Roberts dismissed me in his cabin, he again gave me his hand and regretted that he could not do so outside four walls. He detailed another naval officer to shepherd me and this man went with me from one authority to another. Finally I was given a proper discharge certificate at an office in Hamburg.

And then I stood in the street, a free man. Hamburg lay in ruins. All around me was emptiness. Most of my comrades were no longer alive, the years of my youth had gone. Like so many others I had given of my best in a war which very few of us had wanted and in which the faith and readiness for sacrifice of the German people and the bravery of its soldiers had been most terribly abused.

Afterword

The question may be asked, what was the attitude of young German naval officers as war with Great Britain became a probability. We were very conscious of the fact that Britain, together with her Empire, accounted for nearly a quarter of the world's population and of the earth's surface. Also that her natural ally would be the United States, the richest country in the world, especially with her great reserves of raw materials. Great Britain, we were also well aware, had by force of her imperial circumstances made herself the world's leading seapower, and her battle fleet was studied as a model — even Nelson's manoeuvres at the Battle of Trafalgar were required to be learnt by heart in German naval schools.

The American battle fleets were by no means underestimated. As a sea cadet I had been invited to visit the heavy cruiser USS *Houston*, and had been impressed not only be the weaponry but also the living conditions enjoyed by American crews, and by the easy relationship between ranks.

When war was declared, first against Great Britain, later against the United States, we in the German Navy saw ourselves as David being sent out to do battle with Goliath. At one point, when there were only 11 U-boats operational in the Atlantic against the enormous battle fleets of our enemies, it took a sort of cheeky gallows humour to put about the 'positive' side of things: 'Ah well, all the more tonnage to be sunk.'

As my story makes clear, for the good of all our countries, the war ended not a moment too soon.

Peter Cremer
August, 1983

German U-Boat Casualties in World War II

Source: *United States Submarine Losses, World War II*
published by
Naval History Division, Office of the Chief of Naval Operations,
Washington, D.C., 1963

Date	U-Boat	Last Comdr.	Cause of sinking	Position
1939				
14 Sep	U 39	Glattes	HMS *Faulknor, Foxhound &* *Firedrake*	58-32 N, 11-49 W
20[22?]Sep*	U 27	Franz	HMS *Fortune & Forester*	58-35 N, 09-02 W
8 Oct	U 12	von der Ropp	Mine	† Straits of Dover
13 Oct	U 40	Barten	Mine	Straits of Dover
13 Oct	U 42	Dau	HMS *Imogen & Ilex*	49-12 N, 16-00 W
14 Oct	U 45	Gehlhaar	HMS *Inglefield, Ivanhoe,* *Intrepid, Icarus*	† 50-58 N, 12-67 W
24 Oct	U 16	Wellner	HMS *Puffin & Cayton Wyke* (damaged by)	† 51-09 N, 01-28 E (Mined & stranded on Goodwins)
29 Nov	U 35	Lott	HMS *Kingston, Kashmir &* *Icarus*	60-53 N, 02-47 E
4 Dec	U 36	Fröhlich	HM Sub. *Salmon*	† 57-00 N, 05-20 E
1940				
30 Jan	U 55	Heidel	HMS *Fowey, Whitshed &* Br. Sqdn. 228	48-37 N, 07-46 W
1 Feb	U 15	Frahm	Rammed by German *Iltis* (DD)	Baltic
5 Feb	U 41	Mugler	HMS *Antelope*	† 49-21 N, 10-04 W
12 Feb	U 33	von Dresky	HMS *Gleaner*	55-25 N, 05-07 W (mining Clyde)
23 Feb	U 53	Grosse	HMS *Gurkha* in North Channel	† 60-32 N, 06-10 W
25 Feb	U 63	Lorentz	HMS *Escort, Narwhal,* *Inglefield & Imogen*	58-40 N, 00-10 W
20 Mar	U 44	Mathes	HMS *Fortune*	† 63-27 N, 0-36 E

---

* - A semiofficial British account (1954) says 20 March.
† - No survivors

Date	U-Boat	Last Comdr.	Cause of sinking	Position
14 Feb	U 54	Kutschmann	Mined	(†) North Sea (?) (wreckage found)
13 Apr	U 64	Schulz	HMS *Warspite's* Sqdn. 700	† 68-29 N, 17-30 E
15 Apr	U 49	von Gossler	HMS *Fearless (& Brazen)*	68-53 N, 16-59 E
16 Apr	U 1	Deecke	HM Sub. *Porpoise*	† 58-18 N, 05-47 E
25 Apr	U 22	Jenisch	Mine	† 57-00 N, 09-00 E
10[29?] Apr	U 50	Bauer	HMS *Amazon & Witherington (Hero?)*	† 62-54 N, 01-56 W
31 May	U 13	Schulte	HMS *Weston*	52-27 N, 02-02 E
3 Jul	U 26	Scherlinger	HMS *Gladiolus* & RAAF Sqdn. 10	48-03 N, 11-30 W
— Jul	U 122	Loof	Unknown	† North SEa
3 Aug	U 25	Beduhn	Mine	54-00 N, 05-00 E
20 Aug	U 51	Knorr	HM Sub. *Cachalot*	47-06 N, 04-51 W
21 Aug?	U 102	von Kloth	Unknown	† North Sea?
3 Sep	U 57	Kühl	Norw. SS *Rona*(rammed)	Baltic
30 Oct	U 32	Jenisch	HMS *Harvester & Highlander*	55-37 N, 12-20 W
2 Nov	U 31	Prellberg	HMS *Antelope* (& RAF*)	56-26 N, 10-18 W
21 Nov	U 104	Jürst	HMS *Rhododendron*	† 56-28 N, 14-13 W
1941				
7 Mar	U 70**	Matz	HMS *Camellia & Arbutus*	60-15 N, 14-00 W
8 Mar	U 47	Prien	HMS *Wolverine*	† 60-47 N, 19-13 W
17 Mar	U 99	Kretschmer	HMS *Walker (& Vanoc?)*	61-00 N, 12-00 W
17 Mar	U 100	Schepke	HMS *Walker & Vanoc*	61-00 N, 12-00 W
23 Mar	U 551	Schrott	HMS *Visenda*	† 62-37 N, 16-47 W
5 Apr	U 76	von Hippel	HMS *Wolverine & Scarborough*	58-35 N, 20-20 W
8 Apr	U 65	Hoppe	HMS *Gladiolus*	† 60-04 N, 15-45 W
9 May	U 110	Lemp	HMS *Aubrietia, Bulldog & Broadway* (captured)	60-31 N, 33-10 W
2 Jun	U 147	Wetjen	HMS *Wanderer & Periwinkle*	† 56-38 N, 10-24 W
18 Jun	U 138	Gramitzky	HMS *Faulknor, Fearless, Forester, Foresight & Foxhound*	36-04 N, 07-29 W
27 Jun	U 556	Wohlfahrt	HMS *Nasturtium, Celandine & Gladiolus*	60-24 N, 29-00 W
29 Jun	U 651	Lohmeyer	HMS *Malcolm, Violet, Scimitar, Arabis & Speedwell*	59-52 N, 18-36 W

** - the most recently published British research suggests *U 47* and *U 70* sinkings should be transposed.

* - Second sinking: sunk 3-11-40, Schillig Rds., by RAF, raised and recommissioned.

Date	U-Boat	Last Comdr.	Cause of sinking	Position
3 Aug	U 401	Zimmermann	HMS *Wanderer, St. Albans* & *Hydrangea*	† 50-27 N, 19-50 W
9 Aug (28 Jul?)	U 144	v. Mittelstaedt	Torpedoed by Russ. Sub. *SC-307*	† Gulf of Bothnia
25 Aug	U 452	March	HMS *Vascama* & Br. Sqdn. 209	† 61-30 N, 15-30 W
27 Aug	U 570*	Rahmlow	Br. Sqdn. 269	62-15 N, 18-35 W
10 Sep	U 501	Förster	HMCS *Chambly* & *Moosejaw*	62-50 N, 37-50 W
11 Sep	U 207	Meyer	HMS *Leamington* & *Veteran*	† 63-59 N, 34-48 W
4 Oct	U 111	Kleinschmidt	HMS *Lady Shirley*	27-15 N, 20-27 W
19 Oct	U 204	Kell	HMS *Mallow* & *Rochester*	† 35-46 N, 06-02 W
11 Nov	U 580	Kuhlmann	Collision	Baltic (off Memel)
15 Nov	U 583	Ratsch	Collision	† Baltic
16 Nov	U 433	Ey	HMS *Marigold*	36-13 N, 04-42 W
28 Nov	U 95	Schreiber	HNM Sub. *0-21*	36-24 N, 03-20 W
30 Nov	U 206	Opitz	RAF Sqdn. 502	† 46-55 N, 07-16 W
11 Dec (Nov?)	U 208	Schlieper	HMS *Bluebell*	† Atlantic, W. of Gibraltar
15 Dec	U 127	Hansmann	HMAS *Nestor*	† 36-28 N, 09-12 W
16 Dec	U 557	Paulssen	Rammed by Ital. Torp. boat *Orione*	† 35-33 N, 23-14 E
17 Dec	U 131	Baumann	HMS *Exmoor, Blankney, Stanley, Stork, Pentstemon & Audacity* [& 802 Sqdn (RN)]	34-12 N, 13-35 W
18 Dec	U 434	Heyda	HMS *Stanley* & *Blankney*	36-15 N, 15-48 W
19 Dec	U 574	Gengelbach	HMS *Stork*	38-12 N, 17-23 W
21 Dec	U 451	Hoffmann	Br. Sqdn. 812	35-55 N, 06-08 W
21 Dec	U 567	Endrass	HMS *Deptford* & *Samphire*	† 44-02 N, 20-10 W
20 Dec	U 79	Kaufmann	HMS *Hasty* & *Hotspur*	32-15 N, 25-19 E
28 Dec	U 75	Ringelmann	HMS *Kipling*	31-50 N, 26-40 E
1942				
9 Jan	U 577	Schauenburg	Br. Sqdn. 230	† 32-22 N, 26-54 E
12 Jan	U 374	v. Fischel	HM Sub. *Unbeaten*	37-50 N, 16-00 E
15 Jan	U 93	Elfe	HMS *Hesperus*	36-40 N, 15-52 W
2 Feb	U 581	Pfeiffer	HMS *Westcott*	39-00 N, 30-00 W
6 Feb	U 82	Rollmann	HMS *Rochester* & *Tamarisk*	† 44-10 N, 23-52 W
1 Mar	U 656	Kröning	VP-82	† 46-15 N, 53-15 W
14 Mar	U 133	Mohr	Mine (her own?)	† 38-00 N, 24-00 W
15 Mar	U 503	Gerhicke	VP-82	† 45-50 N, 48-50 W
24 Mar	U 655	Dumrese	HMS *Sharpshooter*	† 73-00 N, 21-00 W
27 Mar	U 587	Borcherdt	HMS *Leamington, Grove, Aldenham & Volunteer*	† 47-21 N, 21-39 W

*(HMS *Graph* from '42)

Date	U-Boat	Last Comdr.	Cause of sinking	Position
29 Mar	U 585	Lohse	HMS *Fury*	† 72-15 N, 34-22
— Apr	U 702	v. Rabenau	Unknown	† North Sea (?)
14 Apr	U 85	Greger	*Roper (DD-147)*	† 35-55 N, 75-13
14 Apr	U 252	Lerchen	HMS *Stork & Vetch*	† 47-00 N, 18-14
1 May	U 573	Heinsohn	Br. Sqdn. 233	(†)37-00 N, 01-00
2 May	U 74	Friederich	HMS *Wishart, Wrestler* & Br. Sqdn. 202	† 37-32 N, 00-10
9 May	U 352	Rathke	USCGC *Icarus (WPC-110)*	34-12 N, 76-35
28 May	U 568	Preuss	HMS *Eridge, Hero* & *Hurworth*	32-42 N, 24-53
2 Jun	U 652	Fraatz	Br. Sqdn. 815 & 203	31-55 N, 25-13
13 Jun	U 157	Henne	USCGC *Thetis (WPC-115)*	† 24-13 N, 82-03
30 Jun	U 158	Rostin	VP-74	† 32-50 N, 67-28
3 Jul	U 215	Höckner	HMS *Le Tiger*	† 41-48 N, 66-38
5 Jul	U 502	v. Rosenstiel	Br. Sqdn. 172	† 46-10 N, 06-40 W
6 Jul } 13 Jul	U 153	Reichmann	{ US Army Bomb. Sqdn. 59 & *Lansdowne* (DD-486)	12-50 N, 72-20 W † 09-56 N, 81-29 W
7 Jul	U 701	Degen	US Army Bomb. Sqdn. 396	34-50 N, 74-55 W
11 Jul	U 136	Zimmermann	HMS *Spey, Pelican* & RF *Léopard*	† 33-30 N, 22-52 W
15 Jul	U 576	Heinicke	VS-9 & Amer. MS *Unicoi*	† 34-51 N, 75-22 W
17 Jul	U 751	Bigalk	Br. Sqdn. 502 & 61	† 45-15 N, 12-22 W
24 Jul	U 90	Oldörp	HMCS *St. Croix*	† 48-12 N, 40-56 W
31 Jul	U 213	v. Varendorff	HMS *Erne, Rochester* & *Sandwich*	† 36-45 N, 22-50 W
31 Jul	U 588	Vogel	HMCS *Wetaskiwin & Skeena*	† 49-59 N, 36-36 W
31 Jul	U 754	Oestermann	RCAF Sqdn. 113	† 43-02 N, 64-52 W
1 Aug	U 166	Kuhlmann	USCG Sqdn. 212	† 28-37 N, 90-45 W
3 Aug	U 335	Pelkner	HM Sub. *Saracen*	62-48 N, 00-12 W
4 Aug	U 372	Neumann	HMS *Sikh, Zulu, Croome, Tetcott* & Br. Sqdn. 221	32-00 N, 34-00 E
6 Aug	U 210	Lemcke	HMCS *Assiniboine*	54-25 N, 39-37 W
8 Aug	U 379	Kettner	HMS *Dianthus*	57-11 N, 30-57 W
10 Aug	U 578	Rehwinkel	Czech Sqdn. 311	† 45-59 N, 07-44 W
20 Aug	U 464	Harms	VP-73	61-25 N, 14-40 W
22 Aug	U 654	Forster	US Army Bomb. Sqdn. 45	† 12-00 N, 79-56 W
28 Aug	U 94	Ites	HMCS *Oakville* & VP-92	17-40 N, 74-30 W
2 Sep	U 222	v. Jessen	Collision	54-25 N, 19-50 E
3 Sep	U 756	Harney	Br. A/C	† 57-30 N, 29-00 W
3 Sep	U 705	Horn	Br. Sqdn. 77	† 47-55 N, 10-04 W
3 Sep	U 162	Wattenberg	HMS *Vimy, Pathfinder* & *Quentin*	12-21 N, 59-29 W
12 Sep	U 589*	Horrer	HMS *Faulknor*	† 75-04 N, 04-49 E
14 Sep	U 88*	Bohmann	HMS *Onslow*	† 75-40 N, 20-32 E
15 Sep	U 261	Lange	Br. Sqdn. 58	† 59-49 N, 09-28 W

* Latest British study transposes these two sinkings also.

Date	U-Boat	Last Comdr.	Cause of sinking	Position
16 Sep	U 457	Brandenburg	HMS *Impulsive*	† 75-05 N, 43-15 E
23 Sep	U 253	Friedrichs	Br. Sqdn. 210	† 68-19 N, 13-50 W
27 Sep	U 165	Hoffmann	Mine & Sqdn. 825	† 47-50 N, 03-22 W
2 Oct	U 512	Schultze	US Army Bomb. Sqdn. 99	06-50 N, 52-25 W
8 Oct	U 582	Schulte	Br. Sqdn. 209	† 06-41 N, 22-38 W
8 Oct	U 179	Sobe	HMS *Active*	† 33-28 N, 17-05 E
9 Oct	U 171	Pfeffer	Mine	47-30 N, 03-30 W
12 Oct	U 597	Bopst	Br. Sqdn. 120	† 56-50 N, 28-05 W
15 Oct	U 661	v. Lilienfeld	Br. Sqdn. 120	† 53-58 N, 33-43 W
15 Oct	U 619	Makowski	HMS *Viscount*	† 53-42 N, 35-56 W
16 Oct	U 353	Römer	HMS *Fame*	53-54 N, 29-30 W
20 Oct	U 216	Schultz	Br. Sqdn. 224	† 48-21 N, 19-25 W
22 Oct	U 412	Jahrmärker	Br. Sqdn. 179	† 63-55 N, 00-24 W
24 Oct	U 599	Breithaupt	Br. Sqdn. 224	† 46-07 N, 17-40 W
27 Oct	U 627	Kindelbacher	Br. Sqdn. 206	† 59-14 N, 22-49 W
30 Oct	U 520	Schwartzkopf	RCAF Sqdn. 10	† 47-47 N, 49-50 W
30 Oct	U 559	Heidtmann	HMS *Pakenham, Petard, Hero, Dulverton, Hurworth* & Br. A/C	32-30 N, 33-00 E
30 Oct	U 658	Senkel	RCAF Sqdn. 145	† 50-32 N, 46-32 W
[20] Oct	U 116	Grimme	[VP-74]?	† Atlantic
5 Nov	U 132	Vogelsang	Br. Sqdn. 120	† 58-08 N, 33-13 W
5 Nov	U 408	v. Hymmen	VP-84	† 67-40 N, 18-32 W
12 Nov	U 272	Hepp	Collision	Baltic (off Hela)
12 Nov	U 660	Baur	HMS *Lotus* & *Starwort*	36-07 N, 01-00 W
13 Nov	U 605	Schütze	HMS *Lotus* & *Poppy*	† 37-04 N, 02-55 E
14[15?]Nov	U 595	Quaet-Faslem	Br. Sqdn. 500 [dmgd, bchd, scuttle]	36-38 N, 00-30 E
15[14?]Nov	U 259	Köpke	Br. Sqdn. 500	† 37-20 N, 03-05 E
16 Nov	U 173	Schweichel	*Woolsey (DD-437), Swanson (DD-443)* & *Quick (DD-490)*	† 33-40 N, 07-35 W
17 Nov	U 331	v. Tiesenhausen	HMS *Formidable's* Sqdn. 820 & Br. Sqdn. 500*	37-05 N, 02-24 E
19 Nov	U 98	Eichmann	Br. Sqdn. 608	† 35-38 N, 11-48 W
20 Nov	U 184	Dangschat	HNMS *Potentilla*	† 49-25 N, 45-25 W
21 Nov	U 517	Hartwig	HMS *Victorious'* Sqdn. 817	46-16 N, 17-09 W
15 Nov	U 411	Spindlegger	HMS *Wrestler*	† 36-09 N, 07-42 E
8 Dec	U 254	Gilardone	Br. Sqdn. 120, after collision with another U-boat (sunk by HMS *Wrestler?*)	57-25 N, 35-19 W
10 Dec	U 611	v. Jacobs	VP-84	† 58-09 N, 22-44 W
15 Dec	U 626	Bade	USCGC *Ingham*	† 56-46 N, 27-12 W
26 Dec	U 357	Kellner	HMS *Hesperus* & *Vanessa*	57-10 N, 15-40 W
27 Dec	U 356	Ruppelt	HMCS *St. Laurent, Chilliwack, Battleford, Napanee* & *St. John*	† 45-30 N, 25-40 W

* - Damaged by and surrendered to Sqdn. 500, but signals not seen by 820 Sqdn., who then sank her.

Date	U-Boat	Last Comdr.	Cause of sinking	Position
1943				
6 Jan	U 164	Fechner	VP-83	01-58 S, 39-23 W
13 Jan	U 224	Kosbadt	HMCS *Ville de Quebec*	36-28 N, 00-49 E
13 Jan	U 507	Schacht	VP-83	† 01-38 S, 39-52 W
15 Jan	U 337	Ruwiedel	Br. Sqdn. 206	† 57-40 N, 27-10 W
21 Jan	U 301	Körner	HM Sub. *Sahib*	41-27 N, 07-04 E
— Jan	U 553	Thurmann	Unknown	† 53-00 N, 33-00 W
3 Feb	U 265	Aufhammer	Br. Sqdn. 220	† 56-35 N, 22-49 W
4 Feb	U 187	Münnich	HMS *Vimy & Beverley*	50-12 N, 36-34 W
7 Feb	U 609	Rudloff	RF *Lobelia*	† 55-17 N, 26-38 W
7 Feb	U 624	v. Soden-Fraunhofen	Br. Sqdn. 220	† 55-42 N, 26-17 W
10 Feb	U 519	Eppen	US Army A/S Sqdn. 2	† 47-05 N, 18-34 W
12 Feb	U 442	Hesse	Br. Sqdn. 48	† 37-32 N, 11-56 W
14 Feb	U 620	Stein	Br. Sqdn. 202	† 39-27 N, 11-34 W
15 Feb	U 529	Fraatz	Br. Sqdn. 120	† 55-45 N, 31-09 W
17 Feb	U 201	Rosenberg	HMS *Fame*	† 50-36 N, 41-07 W
17 Feb	U 69	Gräf	HMS *Viscount*	† 50-50 N, 40-50 W
17 Feb	U 205	Bürgel	HMS *Paladin* & RSAAF Sqdn. 15	32-56 N, 22-01 W
19 Feb	U 562	Hamm	HMS *Isis, Hursley* & Br. A/C	† 32-57 N, 20-54 E
19 Feb	U 268	Heydemann	Br. Sqdn. 172	† 47-03 N, 05-56 W
21 Feb	U 623	Schröder	RAF Sqdn. 120 (A/C torp.)	† 48-68 N, 29-15 W
21 Feb	U 225	Leimkühler	USCGC *Spencer (WPG-36)*	† 51-25 N, 27-28 W
22 Feb	U 606	Döhler	USCGC *Campbell* & ORP *Burza*	47-44 N, 33-43 W
23 Feb	U 522	Schneider	HMS *Totland*	† 31-27 N, 26-22 W
23 Feb	U 443	v. Puttkamer	HMS *Bicester, Lamerton & Wheatland*	† 36-55 N, 02-25 E
24 Feb	U 649	Tiesler	Collision with *U 232*	
4 Mar	U 83	Wörishoffer	RAF Sqdn. 500	† 37-10 N, 00-05 E
4 Mar	U 87	Berger	HMCS *Shediac & St. Croix*	† 41-36 N, 13-31 W
7 Mar	U 633	Müller	Br. Sqdn. 220	† 57-14 N, 26-30 W
8 Mar	U 156	Hartenstein	VP-53	† 12-38 N, 54-39 W
11 Mar	U 432	Eckhardt	RF *Aconit*	51-35 N, 28-20 W
11 Mar	U 444	Langfeld	HMS *Harvester* & RF *Aconit*	51-14 N, 29-18 W
12 Mar	U 130	Keller	*Champlin (DD-601)*	† 37-10 N, 40-21 W
19 Mar	U 5	Rahn	Collision	54-25 N, 19-50 E
20 Mar	U 384	v. Rosenberg-Gruszcynski	Br. Sqdn. 201	† 54-18 N, 26-15 W
21 Mar	U 163	Engelmann	*Herring (SS-233)*	† 44-13 N, 08-23 W (lv. Lorient, 3-10)
22 Mar	U 665	Haupt	Br. Sqdn. 172	† 46-47 N, 09-58 W
22 Mar	U 524	v. Steinaecker	US Army A/S Sqdn. 1	† 30-15 N, 18-13 W
25 Mar	U 469	Claussen	Br. Sqdn. 206	† 62-12 N, 16-40 W
27 Mar	U 169	Bauer	Br. Sqdn. 206	† 60-54 N, 15-25 W
28 Mar	U 77	Hartmann	Br. Sqdns. 233 & 48	37-42 N, 00-10 E
2 Apr	U 124	Mohr	HMS *Stonecrop & Black Swan*	† 41-02 N, 15-39 W

Date	U-Boat	Last Comdr.	Cause of sinking	Position
6 Apr	U 167	Sturm	Br. Sqdn. 233 (5 Apr; scuttled, 6th)	27-47 N, 15-00 W
6 Apr	U 635	Eckelmann	HMS *Tay*	† 58-25 N, 19-22 W
6 Apr	U 632	Karpf	Br. Sqdn. 86	† 58-02 N, 28-42 W
7 Apr	U 644	Jensen	HM Sub. *Tuna*	† 69-38 N, 05-40 W
10 Apr	U 376	Marks	Br. Sqdn. 172	† 46-48 N, 09-00 W
14 Apr	U 526	Möglich	Mine	47-30 N, 03-45 W
17 Apr	U 175	Bruns	USCGC *Spencer (WPG-36)*	48-50 N, 21-20 W
23 Apr	U 602	Schüler	Br. Sqdn. 500 (off Oran)	(†) Mediterranean
23 Apr	U 189	Kurrer	Br. Sqdn. 120	† 59-50 N, 34-43 W
23 Apr	U 191	Fiehn	HMS *Hesperus*	† 56-45 N, 34-25 W
24 Apr	U 710	v. Carlowitz	Br. Sqdn. 206	† 61-25 N, 19-48 W
25 Apr	U 203	Kottmann	HMS *Biter's* Sqdn. 811 HMS *Pathfinder*	55-05 N, 42-25 W
27 Apr	U 174	Grandefeld	VP-125	43-35 N, 56-18 W
30 Apr	U 227	Kuntze	RAAF Sqdn. 455	† 64-05 N, 06-40 W
2 May	U 332	Hüttemann	RAAF Sqdn. 461	† 44-48 N, 08-58 W
3 May	U 659	Stock	Collision with *U-439*	43-32 N, 13-20 W
3 May	U 439	v.Tippelskirch	Collision with *U 659*	43-32 N, 13-20 W
4 May	U 630	Winkler	RCAF Sqdn. 5	† 56-38 N, 42-32 W
7 May	U 465	Wolf	RAAF Sqdn. 10	† 47-06 N, 10-58 W
5 May	U 192	Happe	HMS *Pink*	† 54-56 N, 43-44 W
5 May	U 638	Staudinger	HMS *Loosestrife*	† 53-06 N, 45-02 W
6 May	U 125	Folkers	HMS *Vidette*	† 52-31 N, 44-50 W
6 May	U 531	Neckel	HMS *Oribi*	† 52-31 N, 44-50 W
6 May	U 438	Heinsohn	HMS *Pelican*	† 52-00 N, 45-10 W
7 May	U 447	Bothe	Br. Sqdn. 233	† 35-30 N, 11-55 W
4 May	U 109	Schramm	Br. Sqdn. 86	† 47-22 N, 22-40 W
7 May	U 663	Schmid	Br. Sqdn. 58	† 46-33 N, 11-12 W
11 May	U 528	v. Rabenau	HMS *Fleetwood* & Br. Sqdn. 58	46-55 N, 14-44 W
12[14?]May	U 186	Hesemann	HMS *Hesperus*	† 41-54 N, 31-49 W
12[14]May	U 89	Lohmann	HMS *Biter's* Sqdn. 811, HMS *Broadway* & *Lagan*	† 46-30 N, 25-40 W
13 May	U 456	Teichert	HMS *Lagan*, HMS *Drumheller* & Br. Sqdn. 423	† 48-37 N, 22-39 W
14 May	U 266	v. Jessen	Br. Sqdn. 86	† 47-45 N, 26-57 W
14 May	U 640*	Nagel	VP-84	† 60-10 N, 31-52 W
15 May	U 753	v. Mannstein	Unknown	† 47-00 N, 22-00 W
15 May	U 176	Dierksen	VS-62 & Cuban *SC-13*	† 23-21 N, 80-18 W
15 May	U 463	Wolfbauer	Br. Sqdn. 58	† 45-28 N, 10-20 W
16[15]May	U 182	Clausen	*Mackenzie (DD-614)*	† 33-55 N, 20-35 W
17[28?]May	U 128	Steinert	VP-74, *Moffet (DD-362)* & *Jouett (DD-396)*	10-00 S, 35-35 W
17 May	U 657*	Göllnitz	HMS *Swale*	† 58-54 N, 42-33 W
17 May	U 646	Wulff	Br. Sqdn. 269	† 62-10 N, 14-30 W
19 May	U 954	Löwe	Br. Sqdn. 120	† 55-09 N, 35-18 W
19 May	U 209	Brodda	HMS *Jed* & *Sennen*	† 54-54 N, 34-19 W
19 May	U 273	Rossmann	Br. Sqdn. 269	† 59-25 N, 24-33 W

* Br. Admiralty advises *U 640* and *657* should be transposed.

Date	U-Boat	Last Comdr.	Cause of sinking	Position
19 May	U 381	v. Pückler u. Limpurg	HMS *Duncan & Snowflake*	† 54-41 N, 34-45 W
20 May	U 258	v. Mäszen-hausen	Br. Sqdn. 120	† 55-18 N, 27-49 W
21 May	U 303	Heine	HM Sub. *Sickle*	42-50 N, 06-00 E
22 May	U 569	Johannsen	VC-9 from *Bogue (CVE-9)*	50-40 N, 35-21 W
23 May	U 752	Schröter	HMS *Archer's* A/C	51-40 N, 29-49 W
25 May	U 414	Huth	HMS *Vetch*	† 36-31 N, 00-40 E
26 May	U 467	Kummer	VP-84	† 62-25 N, 14-52 W
26 May	U 436	Seibicke	HMS *Test & Hyderabad*	† 43-49 N, 15-56 W
28 May	U 304	Koch	Br. Sqdn. 120	† 54-50 N, 37-20 W
28 May	U 755	Göing	Br. Sqdn. 608	39-58 N, 01-41 E
31 May	U 563	Borchardt	Br. Sqdn. 58 & 228 & RAAF Sqdn. 10	† 46-35 N, 10-40 W
31 May	U 440	Schwaff	Br. Sqdns. 201	† 45-38 N, 13-04 W
1 Jun	U 202	Poser	HMS *Starling*	56-12 N, 39-52 W
1 Jun	U 418	Lange	Br. Sqdn. 236	† 47-05 N, 08-55 W
2 Jun	U 105	Nissen	Fr. Sqdn. 141	† 14-15 N, 17-35 W
2 Jun	U 521	Bargsten	*PC-565*	37-43 N, 73-16 W
4 Jun	U 308	Mühlenpfordt	HM Sub. *Truculent*	† 64-28 N, 03-09 W
4 Jun	U 594	Mumm	Br. Sqdn. 48	† 35-55 N, 09-25 W
5 Jun	U 217	Reichenbach-Klinke	VC-9 from *Bogue (CVE-9)*	† 30-18 N, 42-50 W
11 Jun	U 417	Schreiner	Br. Sqdn. 206	† 63-20 N, 10-30 W
12 Jun	U 118	Cygan	VC-9 from *Bogue (CVE-9)*	30-49 N, 33-49 W
14 Jun	U 334	Ehrich	HMS *Jed & Pelican*	† 58-16 N, 28-20 W
14 Jun	U 564	Fiedler	Br. Sqdn. 10	44-17 N, 10-25 W
16 Jun	U 97	Trox	RAAF Sqdn. 459	33-00 N, 34-00 E
20 Jun	U 388	Sues	VP-84	† 57-36 N, 31-20 W
24 Jun	U 119	v. Kameke	HMS *Starling*	† 45-00 N, 11-59 W
24 Jun	U 194	Hesse	Br. Sqdn. 120	† 58-15 N, 25-25 W
24 Jun	U 200	Schonder	VP-84	† 59-00 N, 26-18 W
24 Jun	U 449	Otto	HMS *Wren, Woodpecker, Kite & Wild Goose*	† 45-00 N, 11-59 W
3 Jul	U 126	Kietz	Br. Sqdn. 172	† 46-02 N, 11-23 W
3 Jul	U 628	Hasenschar	Br. Sqdn. 224	† 44-11 N, 08-45 W
5 Jul	U 535	Ellmenreich	Br. Sqdn. 53	† 43-38 N, 09-13 W
7 Jul	U 951	Pressel	US Army A/S Sqdn. 1	† 37-40 N, 15-30 W
8 Jul	U 514	Auffermann	Br. Sqdn. 224	† 43-37 N, 08-59 W
8 Jul	U 232	Ziehm	US Army A/S Sqdn. 2	† 40-37 N, 13-41 W
9 Jul	U 435	Strelow	Br. Sqdn. 179	† 39-48 N, 14-22 W
9 Jul	U 590	Kruer	VP-94	† 03-22 N, 48-38 W
12 Jul	U 409	Massmann	HMS *Inconstant*	37-12 N, 04-00 E
12 Jul	U 506	Würdemann	US Army A/S Sqdn. 1	42-30 N, 16-30 W
12 Jul	U 561	Henning	HM *MTB-81*	38-16 N, 15-39 E
13 Jul	U 607	Jeschonnek	Br. Sqdn. 228	45-02 N, 09-14 W
13 Jul	U 487	Metz	VC-13 from *Core (CVE-13)*	27-15 N, 34-18 W
14 Jul	U 160	v. Pommer-Esche	VC-29 from *Santee (CVE-29)*	† 33-54 N, 27-13 W
15 Jul	U 159	Beckmann	VP-32	† 15-58 N, 73-44 W
15 Jul	U 135	Luther	HMS *Rochester, Mignonette & Balsam* & VP-92	28-20 N, 13-17 W

Date	U-Boat	Last Comdr.	Cause of sinking	Position
15 Jul	U 509	Witte	VC-29 from *Santee* (*CVE-29*)	† 34-02 N, 26-02 W
16 Jul	U 67	Müller-Stöckheim	VC-13 from *Core* (*CVE-13*)	30-05 N, 44-17 W
19 Jul	U 513	Guggenberger	VP-74	27-17 S, 47-32 W
20 Jul	U 558	Krech	US Army A/S Sqdn. 19	45-10 N, 09-42 W
21 Jul	U 662	Müller	VP-94	03-56 N, 48-46 W
23 Jul	U 527	Uhlig	VC-9 from *Bogue* (*CVE-9*)	35-25 N, 27-56 W
23 Jul	U 613	Köppe	*Badger* (*DD-126*)	† 35-32 N, 28-36 W
23 Jul	U 598	Holtorf	VB-107	04-05 S, 33-23 W
24 Jul	U 459	v.Wilamowitz-Möllendorf	Br. Sqdn. 172	45-53 N, 10-38 W
24 Jul	U 622	Karpf	US Army air raid	63-27 N, 10-23 E
26 Jul	U 759	Friedrich	VP-32	† 18-06 N, 75-00 W
28 Jul	U 359	Förster	VP-32	† 15-57 N, 68-30 W
28 Jul	U 404	Schönberg	US Army A/S Sqdn. 4 & Br. Sqdn. 224	† 45-53 N, 09-25 W
29 Jul	U 614	Sträter	Br. Sqdn. 172	† 46-42 N, 11-03 W
30 Jul	U 591	Ziesmer	VB-127	08-36 S, 34-34 W
30 Jul	U 504	Luis	HMS *Kite, Woodpecker, Wren, Wild Goose*	† 45-33 N, 10-47 W
30 Jul	U 43	Schwandtke	VC-29 from *Santee* (*CVE-29*)	34-57 N, 35-11 W
30 Jul	U 461	Stiebler	RAAF Sqdn. 461	45-42 N, 11-00 W
30 Jul	U 462	Vowe	Br. Sqdn. 502	45-08 N, 10-57 W
30 Jul	U 375	Koenenkamp	*PC-624*	† 36-40 N, 12-28 E
31 Jul	U 199	Kraus	VP-74 & Brazilian A/C	23-54 S, 42-54 W
1 Aug	U 383	Kremser	Br. Sqdn. 228	† 47-24 N, 12-10 W
1 Aug	U 454	Hackländer	RAAF Sqdn. 10	45-36 N, 10-23 W
2 Aug	U 706	v. Zitzewitz	US Army A/S Sqdn. 4	46-15 N, 10-25 W
2 Aug	U 106	Damerow	RAAF Sqdn. 461 & Br. Sqdn. 228	46-35 N, 11-55 W
3 Aug	U 572	Kummetat	VP-205	† 11-35 N, 54-05 W
3 Aug	U 647	Hertin	Unknown	(†) Iceland-Faroes
4 Aug	U 489	Schmandt	RCAF Sqdn. 423	61-11 N, 14-38 W
5 Aug	U 34	Aust	Collision with Ger. sub-tender *Lech*	Off Memel
7 Aug	U 615	Kapitzky	VP-205, VP-204, VB-130 & US Army Bomb. Sqdn. 10	12-57 N, 64-34 W
7 Aug	U 117	Neumann	VC-1 from *Card* (*CVE-11*)	† 39-32 N, 38-21 W
9 Aug	U 664	Graef	VC-1 from *Card* (*CVE-11*)	40-12 N, 37-29 W
11 Aug[3?]	U 604	Höltring	Scuttled as result of attacks by VB-129, VB-107 & *Moffet* (*DD-362*)	05-00 S, 20-00 W [9-10 S, 29-43 W]
11 Aug	U 468	Schamong	Br. Sqdn. 200	12-20 N, 20-07 W
11 Aug	U 525	Drewitz	VC-1 from *Card* (*CVE-11*)	† 41-29 N, 38-55 W
17 Aug	U 403	Heine	Br. Sqdn. 200 & Fr. Sqdn. 697	14-11 N, 17-40 W
20 Aug	U 197	Bartels	Br. Sqdn. 265 & 259	† 28-40 S, 42-36 E
21 Aug	U 670	Hyronimus	Collision	Baltic
22 Aug	U 458	Diggins	HMS *Easton* & HHMS *Pindos*	36-25 N, 12-39 E

223

Date	U-Boat	Last Comdr.	Cause of sinking	Position
24 Aug	U 134	Brosin	Br. Sqdn. 179	† 42-07 N, 09-30 W
24[30?]Aug	U 185	Maus	VC-13 from *Core (CVE-13)*	27-00 N, 37-06 W
24[26?]Aug	U 84	Uphoff	VC-13 from *Core (CVE-13)*	† 27-09 N, 37-03 W
25 Aug	U 523	Pietzsch	HMS *Wanderer &*	42-03 N, 18-02 W
			Wallflower	
27 Aug	U 847	Kuppisch	VC-1 from *Card (CVE-11)*	† 28-19 N, 37-58 W
30 Aug	U 634	Dahlhaus	HMS *Stork & Stonecrop*	† 40-13 N, 19-24 W
30 Aug	U 639	Wichmann	Russian Sub. *S-101*	† Kara Sea
7 Sep	U 669	Köhl	RCAF Sqdn. 407	† 45-36 N, 10-13 W
8 Sep	U 983	Reimers	Collision	Baltic
8 Sep	U 760	Blum	Damaged by HMS	Interned in Spain;
			Wellington's Sqdn. 179	surrendered in '45
11[12?]Sep	U 617	Brandi	Br. Sqdn. 179,	35-38 N, 03-27 W
			HMS *Hyacinth, Haarlem*	
			& HMAS Woolongong	
19 Sep	U 341	Epp	RCAF Sqdn. 10	† 58-40 N, 25-30 W
20 Sep	U 338	Kinzel	Br. Sqdn. 120	† 57-40 N, 29-48 W
20 Sep	U 346	Leisten	Marine casualty	† 54-25 N, 19-50 E
			(diving accident)	
22 Sep	U 229	Schetelig	HMS *Keppel*	† 54-36 N, 36-25 W
27 Sep	U 161	Achilles	VP-74	† 12-30 S, 35-35 W
27 Sep	U 221	Trojer	Br. Sqdn. 58	† 47-00 N, 18-00 W
4 Oct	U 279	Finke	Br. Sqdn. 120	† 60-51 N, 28-26 W
4 Oct	U 336	Hunger	VB-128	† 60-40 N, 26-30 W
4 Oct	U 422	Poeschel	VC-9 from *Card (CVE-11)*	† 43-18 N, 28-58 W
4 Oct	U 460	Schnorr	VC-9 from *Card (CVE-11)*	43-13 N, 28-58 W
5 Oct	U 389	Heilmann	Br. Sqdn. 269	† 62-43 N, 27-17 W
8 Oct	U 643	Speidel	Br. Sqdn. 86 & 120	56-14 N, 26-55 W
8 Oct	U 610	v. Freyberg	RCAF Sqdn. 423	† 55-45 N, 24-33 W
8 Oct	U 419	Giersberg	Br. Sqdn. 86	56-31 N, 27-05 W
13 Oct	U 402	v. Forstner	VC-9 from *Card (CVE-11)*	† 18-56 N, 29-41 W
16 Oct	U 470	Grave	Br. Sqdn. 59 & 120	58-20 N, 29-20 W
16 Oct	U 533	Hennig	Br. Sqdn. 244	25-28 S, 56-50 E
16 Oct	U 844	Möller	Br. Sqdns. 86 & 59	† 58-30 N, 27-16 W
16 Oct	U 964	Hummer	Br. Sqdn. 86	† 57-27 N, 28-17 W
17 Oct	U 631	Krüger	HMS *Sunflower*	† 58-13 N, 32-29 W
17 Oct	U 841	Bender	HMS *Byard*	59-57 N, 31-06 W
17 Oct	U 540	Kasch	Br. Sqdns. 59 & 120	† 58-38 N, 31-56 W
20 Oct	U 378	Mäder	VC-13 from *Core (CVE-13)*	47-40 N, 28-27 W
23 Oct	U 274	Jordan	HMS *Duncan, Vidette &*	† 57-14 N, 27-50 W
			Br. Sqdn. 224	
24 Oct	U 566	Hornkohl	Br. Sqdn. 179	41-12 N, 09-31 W
26 Oct	U 420	Reese	RCAF Sqdn. 10	† 50-49 N, 41-01 W
28 Oct	U 220	Barber	VC-1 from *Block Island*	† 48-53 N, 33-30 W
			(CVE-106)	
29 Oct	U 282	Müller	HMS *Vidette, Duncan &*	† 55-28 N, 31-57 W
			Sunflower	
30 Oct	U 431	Schöneboom	HM Sub. *Ultimatum*	† 43-04 N, 05-57 E
31 Oct	U 306	v. Trotha	HMS *Whitehall & Geranium*	† 46-19 N, 20-44 W
31 Oct	U 584	Deecke	VC-9 from *Card (CVE-11)*	† 49-14 N, 31-55 W
31 Oct	U 732	Carlsen	HMS *Imperialist & Douglas*	35-54 N, 05-52 W

Date	U-Boat	Last Comdr.	Cause of sinking	Position
1 Nov	U 340	Klaus	HMS *Fleetwood, Active, Witherington* & Br. Sqdn. 179	35-33 N, 06-37 W
1 Nov	U 405	Hopmann	*Borie (DD-215)*	† 49-00 N, 31-14 W
5 Nov	U 848	Rollmann	VB-107 & US Army 1st Compron	10-09 S, 18-00 W
6 Nov	U 226	Gange	HMS *Starling, Woodcock* & *Kite*	† 44-49 N, 41-13 W
6 Nov	U 842	Heller	HMS *Starling* & *Wild Goose*	† 43-42 N, 42-08 W
9 Nov	U 707	Gretschel	Br. Sqdn. 220	† 40-31 N, 20-17 W
10 Nov	U 966	Wolf	VB-103, VB-110 & Czech Sqdn. 311	44-00 N, 08-30 W
12 Nov	U 508	Staats	VB-103	† 46-00 N, 07-30 W
16 Nov	U 280	Hungers-hausen	Br. Sqdn. 86	† 49-11 N, 27-32 W
18 Nov	U 718	Wieduwilt	Collision	Baltic
19 Nov	U 211	Hause	Br. Sqdn. 179	† 40-15 N, 19-18 W
20 Nov	U 536	Schauenburg	HMS *Nene, Snowberry* & HMCS *Calgary*	43-50 N, 19-39 W
20 Nov	U 768	Buttjer	Collision	Baltic
21 Nov	U 538	Gossler	HMS *Foley* & *Crane*	† 45-40 N, 19-35 W
23 Nov	U 648	Stahl	HMS *Bazley, Blackwood* & *Drury*	† 42-40 N, 20-37 W
25 Nov	U 849	Schultze	VB-107	† 06-30 S, 05-40 W
25 Nov	U 600	Zurmühlen	HMS *Bazley* & *Blackwood*	† 40-31 N, 22-07 W
28 Nov	U 542	Coester	Br. Sqdn. 179	† 39-03 N, 16-25 W
29 Nov	U 86	Schug	VC-19 from *Bogue (CVE-9)*	† 39-33 N, 19-01 W
13[12?]Dec	U 172	Hoffmann	VC-19 from *Bogue (CVE-9), George E. Badger (AVD-3), DuPont (DD-152), Clemson (DD-186 & George W. Ingram (DE-62)*	26-19 N, 29-58 W
13 Dec	U 345	Knackfuss	Mine	† 54-06 N, 12-09 E
13 Dec	U 391	Dültgen	Br. Sqdn. 53	† 45-45 N, 09-38 W
13 Dec	U 593	Kelbling	*Wainwright (DD-419),* HMS *Calpe*	37-38 N, 05-58 E
16 Dec	U 73	Deckert	*Woolsey (DD-437)* & *Trippe (DD-403)*	36-07 N, 00-50 W
20 Dec	U 850	Ewerth	VC-19 from *Bogue (CVE-9)*	† 32-54 N, 37-01 W
21 Dec	U 284	Scholz	Scuttled	55-04 N, 30-23 W
24 Dec	U 645	Ferro	*Schenck (DD-159)*	† 45-20 N, 21-40 W
1944				
8 Jan	U 426	Reich	RAAF Sqdn. 10	† 46-47 N, 10-42 W
8 Jan	U 757	Deetz	HMS *Bayntun* & HMCS *Camrose*	† 50-33 N, 18-03 W
9 Jan	U 81	Krieg	US Army A/C	Pola
9 Jan	UIT 19	-(unknown)-	US Army A/C	Pola
13 Jan	U 231	Wenzel	Br. Sqdn. 172	44-15 N, 20-38 W
— Jan	U 377	Kluth	Unknown	(†) Atlantic
16 Jan	U 544	Mattke	VC-13 from *Guadalcanal (CVE-60)*	† 40-30 N, 37-20 W

Date	U-Boat	Last Comdr.	Cause of sinking	Position
17 Jan	U 305	Bahr	HMS *Wanderer & Glenarm*	† 49-39 N, 20-10 W
19 Jan	U 641	Rendtel	HMS *Violet*	† 50-25 N, 18-49 W
— Jan	U 972	König	Unknown	† Atlantic
20 Jan	U 263	Nölke	Mine	† 46-10 N, 01-14 W
28 Jan	U 571	Lüssow	RAAF Sqdn. 461	† 52-41 N, 14-27 W
28 Jan	U 271	Barleben	VB-103	† 53-15 N, 15-52 W
30 Jan	U 314	Basse	HMS *Whitehall & Meteor*	† 73-45 N, 26-15 E
30 Jan	U 364	Sass	Br. Sqdn. 172	† 45-25 N, 05-15 W
31 Jan	U 592	Jaschke	HMS *Starling, Wild Goose &* *Magpie*	† 50-20 N, 17-29 W
4 Feb	U 854	Weiher	Mine	53-55 N, 14-17 E
6 Feb	U 177	Buchholz	VB-107	10-35 S, 23-15 W
8 Feb	U 762	Pietschmann	HMS *Woodpecker, (Wild* *Goose & Starling)*	† 49-02 N, 16-58 W
9 Feb	U 238	Hepp	HMS *Kite, Magpie & Starling*	† 49-44 N, 16-07 W
9 Feb	U 734	Blauert	HMS *Wild Goose & Starling*	† 49-43 N, 16-23 W
10 Feb	U 545	Mannesmann	Br. Sqdn. 612	58-17 N, 13-22 W
10 Feb	U 666	Willberg	HMS *Fencer's* A/C	† 53-56 N, 17-16 W
11 Feb	U 424	Lüders	HMS *Wild Goose &* *Woodpecker*	† 50-00 N, 18-14 W
11 Feb	U 283	Ney	RCAF Sqdn. 407	† 60-45 N, 12-50 W
14 Feb	U 738	Hoffmann	Diving accident	54-31 N, 18-33 E
14 Feb	UIT 23	Striegler	HM Sub. *Tally Ho*	† 04-25 N, 100-09 E
18 Feb	U 406	Dieterichs	HMS *Spey*	† 48-32 N, 23-36 W
18 Feb	U 7	Loeschke	Collision	54-25 N, 19-50 E
19 Feb	U 264	Looks	HMS *Woodpecker & Starling*	48-31 N, 22-05 W
19 Feb	U 386	Albrecht	HMS *Spey*	48-51 N, 22-41 W
24 Feb	U 257	Rahe	HMCS *Waskesiu*	47-19 N, 26-00 W
24 Feb	U 713	Gosejacob	HMS *Keppel*	† 69-27 N, 04-53 E
24 Feb	U 761	Geider	VP-63, VB-127, Br. Sqdn. 202, HMS *Anthony &* *Wishart*	35-55 N, 05-45 W
25 Feb	U 601	Hansen	Br. Sqdn. 210	† 70-26 N, 12-40 E
25 Feb	U 91	Hungerhausen	HMS *Affleck, Gore & Gould*	49-45 N, 26-20 W
1 Mar	U 358	Manke	HMS *Affleck, Gould, Garlies* *& Gore*	45-46 N, 23-16 W
1 Mar	U 709	Ites	*Thomas (DE-102), Bostwick* *(DE-103) & Bronstein* *(DE-189)*	† 49-10 N, 26-00 W
1 Mar	U 603	Bertelsmann	*Bronstein (DE-189)*	† 48-55 N, 26-10 W
4 Mar	U 472	v. Forstner	HMS *Chaser's* Sqdn. 816 & HMS *Onslaught*	73-05 N, 26-40 W
5 Mar	U 366	Langenberg	HMS *Chaser's* Sqdn. 816	† 72-10 N, 14-45 E
6 Mar	U 744	Blischke	HMCS *St. Catherine's,* *Chilliwack, Gatineau,* *Fennel, Chaudière,* HMS *Icarus & Kenilworth Castle*	
6 Mar	U 973	Paepenmöller	HMs *Chaser's* Sqdn. 816	70-04 N, 05-48 E
10 Mar	U 450	Böhme	HMS *Exmoor, Blankney,* *Blencathra & Brecon*	40-11 N, 12-27 E
10 Mar	U 343	Rahn	HMS *Mull*	† 38-07 N, 09-41 E
10 Mar	U 625	Straub	RCAF Sqdn. 422	† 52-35 N, 20-19 W

Date	U-Boat	Last Comdr.	Cause of sinking	Position
10 Mar	U 845	Weber	HMS *Forester;* HMCS *St. Laurent, Owen Sound & Swansea*	48-20 N, 20-33 W
11 Mar	UIT 22 [ex-*Alpino Attilio Bagnolini*]	Wunderlich	RSAAF Sqdns. 279 & 262	† 41-28 S, 17-40 E
11 Mar	U 380	Brandi	US Army A/C	Toulon
11 Mar	U 410	Fenski	US Army A/C	Toulon
13 Mar	U 575	Boehmer	VC-95 from *Bogue (CVE-9);* Br. Sqdns. 172 & 206, *Haverfield (DE-393), Hobson (DD-464),* HMCS *Prince Rupert &* Br. Sqdn. 220	46-18 N, 27-34 W
15 Mar	U 653	Kandler	HMS *Vindex's* A/C, HMS *Starling & Wild Goose*	† 53-46 N, 24-35 W
16 Mar	U 392	Schümann	VP-63, HMS *Affleck & Vanoc*	† 35-55 N, 05-41 W
16 Mar	U 801	Branz	VC-6 from *Block Island (CVE-106); Corry (DD-463) & Bronstein (DE-189)*	16-42 N, 30-28 W
17 Mar	U 1013	Linck	Collision	Baltic
19 Mar	U 1059	Leupold	VC-6 from *Block Island (CVE-106)*	13-10 N, 33-44 W
25 Mar	U 976	Tiesler	Br. Sqdn. 248	46-48 N, 02-43 W
— Mar	U 851	Weingaertner	Unknown	(†) Atlantic
29 Mar	U 961	Fischer	HMS *Starling*	† 64-31 N, 03-19 W
30 Mar	U 223	Gerlach	HMS *Laforey, Tumult, Hambledon & Blencathra*	38-48 N, 14-10 E
— Mar	U 28	Sachse	Marine casualty	Baltic (Neustadt)
1 Apr	U 355	La Baume	HMS *Tracker's* Sqdn. 846 & HMS *Beagle*	† 73-07 N, 10-21 E
2 Apr	U 360	Becker	HMS *Keppel*	† 73-28 N, 13-04 E
3 Apr	U 288	Meyer	HMS *Tracker's* Sqdn. 846 & HMS *Activity's* Sqdn. 819	† 73-44 N, 27-12 E
6 Apr	U 302	Sickel	HMS *Swale*	† 45-05 N, 35-11 W
6 Apr	U 455	Scheibe	Unknown	† 44-04 N, 09-51 E
7 Apr	U 856	Wittenberg	*Champlin (DD-601) & Huse (DE-145)*	40-18 N, 62-22 W
8 Apr	U 2	Schwarzkopf	Collision	Baltic (W. of Pillau)
8 Apr	U 962	Lieseberg	HMS *Crane & Cygnet*	† 45-43 N, 19-57 W
9 Apr	U 515	Henke	VC-58 from *Guadacanal (CVE-60); Pope (DD-225), Pillsbury (DE-133), Chatelain (DE-149) & Flaherty (DE-135)*	34-35 N, 19-18 W
10 Apr	U 68	Lauzemis	VC-58 from *Guadalcanal (CVE-60)*	33-25 N, 18-59 W

Date	U-Boat	Last Comdr.	Cause of sinking	Position
14 Apr	U 448	Dauter	HMCS *Swansea* & HMS *Pelican*	46-22 N, 19-35 W
16 Apr	U 550	Hänert	*Gandy (DE-764), Joyde (DE-317)* & *Peterson (DE-152)*	40-09 N, 69-44 W
17 Apr	U 342	Hossenfelder	RCAF Sqdn. 162	† 60-23 N, 29-20 W
17 Apr	U 986	Kaiser	*Swift (AM-122)* & *PC-619*	† 50-09 N, 12-51 W
19 Apr	U 974	Wolff	HNorMSub. *Ula*	59-08 N, 05-23 E
24 Apr	U 311	Zander	RCAF Sqdn. 423	† 50-36 N, 18-36 W
26 Apr	U 488	Studt	*Frost (DE-144), Huse (DE-145), Barber (DE-161)* & *Snowden (DE-246)*	† 17-54 N, 38-05 W
27 Apr	U 803	Schimpf	Mine	53-55 N, 14-17 E
28 Apr	U 193	Abel	Br. Sqdn. 612	† 45-38 N, 09-43 W
29 Apr	U 421	Kolbus	US Army A/C	Toulon
(11?) Apr	U 108	Brünig	US Army & RAF A/C (Decomm., 17th; Scuttled, May '45)	Stettin
1 May	U 277	Lübsen	HMS *Fencer's* Sqdn. 842	† 73-24 N, 15-32 E
2 May	U 674	Muhs	HMS *Fencer's* Sqdn. 842	† 70-32 N, 04-37 E
2 May	U 959	Weitz	HMS *Fencer's* Sqdn. 842	† 69-20 N, 00-20 W
3 May	U 852	Eck	Br. Sqdns. 8 & 621	09-32 N, 50-59 E
4 May	U 371	Fenski	*Pride (DE-323), Joseph E. Campell (DE-70)*, RF *Sénégalais* & HMS *Blankney*	37-49 N, 05-39 E
4 May	U 846	Hashagen	RCAF Sqdn. 407	46-04 N, 09-20 W
5 May	U 473	Sternberg	HMS *Starling, Wren* & *Wild Goose*	49-29 N, 21-22 W
6 May	U 66	Seehausen	VC-55 from *Block Island (CVE-106)* & *Buckley (DE-51)*	17-17 N, 32-29 W
6 May	U 765 (ex-)	Wendt	HMS *Vindex's* Sqdn. 825, *Bickerton, Bligh* & *Aylmer*	52-30 N, 28-28 W
13 May	U 1224 (HIJMS *RO-501)*	Norita	*Francis M. Robinson (DE-220)*	† 18-08 N, 33-13 W
14-17 May	U 616	Koitschka	*Nields (DD-616), Gleaves (DD-423), Ellyson (DD-454), Hilary P. Jones (DD-427), Macomb (DD-458), Hambleton (DD-455), Rodman (DD-456), Emmons (DD-457)* & Br. Sqdn. 36	36-52 N, 00-11 E
15 May	U 1234	Wrede	Collision (later raised)	Off Göteborg
15 May	U 731	Keller	VP-63, HMS *Kilmarnock* & *Blackfly*	† 35-54 N, 05-45 W
16 May	U 240	Link	Nor. Sqdn. 330	† 63-05 N, 03-10 E
18 May	U 241	Werr	Br. Sqdn. 210	† 63-36 N, 01-42 E
19 May	U 960	Heinrich	*Niblack (DD-424), Ludlow (DD-438),* Br. Sqdns. 36 & 500	37-20 N, 01-35 E

Date	U-Boat	Last Comdr.	Cause of sinking	Position
19 May	U 1015	Boos	Collision	† 54-25 N, 19-50 E
21 May	U 453	Lührs	HMS *Termagant, Tenacious* & *Liddesdale*	38-13 N, 16-36 E
24 May	U 476	Niethmann	Br. Sqdn. 210	† 65-08 N, 04-53 E
24 May	U 675	Sammler	Br. Sqdn. 4	† 62-27 N, 03-04 E
25 May	U 990	Nordheimer	Br. Sqdn. 59	† 65-05 N, 07-28 E
27 May	U 292	Schmidt	Br. Sqdn. 59	† 62-37 N, 00-57 E
29 May	U 549	Krankenhagen	*Eugene E. Elmore (DE-686)* & *Ahrens (DE-575)*	† 31-13 N, 23-03 W
31 May	U 289	Hellwig	HMS *Milne*	† 73-32 N, 00-28 E
3 Jun	U 477	Jenssen	RCAF Sqdn. 162	† 63-59 N, 01-37 E
4 Jun	U 505	Lange	Captured by VC-8 from *Guadalcanal (CVE-60)*; *Chatelain (DE-149)*, *Jenks (DE-665)* & *Pillbury (DE-133)*	Now at Chicago Museum of Science & Industry 21-30 N, 19-20 W
7 Jun	U 955	Baden	Br. Sqdn. 201	† 45-13 N, 08-30 W
7 Jun	U 970	Ketels	Br. Sqdn. 228	45-15 N, 04-10 W
8 Jun	U 629	Bugs	Br. Sqdn. 224	† 48-27 N, 05-47 W
8 Jun	U 373	v. Lehsten	Br. Sqdn. 224	48-10 N, 05-31 W
9 Jun	U 740	Stark	Br. Sqdn. 120	† 49-09 N, 08-37 W
10 Jun	U 821	Knackfuss	Br. Sqdns. 206 & 248	† 48-31 N, 05-11 W
11 Jun	U 980	Dahms	RCAF Sqdn. 162	† 63-07 N, 00-26 E
12 Jun	U 490	Gerlach	VC-95 from *Croatan* *(CVE-25); Frost (DE-144)*, *Inch (DE-146)* & *Huse* *(DE-145)*	42-47 N, 40-08 W
13 Jun	U 715	Röttger	RCAF Sqdn. 162	62-45 N, 02-59 W
15 Jun	U 860	Büchel	VC-9 from *Solomons* *(CVE-67)*	25-27 S, 05-30 W
15 Jun	U 987	Schreyer	HM Sub. *Satyr*	† 68-01 N, 05-08 E
16 Jun	U 998	Fiedler	Nor. Sqdn. 333: heavily damaged, scuttled 27th.	61-01 N, 03-00 E
17 Jun	U 423	Hackländer	Nor. Sqdn. 333	† 63-06 N, 02-05 E
18 Jun	U 767	Dankleff	HMS *Fame, Inconstant* & *Havelock*	49-03 N, 03-13 W
18 Jun	U 441	Hartmann	Polish Sqdn. 304	49-03 N, 04-48 W
24 Jun	U 971	Zeplin	HMCS *Haida*, HMS *Eskimo* & Czech Sqdn. 311	49-01 N, 05-35 W
24 Jun	U 1225	Sauerberg	RCAF Sqdn. 162	† 63-00 N, 00-50 W
25 Jun	U 1191	Grau	HMS *Affleck & Balfour*	† 50-03 N, 02-59 W
25 Jun	U 269	Uhl	HMS *Bickerton*	50-01 N, 02-59 W
26 Jun	U 317	Rahlf	Br. Sqdn. 86	† 62-03 N, 01-45 E
26 Jun	U 719	Steffens	HMS *Bulldog*	† 55-33 N, 11-02 W
29 Jun	U 988	Dobberstein	HMS *Essington, Duckworth,* *Domett, Cooke,* & Br. Sqdn. 224	† 49-37 N, 03-41 W
30 Jun	U 478	Rademacher	Br. Sqdn. 86 & RCAF Sqdn. 162	† 63-27 N, 00-50 W
2 Jul	U 543	Hellriegel	VC-58 from *Wake Island* *(CVE-65)*	† 25-34 N, 21-36 W
3 Jul	U 154	Gemeiner	*Inch (DE-146)* & *Frost* *(DE-144)*	† 34-00 N, 19-30 W

Date	U-Boat	Last Comdr.	Cause of sinking	Position
5 Jul	U 390	Geissler	HMS *Wanderer & Tavy*	49-52 N, 00-48 W
5 Jul	U 586	Götze	US Army A/C	Toulon
5 Jul(?)	U 642	Brünning	US Army A/C	Toulon
5 Jul	U 233	Steen	*Card (CVE-11)'s* A/C, *Baker (DE-190)* & *Thomas (DE-102)*	42-16 N, 59-49 W
6 Jul	U 678	Hyronimus	HMCs *Ottawa, Kootenay* & HMS *Statice*	† 50-32 N, 00-23 W
8 Jul	U 243	Märtens	RAAF Sqdn. 10	47-06 N, 06-40 W
11 Jul	U 1222	Bielfeld	Br. Sqdn. 201	† 46-31 N, 05-29 W
14 Jul	U 415	Werner	Mine	48-22 N, 04-29 W
15 Jul	U 319	Clemens	Br. Sqdn. 206	† 57-40 N, 05-00 E
17 Jul	U 361	Seidel	Br. Sqdn. 86	† 68-36 N, 08-33 E
17 Jul	U 347	de Buhr	Br. Sqdn. 210	68-35 N, 06-00 E
18 Jul	U 672	Lawaetz	HMS *Balfour* (Scuttled)	50-03 N, 02-30 W
18 Jul	U 742	Schwassmann	Br. Sqdn. 210	† 68-24 N, 09-51 E
21 Jul	U 212	Vogler	HMS *Curzon & Ekins*	† 50-27 N, 09-51 E
(22) Jul	U 1166	Ballert	Torpedo explosion	Eckernförde
23 Jul	U 239	Vöge	RAF A/C (out of svce., 24 July)	Kiel
23 Jul	U 1164	-(unknown)-	RAF A/C (out of svce., 24 July)	Kiel
26 Jul	U 214	Conrad	HMS *Cooke*	† 49-55 N, 03-31 W
29 Jul	U 2323	Angermann	US Army A/C	Bremen
29 Jul	U 872	Grau	US Army A/C	Bremen
30 Jul	U 250	Schmidt	Russian *M-103* (sub)	Gulf of Finland
31 Jul	U 333	Fiedler	HMS *Starling & Loch Killin*	49-39 N, 07-28 W
4 Aug	U 671	Hegewald	HMS *Stayner & Wensleydale*	50-23 N, 00-06 W
6 Aug	U 736	Reff	HMS *Loch Killin & Starling*	47-19 N, 04-16 W
6 Aug	U 952	Curio	US Army A/C	Toulon
6 Aug	U 471	Klövekorn	US Army A/C	Toulon
6 Aug	U 969	Dobbert	US Army A/C	Toulon
9 Aug	U 608	Reisener	Br. Sqdn. 53 & HMS *Wren*	46-30 N, 03-08 W
11 Aug	U 385	Valentiner	RAAF Sqdn. 461 & HMS *Starling*	46-16 N, 02-45 W
12 Aug	U 981	Keller	Br. Sqdn. 502	45-41 N, 01-25 W
13 Aug	U 270	Schreiber	RAAF Sqdn. 461	46-19 N, 02-56 W
12 Aug	U 198	Heusinger v. Waldegg	HMS *Findhorn* & HMIS *Godavari*	† 03-35 S, 52-49 E
14 Aug	U 618	Faust	Br. Sqdn. 53 & HMS *Duckworth & Essington*	† 47-22 N, 04-39 W
15 Aug	U 741	Palmgren	HMS *Orchis*	50-02 N, 00-36 W
18 Aug	U 107	Fritz	Br. Sqdn. 201	† 46-46 N, 03-39 W
18 Aug	U 621	Stuckmann	HMCS *Ottawa, Kootenay* & *Chaudiére*	† 45-52 N, 02-36 W
19 Aug	U 123	v. Schröter	(Out of Service, 8/44) (RF *Blaison*, '54)	Lorient
19 Aug	U 466	Thater	Scuttled (Blown up?)	Toulon
19 Aug	U 967	Eberbach	Scuttled	Toulon
20 Aug	U 413	Sachse	HMS *Wensleydale, Forester* & *Vidette*	50-21 N, 00-01 W
20 Aug	U 984	Sieder	HMCS *Ottawa, Chaudière* & *Kootenay*	† 48-16 N, 05-33 W

Date	U-Boat	Last Comdr.	Cause of sinking	Position
20 Aug	U 1229	Zinke	VC-42 from *Bogue (CVE-9)*	42-20 N, 51-39 W
20 Aug	U 9	Klapdor	Russian A/C	Constanza
21 Aug	U 230	Eberbach	Scuttled	Toulon
22 Aug	U 180	Riesen	Mine	† 45-00 N, 02-00 W
24 Aug	U 354	Sthamer	HMS *Vindex's* Sqdn. 825, *Mermaid, Loch Dunvegan, Keppel & Peacock*	† 74-54 N, 15-26 E*
22 Aug	U 344	Pietsch	HMS *Vindex's* Sqdn. 825	† 72-49 N, 30-41 E*
24 Aug	U 445	v. Treuberg	HMS *Louis*	† 47-21 N, 05-50 W
25[20?] Aug	U 178	Spahr	Scuttled	Bordeaux
20 Aug	U 188	Lüdden	Scuttled	Bordeaux
25 Aug	UIT 21 [ex-*Giuseppe Finzi*]	-(unknown)-	Scuttled	Bordeaux (out of service after 9/8/43 attack)
25 Aug	U 667	Lange	Mine	† 46-10 N, 01-14 W
25[31?] Aug	U 1000	Müller	Mine	Neustadt (Pillau?)
— Aug	U 766	Wilke	(Out of service, 8/44) (RF *Laubie*, '47)	La Pallice
— Aug	U 129	v. Harpe	(Out of service, 7/44) (later scuttled)	Lorient
25 Aug 10 Sep?	U 18	Fleige	Scuttled (later raised by USSR)	Constanza (Kustendje)
25 Aug	U 24	Lenzmann	Scuttled (later raised by USSR)	Constanza
1 Sep	U 247	Matschulat	HMCS *St. John & Swansea*	† 49-54 N, 05-49 W
2 Sep	U 394	Borger	HMS *Vindex's* Sqdn. 825, *Keppel, Mermaid, Whitehall & Peacock*	† 69-47 N, 04-41 E
4 Sep	UIT 15, 16, 20		(See: Italian sub. chronology, inf.)	
5 Sep	U 362	Franz	Russian Minesweeper *T-116*	† Krakowka I. vicinity
9 Sep	U 743	Kandzlor	HMS *Portchester Castle & Helmsdale*	† 55-45 N, 11-41 W
9 Sep	U 484	Schäfer	HMCS *Dunver, Hespeler* (& RCAF Sqdn. 423?)	† 56-30 N, 07-40 W
10 Sep	U 19	Ohlenburg	Scuttled	Turkish coast
10 Sep	U 20	Grafen	Scuttled	Turkish coast
10 Sep	U 23	Arendt	Scuttled	Turkish coast
19 Sep	U 407	Kolbus	HMS *Troubridge, Terpsichore* & ORP *Garland*	36-27 N, 24-33 E
19 Sep	U 865	Stellmacher	Unknown	† North Sea
19 Sep	U 867	v. Mühlendahl	Br. Sqdn. 224 (or engine failure?)	† 62-15 N, 01-50 E
23 Sep	U 859	Jebsen	HM Sub. *Trenchant*	05-46 N, 100-04 E
24 Sep	U 565	Henning	US Army A/C	Salamis
24 Sep	U 596	Kolbus	US Army A/C	Salamis
24 Sep	U 855	Ohlsen	Br. Sqdn. 224	† 61-00 N, 04-07 E
26 Sep	U 871	Ganzer	Br. Sqdn. 220	† 43-18 N, 36-28 W
29 Sep	U 863	v. d. Esch	VB-107	† 10-45 S, 25-30 W

---

* - Br. Admiralty indicates these two positions should be transposed.

Date	U-Boat	Last Comdr.	Cause of sinking	Position
30 Sep	U 921	Werner	HMS *Campania's* Sqdn. 813	† 72-32 N, 12-55 E
30 Sep	U 1062	Albrecht	*Fessenden (DE-142)* & *Mission Bay (CVE-59)*	† 11-36 N, 34-44 W
30 Sep	U 703	Brünner	Mine	† Iceland (E. coast)
18 Sep	U 925	Knoke	Unknown (Sailed from Bergen 24 Aug)	† Iceland-Faeroes
4 Oct	U 993	Steinmetz	RAF A/C	Bergen
4 Oct	U 228	Engel	RAF A/C (out of service, 12 Oct)	Bergen
4 Oct	U 437	Lamby	RAF A/C (Put out service, 13 Oct)	Bergen
4 Oct	U 92	Brauel	RAF A/C (Put out of service, 12 Oct	Bergen
5 Oct	U 168	Pich	HNMSub. *Zwaardvisch*	06-20 S, 111-28 E
15 Oct	U 777	Ruperti	RAF A/C	Wilhelmshaven
16 Oct	U 1006	Voigt	HMCS *Annan*	60-59 N, 04-49 W
19 Oct	U 957	Schaar	Rammed 19th by Ger. trspt.; out of service, Narvik, 21st.	
23 Oct	U 985	Wolff	Mine (out of service, 15 Nov)	[63-07 N, 07-45 E?] (or Listerfjord?)
24 Oct	U 673	Gerke	Collision w/minesweeper; stranded	59-20 N, 05-53 E
27 Oct	U 1060	Brammer	HMS *Implacable's* 1771 Sqdn., Br. Sqdn. 502 & Czech Sqdn. 311	† 65-24 N, 12-00 E
28 Oct	U 1226	Claussen	Unknown (Schnörkel accident?)	† Atlantic
— Oct	U 2331	Pahl	Marine casualty	Near Hela (Baltic)
9 Nov	U 537	Schrewe	*Flounder (SS-251)*	† 07-13 S, 115-17 E
10 Nov	U 966	Wolf	Collision	Off C. Ortegal, Biscay
11 Nov	U 771	Block	HM Sub. *Venturer*	† 69-17 N, 16-28 E
11 Nov	U 1200	Mangels	HMS *Pevensey Castle, Launceston Castle, Portchester Castle & Kenilworth Castle*	† 50-24 N, 09-10 W
25 Nov	U 322	Wysk	HMS *Ascension* & Norw. Sqdn. 330	† 60-18 N, 04-52 W
28 Nov	U 80	Keerl	Diving accident	54-25 N, 19-50 E
30 Nov	U 196	Striegler	Unknown	† Sunda Straits
— Nov	U 547	Niemeyer	Mine	Baltic
6 Dec	U 297	Aldegarmann	HMS *Loch Insh & Goodall*	† 58-44 N, 04-29 W
9 Dec	U 387	Büchler	HMS *Bamborough Castle*	† 69-41 N, 33-12 E
12 Dec	U 416	Rieger	Raised after collision of 30 March	Baltic (off Pillau)
12 Dec	U 479	Sons	Mine	Eastern Baltic
13 Dec	U 365	Todenhagen	HMS *Campania's* Sqdn. 813	† 70-43 N, 08-07 E
17 Dec	U 400	Creutz	HMS *Nyasaland*	† 51-16 N, 08-05 W
18 Dec	U 1209	Hülsenbeck	Diving accident [struck rock]	49-57 N, 05-47 W
19 Dec	U 737	Gréus	Collision with minesweeper	(60-00 N, 05-00 E)
26 Dec	U 2342	Schad v. Mittelbiberach	Mine	† 53-55 N, 14-17 E

Date	U-Boat	Last Comdr.	Cause of sinking	Position
27 Dec	U 877	Findeisen	HMCS *St. Thomas*	46-25 N, 36-38 W
28 Dec	U 735	Börner	RAF A/C	59-24 N, 10-29 E (Horten)
30 Dec	U 772	Rademacher	RCAF Sqdn. 407	† 50-05 N, 02-31 W
31 Dec	U 906	Unknown	Air attack	Hamburg
31 Dec (Apr	U 2532	Unknown	US Army A/C (& RAF)	Hamburg
31 Dec '45?)	U 2537	Klapdor	US Army A/C	Hamburg

1945

Date	U-Boat	Last Comdr.	Cause of sinking	Position
— Jan	U 650	Zorn	Unknown	† NE of Scotland(?)
10 Jan	U 679	Aust	Mine [Russian A/S vsl. *MO-124?*]	† Baltic
16 Jan	U 248	Loos	*Hayter (DE-212), Otter (DE-210), Varian (DE-798) & Harry E. Hubbard (DD-748)*	† 47-43 N, 26-37 W
16 Jan	U 482	v. Matuschka	HMS *Peacock, hart, Starling,* Loch Craggie & Amethyst	† 55-30 N, 05-53 W
17 Jan (11)	U 2515	Borchers	US Army	Hamburg
17 Jan Mar?)	U 2530	Bockelberg	US Army	Hamburg
17 Jan	U 2523	Ketels	US Army & RAF A/C	Hamburg
21 Jan	U 1199	Stollmann	HMS *Icarus & Mignonette*	49-57 N, 05-42 W
24 Jan	U 763	Schröter	Russian A/C	Koenigsberg
26 Jan	U 1172	Kuhlmann	HMS *Aylmer, Calder, Bentinck & Manners*	† 53-39 N, 05-23 W
27 Jan	U 1051	v. Holleben	HMS *Tyler, Keats & Bligh*	† 52-24 N, 05-42 W
31 Jan	U 3520	Ballert	Mine	† 54-27 N, 09-26 E
— Jan	U 1020	Eberlein	Unknown	(†) 57-50 N, 04-10 W
— Jan	U 382	Wilke	Collision	Baltic
3 Feb	U 1279	Falke	HMS *Bayntun, Braithwaite & Loch Eck*	61-21 N, 02-00 W
4 Feb	U 745	v. Trotha	Unknown	† Eastern Baltic
4 Feb	U 1014	Glaser	HMS *Loch Scavaig, Nyasaland, Papua & Loch Shin*	† 55-17 N, 06-44 W
9 Feb	U 864	Wolfram	HM Sub. *Venturer*	† 60-46 N, 04-35 E
14 Feb	U 989	v. Roithberg	HMS *Bayntun, Braithwaite, Loch Eck & Loch Dunvegan*	† 61-36 N, 01-35 W
15 Feb	U 1053	Lange	Casualty in rocket tests	† 60-22 N, 05-10 E
16 Feb	U 309	Loeder	HMCS *St. John*	† 58-09 N, 02-23 W
17 Feb	U 425	Bentzien	HMS *Lark & Alnwick Castle*	69-39 N, 33-50 E
17 Feb	U 1273	Knollmann	Mine	† 59-30 N, 10-30 E
17 Feb	U 1278	Müller-Bethke	HMS *Bayntun & Loch Eck*	† 61-32 N, 01-36 W
18 Feb	U 2344	Ellerhage	Collision	54-09 N, 11-51 E
19 Feb	U 676	Sass	Mine	† Baltic
20 Feb	U 1208	Hagene	HMS *Amethyst*	† 51-48 N, 07-07 W
22 Feb	U 300	Hein	HMS *Recruit, Evadne & Pincher*	36-29 N, 08-20 W
24 Feb	U 480	Förster	HMS *Duckworth & Rowley*	† 49-55 N, 06-08 W
24 Feb	U 927	Ebert	Br. Sqdn. 179	† 49-54 N, 04-45 W
24 Feb	U 3007	Marbach	US Army A/C	Bremen
27 Feb	U 1018	Burmeister	HMS *Loch Fada*	49-56 N, 05-20 W

233

Date	U-Boat	Last Comdr.	Cause of sinking	Position
27 Feb	U 327	Lemcke	VPB-12, HMS *Labuan*, *Loch Fada* & *Wild Goose*	† 49-46 N, 05-47 W
28 Feb	U 869	Neuerburg	*Fowler (DE-222)* & RF *l'Indiscret*	† 34-30 N, 08-13 W
— Feb	U 923	Frömmer	Mine	† Baltic
2 Mar	U 3519	v. Harpe	Mine	† 54-11 N, 12-05 E
7 Mar	U 1302	Herwartz	HMCS *La Hulloise*, *Strathadam* & *Thetford Mines*	† 52-19 N, 05-23 W
10 Mar	U 275	Wehrkamp	Mine	† 50-36 N, 00-04 E
11 Mar	U 681	Gebauer	VPB-103	49-53 N, 06-31 W
12 Mar	U 683	Keller	HMS *Loch Ruthven* & *Wild Gosse*	† 49-52 N, 05-52 W
12 Mar	U 260	Becker	Mine	51-15 N, 09-05 W
14 Mar	U 714	Schebcke	HMSAS *Natal*	† 55-57 N, 01-57 W
15 Mar	U 367	Stegemann	Mine	† 54-25 N, 19-50 E
18 Mar	U 866	Rogowsky	*Lowe (DE-325)*, *Menges (DE-320)*, *Pride (DE-323)* & *Mosley (DE-321)*	† 43-18 N, 61-08 W
20 Mar	U 905	Schwarting	Br. Sqdn. 86	† 59-42 N, 04-55 W
20 Mar	U 1003	Strübing	HMCS *New Glasgow* [rammed]*	55-25 N, 06-53 W
22 Mar	U 296	Rasch	Br. Sqdn. 120	† 55-23 N, 06-40 W
26 Mar	U 399	Buhse	HMS *Duckworth*	49-56 N, 05-22 W
27 Mar	U 965	Unverzagt	HMS *Conn*, *(Rupert & Deane)*	† 58-34 N, 05-46 W
27 Mar	U 722	Reimers	HMS *Fitzroy, Redmil* & *Byron*	† 57-09 N, 06-55 W
29 Mar	U 246	Raabe	HMS *Duckworth*	† 49-58 N, 05-25 W
29 Mar	U 1106	Bartke	Br. Sqdn. 224	† 61-46 N, 02-16 W
30 Mar	U 1021	Holpert	HMS *Rupert, Conn* *(& Deane)*	† 58-19 N, 05-31 W
4 Mar	U 3508	v. Lehsten	US Army A/C	Wilhelmshaven
30 Mar	U 429 (ex RS *S-2*)	Kuttkat	US Army A/C	Wilhelmshaven
30 Mar	U 96	Rix	US Army A/C	Wilhelmshaven
30 Mar	U 72	Mayer	US Army A/C	Bremen
30 Mar	U 430 (ex RS *S-3*)	Hammer	US Army A/C	Bremen
30 Mar	U 870	Hechler	US Army A/C	Bremen
30 Mar	U 329	-(unknown)-	US Army A/C	Bremen
30 Mar	U 884	Lüders	US Army A/C	Bremen
30 Mar	U 2340	Klusmeier	US Army A/C	Hamburg
30 Mar	U 350	Niester	US Army A/C	Hamburg (D. Werft)
— Mar	U 348	Schunck	US Army A/C	Hamburg
30 Mar	U 1167	Bortfeld	US Army A/C	Hamburg
30 Mar	U 747	Zahnow	US Army A/C	Hamburg
30 Mar	U 886	—	US Army A/C	Bremen (on stocks)

---

* - Scuttled, 23 d.

Date	U-Boat	Last Comdr.	Cause of sinking	Position
31 Mar	U 682	Tienemann	RAF A/C	Hamburg
2 Apr	U 321	Berends	Polish Sqdn. 304	† 50-00 N, 12-57 W
3 Apr	U 1221	Ackermann	US Army A/C	Kiel
3 Apr	U 2542	Hübschen	US Army A/C	Kiel
3 Apr	U 3505	Willner	US Army A/C	Kiel
3 Apr	U 1276	Wendt	Br. Sqdn. 224	† 61-42 N, 00-24 W
4 Apr	U 749	Huisken	US Army A/C	Kiel
4 Apr	U 237	Menard	US Army A/C	Kiel
4 Apr	U 3003	Kregelin	US Army A/C	Kiel
5 Apr	U 1169	Goldbeck	Mine	† 52-03 N, 05-53 W
6 Apr	U 1195	Cordes	HMS *Watchman*	50-33 N, 00-55 W
7 Apr	U 857	Premauer	*Gustafson (DE-182)*	† 42-22 N, 69-46 W
8 Apr	U 1001	Blaudow	HMS *Fitzroy & Byron*	† 49-19 N, 10-23 W
8 Apr	U 2509	Schendel	RAF A/C	Hamburg
8 Apr	U 2514	Wahlen	RAF A/C	Hamburg
8 Apr	U 3512	Hornkohl	RAF A/C	Kiel
8 Apr	U 774	Sausmikat	HMS *Calder & Bentinck*	† 49-58 N, 11-51 W
9 Apr	U 804	Meyer	Br. Sqdns. 143, 235 & 248	† 57-58 N, 11-15 E
9 Apr	U 843	Herwartz	Br. Sqdns. 143, 235 & 248	57-58 N, 11-15 E
9 Apr	U 1065	Panitz	Br. Sqdn. 235	† 57-48 N, 11-26 E
10 Apr	U 878	Rodig	HMS *Vanquisher & Tintagel Castle*	† 47-35 N, 10-33 W
12 Apr	U 486	Meyer	HM Sub. *Tapir*	† 60-44 N, 04-39 E
12 Apr	U 1024	Gutteck	Captured by HMS *Loch Glendhu* (towed by *Loch More*, but sank underway)	53-39 N, 05-03 W
14 Apr	U 1206	Schlitt	Diving accident (grounded)	57-21 N, 01-39 W
14 Apr	U 235	Huisken	Ger. escort vessel *T-17*	† 57-44 N, 10-39 E
15 Apr	U 285	Bornhaupt	HMS *Grindall & Keats*	† 50-13 N, 12-48 W
16 Apr	U 1063	Stephan	HMS *Loch Killin*	50-08 N, 05-52 W
15 Apr	U 1235	Barsch	*Stanton (DE-247)*, *& frost (DE-144)*	† 47-54 N, 30-25 W
16 Apr	U 78	Hübsch	Russian forces	Pillau, in dock
16 Apr	U 880	Schötzau	*Stanton (DE-247) & frost (DE-144)*	† 47-53 N, 30-26 W
16 Apr	U 1274	Fitting	HMS *Viceroy*	† 55-36 N, 01-24 W
19 Apr	U 251	Säck	Br. Sqdns. 235, 143, 248 and Norw. Sqdn. 333	56-37 N, 11-51 E
19 Apr	U 879	Machen	*Buckley (DE-51 & Reuben James (DE-153)*	† 42-19 N, 61-45 W
21 Apr	U 636	Schendel	HMS *Bazely, Drury & Bentinck*	† 55-50 N, 10-31 W
21[22?] Apr	U 518	Offermann	*Carter ()DE-112) & Neal A. Scott (DE-769)*	† 43-26 N, 38-23 W
23 Apr	U 183	Schneewind	*Besugo (SS-321)*	† 04-57 S, 112-52 E
23 Apr	U 396	Siemon	Br. Sqdn. 86	† 59-29 N, 05-22 W
24 Apr	U 546	Just	*Flaherty (DE-135), Neunzer (DE-150), Chatelain (DE-149), Varian (DE-798), Harry E. Hubbard (DD-748), Janssen (DE-396), Pills-*	43-53 N, 40-07 W

235

Date	U-Boat	Last Comdr.	Cause of sinking	Position
			bury (DE-133) & Keith (DE-241)	
25 Apr	U 1107	Parduhn	VPB-103	† 48-12 N, 05-42 W
28 Apr	U 56	Miede	US Army & RAF A/C	Kiel
29 Apr	U 1017	Riecken	Br. Sqdn. 120	† 56-04 N, 11-06 W
29 Apr	U 307	Krüger	HMS *Loch Insh*	69-24 N, 33-44 E
29 Apr	U 286	Dietrich	HMS *Loch Shin, Anguilla &* *Cotton*	† 69-29 N, 33-37 E
30 Apr	U 242	Riedel	Unknown	(†) U. K. Area
30 Apr	U 548	Krempl	*Natchez (PF-2), Coffmann* *(DE-191), Bostwick* *(DE-103) and Thomas* *(DE-102)*	† 36-34 N, 74-00 W
30 Apr	U 1055	Meyer	VPB-63	† 48-00 N, 06-30 W
— Apr	U 1227	Altmeier	US Army & RAF A/C	Kiel
— Apr	U 677	Ady	US Army & RAF A/C	Hamburg
— Apr	U 982	Harmann	US Army & RAF A/C	Hamburg
— Apr	U 3525	Gaude	US Army & RAF A/C	Baltic
— Apr	U 2516	Kallipke	US Army & RAF A/C	Hamburg
— Apr	U 1131	Fiebig	US Army & RAF A/C	Kiel
30? Apr	U 325	Dohrn	Unknown	† Eng. Channel (I. of Man)
— Apr	U 326	Matthes	Unknown	(†) United Kingdom area
2 May	U 1007	v. Witzendorff	RAF A/C (later mined)	53-54 N, 11-28 E
2 May	U 2359	Bischoff	Br. Sqdns. 143, 235, 248, RCAF Sqdn. 404 & Norw. Sqdn. 333	† 57-29 N, 11-24 E
3 May	U 3030	Luttmann	RAF A/C	55-30 N, 10-00 E
3 May	U 3032	Slevogt	RAF A/C	55-30 N, 10-00 E
3 May	U 2540	Schultze	RAF A/C	55-30 N, 10-00 E
3 May	U 2524	v. Witzendorff	Br. Sqdns. 254 & 236	55-55 N, 10-45 E
3 May	U 1210	Grabert	RAF A/C	54-27 N, 09-51 E
4 May	U 2503	Wächter	Br. Sqdns. 236 & 254 (damage, beached)	55-37 N, 10-00 E
4 May	U 711	Lange	HMS *Searcher's, Trumpeter's* *& Queen's* Sqdns. 853, 882 & 846	68-48 N, 16-38 E
4 May	U 2338	Kaiser	Br. Sqdns. 254 & 236	55-37 N, 10-00 E
4 May	U 393	Herrle	Br. Sqdns. 254 & 236	55-37 N, 10-00 E
4 May	U 904	Stührmann	RAF bombs ⎫ Scuttled	54-29 N, 09-52 E
4 May	U 746	Lottner	RAF bombs ⎬ after	54-48 N, 09-55 E
4 May	U 876	Bahn	RAF bombs ⎭ damage	54-29 N, 09-52 E
4 May	U 236	Mumm	Br. Sqdns. 236 & 254 [Scuttled later]	55-37 N, 10-00 E
4 May	U 4708	Schulz	A/C	Kiel (Germaniawerft)
4 May	U 4709		A/C	Kiel (Germaniawerft)
4 May	U 4711	Endler	A/C	Kiel (Germaniawerft)
4 May	U 4712	Fleige	A/C	Kiel (Germaniawerft)

Date	U-Boat	Last Comdr.	Cause of sinking	Position
5 May	U 2365	Christiansen	Czech Sqdn. 311	57-27 N, 10-38 E
5 May	U 2367	Schröder	Collision with U-boat; (raised, '56, for Bundesmarine)	Great Belt
5 May	U 534	Nollau	Br. Sqdn. 206	56-59 N, 11-48 E
5 May	U 3523	Müller	Br. Sqdn. 224	† 56-06 N, 11-06 E
5[4?] May	U 2521	Methner	Br. Sqdn. 547	† 56-11 N, 11-08 E
5 May	U 733	Hammer	RAF bombs (Damaged, scuttled)	54-47 N, 09-26 E
5 May	U 3503	Deiring	Br. Sqdn. 86 (Scuttled off Göteborg, 8th)	56-45 N, 10-49 E
5 May	U 579	Schwarzenberg	RAF bombs	† 55-30 N, 10-00 E
6 May	U 1008	Gessner	Br. Sqdn. 86	57-52 N, 10-49 E
6 May	U 2534	Drews	Br. Sqdn. 86	† 57-08 N, 11-52 E
6 May	U 853	Frömsdorf	*Atherton (DE-169) & Moberly (PF-63)*	† 41-13 N, 71-27 E
6 May	U 881	Frischke	*Farquhar (DE-139)*	† 43-18 N, 47-44 W
7 May	U 320	Emmrich	Br. Sqdn. 210	61-32 N, 01-53 E
— May	U 398	Cranz	Unknown	(†) E. Coast
9 May	U 2538	Klapdor	Mine	Off Marstal, SW Aerö I.
16 May	U 873	Steinhoff	Surrendered	Portsmouth, N.H.
3 Jun	U 1277	Stever	Scuttled	W. of Oporto
17 Aug	U 977	Schaeffer	Surrendered	La Plata R., Argentina

N. B.: Over 150 U-boats were scuttled in northern ports the first week in May '45—15 in Wilhelmshaven, 10 at Hamburg, 31 in Travemünde and 26 in Kiel the 2d. and 3d.; 56 in Flensburg alone the 5th. From then till the end of June, approximately an equal number of submarine crews surrendered to the Allies from Narvik to Portsmouth, N. H., and a straggler or two at the River Plate as late as mid-August. To pinpoint terminal date and locale for an individual U-boat, consult the general index, as space in the two paragraphs immediately following permits only a skeleton listing of the 300 U-numbers.

Scuttled, May 1945

U 8, 14, 17, 29, 30, 37, 38, 46, 48, 52, 57, 58, 60, 61, 62, 71, 120, 121, 129, 137, 139, 140, 141, 142, 146, 148, 151, 152, 267, 290, 316, 323, 339, 349, 351, 370, 397, 428, 446, 474, 475, 552, 560, 612, 704, 708, 717, 721, 748, 750, 792, 793, 794, 795, 822, 828, 903, 922, 924, 929, 958, 963, 979, 999, 1002, 1016, 1025, 1056, 1057, 1058, 1101, 1132, 1161, 1162, 1168, 1170, 1192, 1193, 1196, 1204, 1207, 1277, 1303, 1304, 1306, 1308, 1405, 1406, 1407, 2327, 2330, 2332, 2333, 2339, 2343, 2346, 2347, 2349, 2352, 2355, 2357, 2358, 2360, 2362, 2366, 2368, 2369, 2370, 2371, 2501, 2504, 2505, 2508, 2510, 2512, 2517, 2519, 2520, 2522, 2525, 2526, 2527, 2528, 2531, 2533, 2535, 2536, 2539, 2541, 2543, 2544, 2545, 2546, 2548, 2551, 3001, 3002, 3004, 3005, 3006, 3009_3016, 3018_3029, 3031, 3033, 3034, 3037_3040, 3044, 3501, 3502, 3504, 3506, 3507, 3510, 3511, 3513, 3516, 3517, 3518, 3521, 3522, 3524, 3526_3530, 4705, 4707, 4710, UIT 2, 3, 6-14.

Surrendered, May–June, 1945

(Over 100 U-boats, here marked †, were sunk in deep water in the North Atlantic soon after capitulation; this was the British »Operation Deadlight.«)

U 59, 101, 143†, 145†, 149†, 150, 155†, 170†, 190, 218†, 234, 244†, 245†, 255†, 256, 262, 276, 278†, 281†, 291†, 293†, 294†, 295†, 298†, 299†, 310, 312†, 313†, 315, 318†, 324, 328†, 363†, 368†, 369†, 427†, 481†, 483†, 485, 510, 516†, 530, 532†, 539†, 541†, 555, 637†, 668†, 712, 716†, 720†, 739†, 758, 764†, 773†, 775†, 776†, 778†, 779†, 802†, 805, 806, 825†, 826†, 827†, 858, 861†, 868†, 873, 874†, 875†, 883†, 889, 901†, 907†, 926, 928†, 930†, 953, 956†, 968†, 975†, 977, 978†, 991†, 992†, 994†, 995, 997†, 1004†, 1005†, 1009†, 1010†, 1019†, 1022†, 1023†, 1052†, 1054, 1061†, 1064, 1102†, 1103†, 1104, 1105, 1108, 1109, 1110†, 1163†, 1165†, 1171, 1194†, 1197†, 1198†, 1201, 1202, 1203, 1228, 1230†, 1231, 1232, 1233†, 1271, 1272, 1275, 1301†, 1305, 1307†, 2321†, 2322†, 2324†, 2325†, 2326, 2328†, 2329†, 2334†, 2335†, 2336†, 2337†, 2341†, 2345†, 2348†, 2350†, 2351, 2353, 2354†, 2356, 2361†, 2363†, 2502, 2506, 2511, 2513, 2518, 2529, 3008, 3017, 3035, 3041, 3514†, 3515, 4706.

Select bibliography

Beesly, Patrick, *Very Special Intelligence*, London, 1977
Chalmers, W. S., *Max Horton and the Western Approaches*, London, 1954
Dönitz, Karl, *Zehn Jahre und zwanzig Tage*, Bonn, 1958
Harnack, Wolfgang, *Zerstörer unter deutscher Flagge 1934–1945*, Herford, 1978
Heiber, Helmut, *Hitlers Lagebesprechungen, 1942–1945*, Stuttgart, 1962
Lüdde-Neurath, Walter, *Regierung Dönitz*, Göttingen, 1964
McLachlan, Donald, *Room 39, Naval Intelligence in Action, 1939–1945*, London, 1968
Morison, Samuel Eliot, *Battle of the Atlantic, 1939–1943*, Boston, 1951
Picker, Henry, *Hitlers Tischgespräche im Führerhauptquartier 1941–1942*, Stuttgart, 1963
Prager, H. G., *Blohm & Voss*, Herford, 1977
Price, Alfred, *Aircraft Versus Submarine*, London, 1973
Raeder, Erich, *Mein Leben I/II*, Tübingen, 1956
Robertson, T., *Walker R.N.*, London, 1956
Rohwer, Jürgen, *Die U-boot-Erfolge der Achsenmächte 1939–1945*, Munich, 1968
Rohwer, Jürgen/Hümmelchen, Gerhard, *Chronik des Seekrieges, 1939–1945*, Oldenburg, Munich, 1968
Rohwer, Jürgen, *Geleitzugschlachten im März 1943*, Stuttgart, 1975
Rohwer, Jürgen/Jäckel, Eberhard, *Funkaufklärung und ihre Rolle im Zweiten Weltkrieg*, Stuttgart, 1978
Roskill, S. W., *The War at Sea*, Vols I–III, London, 1960
Rutter, Owen, *Red Ensign, A History of Convoy*, London, 1942
Salewski, Michael, *Die Deutsche Seekriegsleitung 1935–1945*, Vols I–III, Munich, 1975
Schramm, Percy Ernst, *Kriegstagebuch des Oberkommandos der Wehrmacht*, Vols I–IV, Frankfurt, 1963
Lagevorträge des Oberbefehlshabers der Kriegsmarine vor Hitler 1939–1945, Munich, 1972
Ministry of Information, *Merchantmen at War*, HMSO, London, 1944
Ministry of Information, *His Majesty's Submarines*, London, 1945
Office of the Chief of Naval Operations, *United States Submarine Losses WWII*, Washington, 1963
OKM 3. Ski — M. Dv. Nr. 135, *Die Handelsflotten der Welt 1942*, — München/Berlin, 1942
Die deutschen Marine-Quadratkarten im Zweiten Weltkrieg

Index

Aboukir, HMS, cruiser, 19
Activity, HMS, carrier, 179
Admiral Hipper, cruiser, 10–14, 53
Admiral Scheer, cruiser, 53
Algonquin, USS, tanker, 38
Altmark, tanker, 10
Amazone, SS, 71
Amethyst, HMS, corvette, 191
'Aphrodite' anti-radar device, 184
Archer, USS, carrier, 132
Ark Royal, HMS, carrier, 33
Athenia, SS, 20
Atlantic transmitter, 96, 123–5, 129, 138, 169, 189
ASV radar, *see* Radar, Airborne
Azores, 119, 147

Balingkar, SS, 92
Barham, HMS, battleship, 27, 33
Barker, USS, destroyer, 144
Beesly, Lt. Cdr. Patrick, 129, 136
Bergen, 50, 187, 201
Bernd von Arnim, destroyer, 11–12
Bethel Shoal, Fla., 68, 70
Biscay, Bay of, 1, 86, 111, 118–19, 138, 147, 179, 181
'Biscay cross', 60, 86, 116
Biter, USS, carrier, 132
Blagrove, Rear Adm., 19
Bleichrodt, Heinrich, 76
Blockade runners, 44–6
Blücher, cruiser, 14
Bogue, USS, carrier, 131, 132, 140, 145, 161
Böhm, Adm., 17
Bold, submarine bubble target, 127–8, 152, 165
Bonatz, Capt. Heinz, 136
Bordeaux, 49, 111, 169, 179
Bormann, Martin, 203
Bremen, 194
Brest, 49, 111, 169, 179, 181
British Prestige, SS, tanker, 64–5
Burwell, HMS, patrol ship, 108

Caledonian Monarch, SS, 41
Calgary, HMS, corvette, 159
Canada, 114–15
Canaris, Adm. Wilhelm, 10, 96
Card, USS, carrier, 140
Caribbean Sea, 52
Carls, Adm. Rolf, 113

Chanticler, HMS, corvette, 159, 165, 175
Cheshire, HMS, cruiser, 87, 92, 93
Churchill, Winston, 10, 49, 53, 164, 191, 197, 201, 202, 209
City of Manila, SS, 93
Clan Skene, SS, 76
Coast Guard, US, 72, 76–7, 81
Coded radio signals, 33, 34, 134–7
Convoy system, 18–20, 35, 72, 79–80, 86, 130–1, 154
Core, USS, carrier, 140, 143, 144, 145, 148
Cossack, HMS, destroyer, 10
Courageous, HMS, carrier, 19
Crane, HMS, 159
Cremer, Peter 'Ali',
   gunnery officer, *Theodore Riedel*, 5–15
   awarded Iron Cross, 14
   given command of U 152, 23
   given command of U 333, 29
      acceptance and training, 30–3
      first patrol, 35–45
      court martial, 45–7
      moved to La Pallice, 48
      second patrol, 56–83
   awarded Knight's Cross, 83
      third patrol, 86–9
      fourth patrol, 95–103
   second staff officer, 3, 113–37
      fifth patrol, 138–48
      sixth patrol, 150–60
      seventh patrol, 169–75
      eighth patrol, 181–5
   given command of U 2519, 186
   given command of anti-tank unit, 199
   given command of Dönitz's bodyguard, 200
   receives discharge, 213
Cressy, HMS, cruiser, 19
Crocus, HMS, corvette, 97–100, 103, 105

Dallas, USS, destroyer, 74–6
Danzig, 24, 194
Dasher, USS, carrier, 132
Deadlight, Operation, 208
Defoe, SS, 93
Delius, SS, 159
Delmer, Sefton, 126

Dietl, Gen. Eduard, 10
Dönitz, Grand Adm. Karl,
  as C-in-C U-boats, 6, 14, 49, 80,
    104, 127, 135, 150, 207
  as C-in-C Navy, 1–4, 113, 133,
    163–4, 181, 200, 202
  and U-boat construction
    programme, 17–18, 81, 192–3,
    197
  and operational orders, 19, 45, 47,
    51–2, 89, 119–21, 145–7, 174,
    178–9, 182
  and U-boat esprit de corps, 27, 85,
    134, 201, 207, 208
  in command of North Germany, 199
  as head of state, 203–5, 210–12
'Drum beat', Operation, 52, 68, 70,
    78, 81
Dunmore, SS, 91

Eclipse, SS, 72, 77
Edelsten, Rear Adm., 130
Eisenhower, Gen., 206
Electro-boat, see U-boat, Type XXI
Emden, 30–1
Empire Heritage, SS, 191
Empire McAlpine, (MAC), 132
Empire Voice, SS, 93
Enigma, see Coded radio signals
Esch, Lt. Cdr. Dietrich von der, 198
Espionage by French Underground,
    49, 138, 168–9, 176
Exe, HMS, frigate, 155–61

Fiedler, Lt. Cdr. Hans, 186–9
Fleming, Cdr. Ian, 126
Flensburg, 129, 204, 209
Florida coast, 9, 51, 66, 68–80
Foley, HMS, 159
Folkestone, HMS, corvette, 87, 91
Food, shipboard, 62, 146, 166
Foord, Brig. Gen., 209
Foxer, anti-torpedo device, 175
Franke, Lt. Cdr. Heinz, 114–15, 151
Friedeburg, Adm. von, 63, 113,
    205–6, 212
Furious, HMS, carrier, 14

'Gap', The Atlantic, 55, 62, 81, 112,
    121, 132, 140
Gates, Group Capt., 213
Geranium, HMS, 152
Gibraltar, 93, 94, 119, 151, 154
Glow-worm, HMS, destroyer, 12–13
'Gnat' torpedo, see Torpedo, acoustic
Gneisenau, battleship, 11
Godt, Rear Adm., 51, 119, 149, 181
Göring, Hermann, 17, 203
Gorleston, HMS, corvette, 87, 91, 93

Graph, HMS, submarine (previously
    U 570), 104–11
Greer, USS, destroyer, 33
Gretton, Vice-Adm., 136
Gretton, Capt., 213
Guadalcanal, USS, 165
Guggenberger, Friedrich, 4, 33, 137,
    148, 149

Hallfried, SS, 151
Halsey, USS, tanker, 71
Hamburg, 187, 193–4, 199–200, 203,
    213
Hans Lüdemann, destroyer, 11
Hardegen, Reinhard, 51
Hart, HMS, sloop, 191
Hartmann, Capt. Erich, 190
Hatarana, SS, 92
Hatteras, Cape, 52, 79
Hedgehog depth charges, 152, 157,
    188
Heimsoht & Rinke, 135
Hein, Fritz, 198
Henke, Werner, 159, 165
Hermann Künne, destroyer, 11
Hessler, Günter, 46, 104, 181
HF/DF (High Frequency Direction
    Finder), 87, 90–1, 94, 133, 140,
    167, 213
Hill, Capt. Ernest, 64
Hitler, Adolf, 1–2, 6, 16, 17, 20, 33,
    48, 53, 113, 117, 127, 134, 164,
    178, 191, 199, 203, 204
Hogue, HMS, cruiser, 19
Holm, Lt. Cdr. J.F., 99–103
Hood, HMS, battleship, 27
Hoover, J. Edgar, 78
Horton, Adm. Sir Max, 82, 112, 121,
    132, 133, 159, 209, 212
Hunter Killer Task Groups, 81, 121,
    132, 139, 140, 145, 161, 171, 191
Hurst Castle, HMS, corvette, 191

Iceland, 33, 105, 106, 108
Infra-red, military uses, 167

Jacksonville, USS, tanker, 191
Japan, 33, 148, 209, 212
Java Arrow, USS, tanker, 70, 77
Jodl, Col. Gen., 206, 212
Johnson, Capt. H.K., 72
Jupiter Inlet (Fla.), 69, 72

Kandler, Hans-Albrecht, 171
Kandzior, Hellmuth, 198
Karlsruhe, cruiser, 14
Kasch, Lt., 101, 160
Kesselring, Field Marshal, 199
Key West, 76
Kiel, 23, 32, 48

King, Adm. Ernest, 80
Kingston Agate, HMS, patrol ship, 108
Kirmse, Dr., 100
Knox, US Navy Secretary Franklin, 33, 78
Königsberg, cruiser, 14
Kowalewski, Maj., 138
Krancke, Adm., 181
Kretschmer, Otto, 19, 27, 29, 31
Kummetat, Heinz, 149
Küpfmüller, Prof., 148, 167
Kuppisch, Herbert, 4, 137, 148
Kurski & Kräger, 135
Kutzscher, Dr. Edgar, 168

Lagan, HMS, 163
La Pallice, 45, 49, 82, 111, 137, 181, 187
La Rochelle, 49
Leberecht Maass, destroyer, 8–9
Legassick, Cmdr. G.V., 159
Leigh light, see Searchlight
Lemp, Fritz, 20, 27
Lionidas M. Kondylis, SS, 42
Loch Craggie, HMS, frigate, 191
Loch Killin, HMS, frigate, 188–9
Lorient, 49, 111, 181
Lüth, Capt. Wolfgang, 211
Lützow, cruiser, 53

Magpie, HMS, 171
Maria Christina, SS, 146
Marriot, Lt. Peter Barnsley, 104–5, 110
Marsa, SS, 159
Marshall, Gen. George, 80
Matuschka, Lt. Cdr., 191, 195, 198
Max Schultz, destroyer, 8–9
McGregor, Flt. Lt. H.A., 183
McLachlan, Donald, 126, 128
Meisel, Adm., 200
Memel, 24, 28
Merchantmen at War, 34
Metox radar warning set, 60, 117, 138, 144, 150, 168
Miami, 69
'Milch cows' (U-tankers), 54, 62, 81, 96, 135, 139, 140, 144, 145, 147
Mine, Magnetic, 7
Monsoon U-boats, see U-boat, Type IX
Montgomery, Field Marshal, 205
Morison, Samuel Eliot, 77, 80
Mountbatten, Lord Louis, 53

Naxos radar warning set, 144, 150, 164, 167, 170, 174
Nelson, HMS, battleship, 27
Nene, HMS, corvette, 159
Niagara, SS, 108

North Channel, 164–74, 191
Northern Chief, HMS, patrol ship, 107–8
Northern Prince, HMS, patrol ship, 108
Norway, 9–15, 28, 34, 52–3, 134, 186, 187, 191, 207, 210
Nurani, SS, 90

Orves, Cdr. d'Estienne d', 96

Pack tactics against convoys, 119–20, 130–1
Paris, 165–6
Patria, SS, 209, 212
PC 450 (US Coast Guard), 73
PC 451 (US Coast Guard), 72–4
Peacock, HMS, sloop, 191
Pentstemon, HMS, corvette, 87, 91, 92
Pinto, SS, 191
Plön, 190, 199, 200, 203, 204
Pocket Book of Navies (Weyer), 5
Pohl, Lt. Wilhelm, 102
Prentice, Cdr. J.D., 132
Price, Alfred, 133
Prien, Günther, 19, 27, 29, 31
Prince Robert, Canadian cruiser, 154
Prinz Eugen, cruiser, 53
Prisoners, Interrogation of U-boat, 109–10, 122–8
Prize regulations, 20
Propaganda, American, 78–9
and see Psychological warfare
Psychological warfare, British, 50, 96, 122–9

Radar, Airborne, 1, 33, 59–60, 81, 86, 95, 116–19, 133, 144, 150, 184
Radio traffic, U-boat, 63, 88, 90, 94, 119, 138–9, 145, 146, 174
Raeder, Grand Adm., 3, 5, 6, 10, 17, 52, 80, 113, 164
Rainbow, Operation, 113
'Rémy', 168, 176
Resistance, French, 49–50, 96, 138, 168–9, 175–6, 188
Ringstad, SS, 42–3
Roberts, Capt. G.H., 212–13
Rock Island, USS, carrier, 140
Rodney, HMS, battleship, 27
Rohwer, Dr. Jürgen, 17, 162–4
Rooks, Maj. Gen., 209, 212
Roope, Lt. Cdr. Gerald, 13
Roper, USS, destroyer, 79
Rösing, Capt. Hans, 186
Roskill, Stephen, 52, 53, 116, 121, 130
Royal Oak, HMS, battleship, 19

Sabotage by French workers, 49–50, 95–6, 168–9
St. Lawrence River, 52

St. Lucie Shoal, 72
St. Nazaire, 49, 111, 113, 169, 181
Santée, USS, carrier, 140, 145
Scapa Flow, 19, 171
Schacht, Harro, 76
Schamong, Klemens, 146
Scharnhorst, battleship, 11
Schepke, Joachim, 19, 29, 31
Schnee, Adalbert, 148, 201–2
Schnorchel (snorkel, snort), 180, 181, 185, 186, 191, 193, 194, 198
Schörner, Field Marshal, 203, 206
Schuhardt, Otto, 19
Schultze, Herbert, 19, 27, 54
Schwaff, Lt. Werner, 113, 116, 137
Searchlight, Airborne, 118–19
Shipwrecked crew rescue, 20, 41–3, 76
Siegmann, Paul, 146
Silver Sandal, SS, 93
Snorkel, *see* Schnorchel
Snowberry, HMS, corvette, 159
Spain, 105, 111, 112, 147–8
Speer, Albert, 3, 204, 205
Spinanger, SS, 191
Spreewald, SS, 44–7
Squid, depth charge, 188–9
Starling, HMS, sloop, 171, 188–9, 191
Steiger, Lt. 143
Steinbauer, Lt. Cdr., 121
Steward, Capt. Valentine, 41
Stummel, Rear Adm., 136
Submarine deployment, British, 104–5, 111
Suhren, Reinhard, 72, 76, 83, 187

Teuffer, Gottfried, 122
Thames estuary, 7
Thane, HMS, carrier, 191
Theodore Riedel, destroyer, 5–15
Thetis, HMS, submarine, 18
Thompson, Sqd. Ldr. J., 106
Thunderbolt, HMS, submarine, 18
Tiesenhausen, H. D. von, 33, 59
Tirpitz, battleship, 53
Torpedo,
  its functioning, 25
  G7a oil-air, 25
  G7e electric, 25, 27, 161
  failures, 26–7, 161–2, 185, 198
  acoustic 'Gnat' or 'Wren', 28, 150–4, 161–4, 165, 175, 198
  quantity carried, 31, 54, 196
  Fido, 164, 213
  false tracks, 9, 72
Tracker, HMS, carrier, 179
Treaty, Anglo-German Naval, 16, 17
Trigg, Fl. Off. L., 146
Triton, SS, 90
Trondheim, 13, 14, 28, 53
Trotha, Claus von, 152

Truskow, Maj. Gen., 212

U-boat,
  construction programme, 2, 16–18, 53, 81, 193, 196–7, 202
  its functioning, 21–3, 31–2, 142, 192
  crews, 23, 67, 134, 208
  Type II-D, 23
  Type VII-C, 31, 53–4, 105, 111, 174, 192–3, 194
  AA gun, 33, 143, 147, 150, 183–4
  deployment, 34, 51–3, 80, 131, 133, 179, 181
  chart for, 35, 46, 87
  Type IX, 51, 54, 144, 146
  Walter, 133, 192–3, 195, 197
  Type XXI, 186, 192–7, 201, 208
  Type XXIII, 197, 201
  Type XXVI, 192, 208
  Type XXVII, 192
  Fleet scuttled, 207
U 333,
  trials, 30–3
  first patrol (Cremer), 35–45
  second patrol (Cremer), 56–83
  rammed by *British Prestige*, 64–6
  third patrol (Cremer), 86–9
  fourth patrol (Cremer), 95–103
  battle with *Crocus*, 96–103
  fifth patrol (Schwaff), 113–16, 120
  sixth patrol (Schwaff), 116–37
  seventh patrol (Cremer), 138–48
  eighth patrol (Cremer), 150–60
  attacked by *Exe*, 155–9
  ninth patrol (Cremer), 169–75
  tenth patrol (Cremer), 181–5
  last patrol (Fiedler), 188–9
U 9, 19
U 25, 27
U 30, 20, 27
U 37, 27
U 38, 27
U 46, 27
U 47, 19, 27, 29
U 56, 27
U 81, 33
U 85, 79
U 86, 161
U 99, 29
U 100, 29
U 105, 45
U 109, 76
U 120, 187
U 129, 147
U 152, 23–9, 198
U 159, 118
U 160, 145
U 169, 132
U 211, 159
U 214, 92

U 230, 146
U 262, 114–15, 151
U 300, 198
U 306, 152
U 331, 33, 59
U 406, 93
U 440, 137
U 459, 62, 100, 135, 140
U 468, 146
U 469, 132
U 482, 191
U 487, 144, 145
U 502, 118
U 507, 76
U 513, 148
U 515, 159, 165
U 536, 159
U 538, 159
U 540, 160
U 542, 161
U 564, 76, 83, 187
U 570, 104–12, 125
U 571, 195
U 572, 138, 149
U 575, 46
U 600, 145, 161
U 618, 145
U 648, 161
U 653, 171
U 657, 132
U 701, 37
U 743, 198
U 752, 132
U 847, 148
U 863, 198
U 954, 133
U 998, 187
U 2511, 201–2
U 2519, 187, 190, 193–5, 198, 207
U 2552, 194
UB 48, 121

UB 68, 121
Ultra, see Coded radio signals,
United States declaration of war, 33
United States, Submarine Losses, World
    War II, 34, 185

Vanoc, HMS, destroyer, 29
Vassilios A. Polemis, SS, 41
Veendam, SS, 195
Vigilant, USS, destroyer, 72–4
Vindex, HMS, carrier, 171, 179
Voltz, Maj. Gen., 199, 205

Walker, HMS, destroyer, 29
Walker, Capt. F.J., 132, 161, 171,
    188, 191
Walter U-boat, see U-boat, Walter
Warspite, HMS, battleship, 14, 27
Wastwater, HMS, trawler, 108
Weddingen, Otto, 19
Wellington, HMS, corvette, 87, 91
Weser, Exercise, 9–14, 27
Whimbrel, HMS, 171
Whitehall, HMS, 152
Wilamowitz-Möllendorf, Georg, von,
    62, 100, 135, 140, 161
Wild Goose, HMS, 171
Wilfred, Operation, 12
Wilhelm Heidkamp, destroyer, 11
Wilhelmshaven, 5–7, 9, 14, 48
Williams, Lt., 143–4
Winchelsea, HMS, corvette, 159
Windermere, HMS, trawler, 108
Winn, Cdr. Roger, 181
Wolf packs, see Pack tactics
Wolverine, HMS, destroyer, 29
Wren, HMS, 171
'Wren', see Torpedo, acoustic

Zahn, Wilhelm, 27
Zetland, HMS, destroyer, 93